"*Tribal Leadership* is a seminal work,** the cutting edge of a new genre of books on corporate culture and the understanding of networks in organizations. It is **a must read for every student of organization behavior, communications, and leadership development.**"
—Samuel M. Lam, president, Linkage Asia

"**I loved your book and highly recommend reading it,** as it describes the best run companies I know. . . ."
—Jim Clifton, chairman and CEO, The Gallup Organization

"Forget silos, think tribal. A silo insulates groups of people from others where no one inside grows together enough to make it up and out into the world; a tribe grows and expands from the inside out with a deep culture and language and much more potential . . . to grow. *Tribal Leadership* is your best guide to succeeding in a global world where silos are doomed to fail.**"
—Dr. Mark Goulston, "Leading Edge" columnist at Fast Company magazine and bestselling author of *Get Out of Your Own Way at Work*

"*Tribal Leadership* identifies the true source of exceptional leadership.** Logan, King, and Fischer-Wright have clearly traced the emergence of great leaders from the dynamics of the team. They have not only identified the source of leadership, but outline the steps necessary to achieve both personal and team excellence."
—Jim Keyes, CEO, Blockbuster stores and former CEO, 7-Eleven

"**I cannot think of a more timely book,** not just for the corporate world, but for nation-states as well. . . . **The insights in this book don't just have the power to change organizations; they can touch the human heart. That makes them very powerful indeed.**"
—from the foreword by Warren Bennis

"*Tribal Leadership* shares with all of us the impact that culture has on an organization.** With all the leadership training in today's world and all the books and courses on leadership, great organizations still must build a great culture to succeed. Having spent the last 42 years building an organization, I can vouch for the fact that a great culture has proved to be the most important element of our success. Even after hiring great people with great talent, it is critical that they work in unison. The culture of teams strengthens and creates a great organization. **You'll certainly learn how to build an organization with a solid culture by reading *Tribal Leadership.*"**
—Art Gensler, founder and chairman, Gensler

"**This is an important book. It changed the way I think about organizations.**"
—Michael C. Jensen, Jesse Isidor Straus emeritus professor of Business Administration, Harvard Business School

"*Tribal Leadership* is an extraordinary early insight into the de rigueur leadership regime of our near-future business culture—a uniquely humane and systemic approach to delivering successful engagements, based on profound depths of collectively derived values and sustainable change. **Logan, King, and Fischer-Wright's *Tribal Leadership* stands to become a key gospel for New Management.**"
—Lewis Pinault, author, *Consulting Demons* and *The Play Zone,* and chairman and founder of BOX at the London School of Economics

"Leaders of any group will find *Tribal Leadership* a fascinating read and an excellent resource for determining where one's organization lies in the hierarchy of effectiveness. Whether for the leader of a corporation, foundation, military unit, or sports team, the book applies the basic building blocks of a "tribe" in assessing human effort and determining how to improve performance. . . . [it] is not only applicable to corporate business competition, but also to foreign diplomatic relations and military operations."
—Brig. Gen. David L. Grange, U.S. Army (ret.), CEO, Robert R. McCormick Tribune Foundation

"A well-researched and highly readable book. *Tribal Leadership* **is a plain speak road map enabling transformation into operational excellence.** The authors have nailed how organizations and societies actually work!"
—Dr. Scott M. Shemwell, CEO, Strategic Decision Sciences

"Dave Logan and John King shine a light on leadership—and how leaders and groups influence each other. Their observations can take an organization from good to great."
—Roxanne Spillett, president, Boys & Girls Clubs of America

"Logan, King, and Fischer-Wright have described business cultural leadership thru a new and provocactive metaphor. 'The Tribe.' *Tribal Leadership* **is particularly valuable** because it focuses on creating an environment where members of the 'tribe' (employees) enhance the quality of their lives as well as the performance of the enterprise. Even more promising, *Tribal Leadership offers* a prescription for the struggling segments of our society, who live without a hopeful vision of the future."
—Jim Copeland, former CEO, Deloitte Touche Tohmatsu

"*Tribal Leadership* **presents a clear road map for the new reality of managing organizations, careers, and life.** This book points to a new paradigm in not just information technology, but also business. It explains what to do in a world where every professional will have an electronic shingle on the Internet to create a vibrant, active, network."
—Reid Hoffman, cofounder, LinkedIn

TRIBAL
LEADERSHIP

COLLINS BUSINESS

An Imprint of HarperCollins*Publishers*

TRIBAL
LEADERSHIP

Leveraging Natural Groups to
Build a Thriving Organization

**Dave Logan, John King,
and Halee Fischer-Wright**

HarperCollins books may be purchased for educational, business, or sales promotional use. For information, please write Special Markets Department, HarperCollins Publishers, 10 East 53rd Street, New York, NY 10022.

FIRST EDITION

Designed by Jaime Putorti

Library of Congress Cataloging-in-Publication Data

Logan, David (David Coleman)

    Tribal leadership : how successful groups form great organizations / Dave Logan, John King, and Halee Fischer-Wright.

    p. cm.

    Includes index.

    ISBN 978-0-06-125130-6

    1. Leadership. 2. Organizational behavior. 3. Teams in the workplace.

I. King, John Paul, 1941–   II. Fischer-Wright, Halee.   III. Title.

HD57.7.L643 2007

658.4'092—dc22

2007023625

09 10 11 12 WB/RRD 10 9 8

We dedicate this book to Tribal Leaders:
The future of the business world depends on you.

Contents

PART IV:
Toward Vital Work Communities (Stage Five)

●　●　●　●　●　●

Acknowledgments

This book would not be possible without a list of people we're honored to consider part of our tribe.

First, the heart of our tribe is Jack Bennett, COO of our consulting firm, but more importantly, a constant friend and advocate. He kept the company running so we could take time to research, teach, and write. There was never a job too big or too small; if it advanced the cause, Jack was there doing it before we could ask. On the next page is our core team: left to right, Dave, Halee, John, and Jack.

We are grateful to the people who granted us interviews, turning cold research findings into stories. The list includes Scott Adams, Don Beck, Carol Burnett, Gordon Binder, Kathy Calcidise, Jim Clifton, Gary Cole, Glen Esnard, Werner Erhard, Mike Eruzione, Brian France, Danny Kahneman, David Kelley, Bob Klitgaard, Marty Koyle, Frank Jordan, Tom Mahoney, Barney Pell, Sandy Rueve, Mark Rumans, Steven Sample, Brian Sexton, Bob Tobias, Charise Valente, Ken Wilber, George Zimmer, the leaders of Griffin Hospital, and the tribe around Design for You in Chicago (especially William and Morgon).

To our "review committee"—a group of people who read through our often agonizing rough drafts and helped us figure out what we were saying. The list includes Marcus Berry, Grace Cheng, Jim Crupi, Loree Goffigan, Gretchen Knudsen, Jay Iinuma, Anna

Photo credit: MelindaKelley.com

Maria Larsen, Megan O'Donnell, Robert Richman, Jody Tolan, and Greg Vorwaller.

At USC, we're indebted to years of students in the Executive MBA, Master of Medical Management, Master of Accounting, and Marshall MBA. The students at USC helped refine and shape our ideas, with many emerging as Tribal Leaders. This book would not have been possible without the mentoring and "safe space" USC provided, and we acknowledge the faculty and staff of the Marshall School of Business.

A special thanks to our agent, Bonnie Solow. Bonnie, this book would not have come together were it not for your absolute professionalism, support, and advice. We will always remember our meetings with you, and with LuLu, a special friend.

Bonnie introduced us to Ethan Friedman, our editor. Thank you for taking this project to the next level through your comments and encouragement, and for introducing us to the tribe at HarperCollins who literally made this book happen. That list includes Sarah Brown, Ruth Mannes, Georgia Morrissey, Victor Mingovits, Helen Song, Anna Chapman, Leah Carlson-Stanisic, and Nyamekye Waliyaya.

We wrote Tribal Leadership as the voice of one tribe, but there are several people that Dave, John, and Halee thank personally.

John's list of Tribal Leaders and partners includes Paul Buss, Rick Chichester, Mike Fitz-Gerald, George Kallis, Scott Kaplan, Randy McNamara, Marsha Morton, Dene Oliver, Craig Robbins, and Candace Shivers Morgan. John sends his appreciation to the thinkers and educators at the Santa Fe institute for inspiring him to merge Chaos and Complexity theory with the human sciences. He would like to acknowledge Landmark Education for cocreating the context for the central interests of his life. On a personal level, John thanks J.H. Vandapool, his first mentor. John says: "Van always saw the dream and aspirations of young people and dedicated his life to training and developing young leaders to attain the impossible. He touched thousands of young lives and his influence on me is present daily." Beyond Van, my family, particularly my mother, Mary King, a woman grounded in core values and the relationship realities of life, and at 93, still teaching her gentle and intelligent philosophy of human interactions. And, lastly, thanks profoundly to my daughter, Krista, her husband Mark, and their three beautiful daughters, Kyra, Juliet, and Keely.

Halee's list includes many strong female tribal leaders that are her mentors in medicine, business, life and friendship, including Grace Caputo, Dale Singer, Lisa Wetherbee, Tracy Beranek, Julie Zimbelman, Pat Mattews, Josie James, and her grandmother, Ida Fischer. She sends a special thank you to her role models: A.D. Jacobson, Walt Haggerty, and Mark Rumans. Halee adds: "I send special love, gratitude, and appreciation to my parents. My most important acknowledgment goes to my husband, Michael. He is a steadfast companion, giving love, humor, and an occasional kick in the butt—a truly extraordinary man."

For Dave, the list includes partners and Tribal Leaders: Skip Beebe, Karla Wiseman Bright, Rich Callahan, Bob Myrtle, and John Ollen, as well as mentors in business and academia, including Tim Campbell, Dave Carter, Mike Duffy, Bill Cohen, Tom Cummings, Warren Bennis, Beverly Kaye, Peter Marston, Patricia Riley, and Bernie Schnippert. Dave would like to acknowledge a debt of thanks to the Barbados Group, notably Michael Jensen and Steve Zaffron—both friends and teachers. There are two people worthy of special thanks: Ken Wilber, who took time from his busy schedule, and significant health problems, to guide us in the last stages of our research; and Werner Erhard. Dave is grateful for Werner's friendship, "listening," "outside the box" thinking, and encouragement. Dave's most important acknowledgment goes to Harte. He says: "You are not only my wife and strongest supporter, yours were the first eyes to see our proposal and chapter drafts. Much of this book was worked out in our long talks on the beach, and without you, we wouldn't have found Bonnie. You are a constant champion, my best friend, and yes, a Tribal Leader."

Foreword

About five years ago, I had lunch with Dave Logan, then a new associate dean at USC. He was the head honcho of USC's executive development programs and had been thinking about writing a book based on his experiences teaching and consulting for top executives. Just as dessert was being served, he leaned forward to ask me a question: "Who's the audience for the book I have in mind?" I thought that this was the key question every author should ask, and I suggested that he learn to write for impact and for the audience of business professionals. I said that he should write about what he not only knows best but what, in his view, would be the most important issue facing leaders, say, five years from now. *Tribal Leadership*, he, John King, and Halee Fischer-Wright tell me, is an outgrowth of that chat over crème brûlée. The three of them have written a book that both adds to what we know about leadership, and challenges some conventional wisdom. I have to confess that five years ago I had no idea of Dave, John, and Halee's prescience. I cannot think of a more timely book, not just for the corporate world but for nation-states as well.

This book points to a fact that is so ubiquitous it's invisible: human beings form tribes. Logan, King, and Fischer-Wright point to the relationship between leadership in tribes, and those who lead them.

They assert that this connection raises important questions about how leaders develop, become great, and leave a legacy. As the leaders build the tribes, the leader develops the tribe. This action in turn contributes back to the leader; the leader surrenders himself to the tribe and becomes far greater than an individual alone could ever become.

This book is the result of a ten-year field study of twenty-four thousand people in two dozen organizations. Instead of bringing us tables of numbers, the authors found people to epitomize their findings, giving us a book that is both interesting and informed. They learned that what separates average tribes from those that excel is culture. Furthermore, tribal culture exists in stages, going from undermining to egocentric to history making. Their work explains why some tribes reject any discussion of values, character, or nobility, while others demand these conversations. One of the most compelling interviews is with Gordon Binder, the former CEO of Amgen. Binder is the model of what a Tribal Leader should be: someone who artfully builds his corporate tribes, then gets out of the way so people can achieve greatness.

This work addresses several intriguing questions. Why do great leaders often fail in a new environment? Why do average leaders sometimes seem better than they really are? Why do great strategies fail more often than they succeed? The authors argue that the answer is the relationship between leaders and tribes. Great leaders build great tribes and engage in history-making efforts as they also recognize their great leaders.

About two years ago, I watched a video of a final leadership project for a class I co-teach with USC President Steven Sample. One of the student groups raised funds to fly high school students from economically disadvantaged neighborhoods to Sacramento to be trained by leaders in the California state government. While there, they worked with John King. The video highlighted King's message, which was that a leader's behavior is shaped by an unwavering commitment to personal and tribal values. The students were moved as they found ways to become leaders of their own tribes. The insights in this book don't just have the power to change organizations; they can touch the human heart. That makes them very powerful, indeed.

Warren Bennis

TRIBAL
LEADERSHIP

PART I

The Tribal Leadership System

CHAPTER 1

Corporate Tribes

Every organization is really a set of small towns. If you're from a small town, think of the people there. If you're not, think of, as Don Henley sings, "that same small town in each of us." There are the business executive and the sheriff. There's the town scandal—the preacher's wife and the schoolteacher. There's talk of who will be the next mayor, who will move away, and the price of grain (or oil or the Wal-Mart starting wage). There's the high school, where the popular kid, the son of the town's sheriff, throws a party the weekend his father is away. There are the church crowd, the bar friends, the single people, the book club, the bitter enemies. There are also the ones who are the natural leaders, who explain why the party at the sheriff's house seemed like a good idea at the time and how sorry they are for the beer stains on the carpet.

The people are different in every town, and the roles are never exactly the same. But there are more similarities than differences, and the metaphor itself always holds, from companies in Nebraska to ones in New York or Kuala Lumpur.

We call these small towns tribes, and they form so naturally it's as though our tribe is part of our genetic code. Tribes helped humans survive the last ice age, build farming communities, and, later, cities. Birds flock, fish school, people "tribe."

A tribe is a group between 20 and 150 people. Here's the test for whether someone is in one of your tribes: if you saw her walking down the street, you'd stop and say "hello." The members of your tribe are probably programmed into your cell phone and in your e-mail address book. The "150" number comes from Robin Dunbar's research, which was popularized in Malcolm Gladwell's *The Tipping Point*. When a tribe approaches this number, it naturally splits into two tribes.

Some of the corporate tribes we've seen include the high-potential managers of one of the world's largest financial services companies; the doctors, nurses, and administrators of one of America's most respected healthcare institutions; the research and development division of a mammoth high-tech firm; the operational executives of a major drug company; and the students of the executive MBA program at the University of Southern California.

Tribes in companies get work done—sometimes a lot of work—but they don't form because of work. Tribes are the basic building block of any large human effort, including earning a living. As such, their influence is greater than that of teams, entire companies, and even superstar CEOs. In companies, tribes decide whether the new leader is going to flourish or get taken out. They determine how much work gets done, and of what quality.

Some tribes demand excellence for everyone, and are constantly evolving. Others are content to do the minimum to get by. What makes the difference in performance? Tribal Leaders.

Tribal Leaders focus their efforts on building the tribe—or, more precisely, upgrading the tribal culture. If they are successful, the tribe recognizes them as the leaders, giving them top effort, cultlike loyalty, and a track record of success. Divisions and companies run by Tribal Leaders set the standard of performance in their industries, from productivity and profitability to employee retention. They are talent magnets, with people so eager to work for the leader that they will take a pay cut if necessary. Tribal Leaders receive so many promotions in such a short time that people often spread buzz that they will be the next CEO. Their efforts seem effortless, leaving many people puzzled by how they do it. Many Tribal Leaders, if asked, can't articulate what they are doing that's different, but after reading this book, you will be able to explain and duplicate their success.

A Tribal Leader many of us know from history is George Washington. His single major contribution was in changing thirteen diverse colonies into one people. If we look into what Washington actually did, he built a single identity (measurable by what people said) to a series of networked tribes. One was the affluent class in Virginia society, perhaps fewer than a hundred people. Another was the Continental Congress, originally fifty-five delegates. The third was the officer class of the Continental Army. Each time, Washington led the group to unity by recognizing its "tribalness," by getting its members to talk about what unified them: valuing freedom, hating the king's latest tax, or wanting to win the fight. As he built the common cause in each tribe, a mission gelled and they embraced "we're great" language. Washington's brilliance in each case was that the man and the cause became synonymous, with the leader shaping the tribe and the tribe calling forth the leader. This is how Tribal Leadership works: the leader upgrades the tribe as the tribe embraces the leader. Tribes and leaders create each other.

● ● ●

Before we move on, a few words about our method. We're at the end of a ten-year set of research studies that involved twenty-four thousand people in two dozen organizations, with members around the world.

We derived each concept, tip, and principle in this book from this research. What moved us, and what we hope moves you, is not the statistical side of the analysis but the people we met along the way—people who live the principles, who make life better for millions of employees, customers, and residents of their communities. As a result, we've written this book around the individuals who moved us.

Our guiding metaphor is this: most popular business books are like log cabins, cozy and warm with a blazing fire. They're comfortable, life affirming, and filled with snapshots of people and moments. They're fun to read, and the principles in them resonate within our experiences as true. The log cabin is built on anecdotes, however, and as we look back to fifty years of them, many have collapsed as times and economic cycles change. Although comfortable, they need structural reinforcement. Another set of books rests on statistical evidence, and while we trust their conclusions, reading them is like visiting a skyscraper with cubicles built in the 1970s, containing steel desks under fluorescent lights that flicker. Their structural integrity stands up during storms, but we find being in them tiring and draining.

We have attempted to put together a book that has the structural integrity of the skyscraper but with Persian rugs, cherrywood tables, floor-to-ceiling windows, perhaps even a stone fireplace or two. In short, you'll be reading about people, but with the assurance that the principles behind the stories are based on research. In presenting our findings, we have done our best to avoid academic concepts like theoretic frameworks and research agendas. When it was necessary to bring in others' research, we went and sat with them (when possible), to bring their personalities into the story as well as their findings. When our research gave us solid conclusions, we sought out people who epitomized what we were seeing in the data, to give a human face to the main points of this book. As you take this journey with us you'll meet former Amgen CEO Gordon Binder; NASCAR Chairman, Brian France; IDEO Founder, Dave Kelley; Gallup CEO, Jim Clifton; authors Ken Wilber and Don Beck; *Dilbert* creator, Scott Adams; actress Carol Burnett; Nobel Laureate Danny Kahneman; and Mike Eruzione, captain of the 1980 Olympic Gold Medal U.S. Hockey team—the basis of the movie *Miracle*.

We are indebted to these individuals and many others, and to a lineage of research that is fairly new to business. If you want to see the academic side of our research, you might start with Appendix B, which is about the story of our methodology. Simply put, it's that tribes emerge from the language people use to describe themselves, their jobs, and others. For most people, language is something they just live with and don't think about. Tribal Leaders know how to nudge language in a way that makes it morph—just as Washington's efforts created a common tribal language in the colonies, the army, and the Continental Congress. Change the language in the tribe, and you have changed the tribe itself.

As we derived principles and tools we put them to work in companies and organizations that were willing to test new methods. Some worked and some failed. We folded these lessons learned back into our studies, so that what you're reading has a basis in both research and practical experience.

A Road Map to Tribal Leadership

Most people describe Tribal Leadership as a journey, in which they understand themselves and the people around them better and, as a result, know exactly what actions will affect their workplaces.

Most people are blind to tribal dynamics. Our clients have described the moment when it all clicked for them, when they were able to see their company as a tribe, and suddenly they saw exactly what do to, in the same way George Washington somehow knew what to do more than two hundred years ago. The first part of this book will give you the insights and vocabulary of a Tribal Leader. Chapter 2 introduces the main thrust of this book: tribal stages.

The tribal stages operate like a slow conveyor belt that keeps sticking. When the belt is moving, people naturally move from one stage to the next. The early chapters in this book will remind you of the early stages of your career—the days right after college when you didn't know people and it was hard to find traction for your ideas. You'll recognize some clusters of people who have gotten stuck at this stage and built their part of the tribe accordingly. The vast majority of people become stuck in the middle stages, then seek out tribes that speak their language and do things in a familiar way. The later chapters will describe you on your best days and give you insight into people you know who can make things happen wherever they go.

After the five stages are introduced, later chapters go into each stage, highlighting exactly what actions will affect it and how to know when you're succeeding. Because each stage has a unique set of "leverage points" that will unstick it, it's critical to understand each one. Apply the leverage points incorrectly, and you'll reinforce tribal mediocrity.

This book is written at three different levels. First is the story—the main text of the book. Second are the "technical notes" in the margins, which answer the many questions we've been asked as we explain the Tribal Leadership system; those of you who like detail and fine gradations, we hope, will find these points useful. Third are the "coaching tips," which are specific steps that will accomplish the main goals of the chapter. Also, if you like summaries, turn to

Appendix A—a "cheat sheet" for Tribal Leaders; it gives the key action steps that will help you build great tribes.

We've written this book to share everything we've learned along the way. The goal of this book is for you to become a Tribal Leader without our help. The lessons we offer are ones we observed around us, so we believe we are students of Tribal Leadership, the same as everyone. That said, we hope you'll share your successes and failures with us, so that we can learn with you. Appendix C gives our contact information. What we learn from you we'll make available through our Web site (www.triballeadership.net), articles, classes (many of them through the Universities), and speeches.

The Goal of Tribal Leadership

The goal of this book is to give you the perspective and tools of a Tribal Leader: someone who can unstick the conveyor belt—and make it run faster—for whole groups of people, no matter which stage they're in. The result is more effective workplaces, greater strategic success, less stress, and more fun. In short, the point of this book is for you to build a better organization in which the best people want to work and make an impact.

The means to building great organizations is the use of these "leverage points," which are ways of unsticking people so that they naturally glide to the next stage. Unstick enough people, and you've swapped one set of tribal dynamics for a higher-performing set and a more capable tribe. Each stage gets more done and has more fun than the one before it. The ultimate expression of Tribal Leadership is companies filled with people who know how to unstick themselves and others—a tribe of Tribal Leaders.

We now turn to the main thrust of how to build greater organizations: the five tribal stages.

Key Points from This Chapter

◆ A tribe is any group of people between about 20 and 150 who know each other enough that, if they saw each other walking down the street, would stop and say "hello."

◆ They are likely people in your cell phone and in your e-mail address book.

◆ A small company is a tribe, and a large company is a tribe of tribes.

CHAPTER 2

The Five Tribal Stages

Entering Griffin Hospital in Derby, Connecticut, is like going to Nordstrom's for healthcare. The first clue that this isn't a normal healthcare company is the valet who squeegees car windows and knows many patients by name. Walk through the front entrance, and the first thing you notice is piano music, soft and elegant, coming from the baby grand in a niche just beside the front door. The second thing you notice is the smell: fresh flowers and wood. In recent years, Griffin has drawn international attention as not only a great hospital but a great employer—ranking fourth on the *Fortune* list of best places to work in its seventh year on that list.

There are many heroes in the Griffin Hospital story, but two stand out as Tribal Leaders because their efforts have gone a long way to upgrade the tribal culture. The first is President and CEO Patrick Charmel. Tall, lean, midforties, dark hair, soft-spoken, self-effacing, a caring tone in his voice, he seems a cross between a high-tech entrepreneur and a priest. Charmel started with Griffin as an intern while attending a local university, then went to Yale for his master of public health degree and returned as a full-time employee. "Some people still remember me as someone who is nineteen years old," he says. "No matter what their position, they don't mind telling me when I mess up."

The second hero is Vice President Bill Powanda, midsixties, gray, fast-talking, and charming. He is easily moved by the human side of the story. Although Griffin has many lines of communication with the community, Powanda is the perfect person to carry the flame to the outside world. He was born at Griffin and is a former state senator and former board chair of the local Chamber of Commerce. Charmel started as Powanda's intern, and they have worked together for twenty-eight years.

Today's success is far different from what long-time Griffin employees call the "perfect storm" of the mid-1980s, when the hospital had the oldest physical plant in the state, falling patient satisfaction and market share, and difficulty recruiting staff and physicians. The community was transforming from a manufacturing town in decline to a bedroom community with an influx of young, educated, mobile residents with higher expectations for their healthcare. Griffin's board authorized a community perception survey and asked local residents this question: "If there is a hospital you'd avoid, please name it." Of those who responded, 32 percent handwrote "Griffin." The hospital, it seemed, was doomed, and without any resources to stop the death spiral.

As we see again and again with Tribal Leaders, Charmel and Powanda didn't save the hospital Superman-style, swooping in to save the day. Rather, they galvanized the tribe of employees, volunteers, board members, and community leaders whose opinions mattered, and the turnaround was a tribal effort. In a sense, Charmel didn't lead it; he nudged it and then was led by it, and he humbly credits the entire Griffin team for its success. "Our success really is a testament to our culture," he said. "Looking back, it's clear that we never could have accomplished this without engaging our employees and getting them involved in the process. I think that's what distinguishes the approach."

It started with the question whether Griffin should remain independent or join another healthcare system. Powanda, glancing out
the window of his office, says, "We are a fiercely independent and
competitive community, and people are used to getting everything
they need *here,* from shopping to church."

As Griffin administrators went through their options, several
executives had their own personal "perfect storms." Charmel's father
had open-heart surgery at a New Jersey hospital. Another vice president was hospitalized after a car accident. Powanda's father-in-law
was admitted to Griffin with inoperable stomach cancer. Although
the cancer was stable, he was bleeding from what the physicians said
were inoperable ulcers located behind the tumors. For over thirty
days he sat in the critical care unit. "He lost blood and they'd put it
back in," Powanda told us, and after thirty-seven days, his surgeon
said, "Today's the day we shut off your blood supply." The patient's
wife went after him with her cane, shouting, "Don't ever come back
to this room again!" The family and their longtime primary care
doctor finally convinced a young surgeon to attempt to suture off the
ulcer. The surgery was successful, and the man went home and lived
another fourteen months before succumbing to the cancer.

"The experience was a personal life-altering event," Powanda
recalled. "It became a passion to ensure that others avoided a similar experience by creating a more humane and patient sensitive care
model for the patient and family."

Griffin decided to remain independent and to rebuild itself into a
hospital that would put the patient first. One operation at a time,
Griffin executives focused the staff on the problem and facilitated
their finding the solution. A board member argued that if the institution created satisfied patients in the maternity ward, Griffin would
keep many of them for years. But what did they want? "Let's ask
them," the board member advised.

"We went on a marketing research tear," Powanda said. "We were pioneers in the industry." Griffin launched surveys and focus groups, and Charmel and a staff member posed as husband and pregnant wife (thanks to a pillow) and toured maternity wards at nearby hospitals. "We put together a long list of what young parents wanted," Powanda recalled. It included a separate hospital entrance—since expectant mothers said they weren't sick and didn't want to be around sick people—double beds, a Jacuzzi for pain relief in early labor, family rooms with kitchens, 24/7 visiting hours, fresh flowers, a spalike atmosphere, and personalized treatment by pleasant staff.

With this long list in hand, the executives sat down to prioritize the enhancements they would offer. In a move that revealed Charmel's tribal orientation, he stopped the process and asked, an atypical edge in his voice, "What are we doing?" After an awkward moment, he continued, "We know what they want—let's give it *all* to them." Griffin's leaders agreed, and design work started on a maternity ward that would set the new standard in the Northeast.

The challenge was to involve the staff as partners, in the same way that the executives and board members were collaborating. Instead of telling employees the new vision, Charmel, then assistant to the president, and other executives led a series of all-day staff retreats, taking one twelfth of the employees at a time. In the morning, one of the executives would describe the "perfect storm." Then they would ask the staff to take the perspective of patients and to answer the question, What would you want your hospital experience to be? As Powanda says, "Lo and behold, they described a scene dramatically different from Griffin and the nation's hospitals. Open visiting, more information about their medical condition, caring staff—and they were the staff! It was an awakening for everyone." Almost every one of the twelve groups came up with the same list of what they'd want, and the chatter at the hospital began to turn toward quality, service, respect, and dignity—now the pillars of Griffin's core values.

During one part of the new building design process, Charmel suggested that Griffin build a full-scale mock-up of the critical components of the new design in a warehouse. Staff members all made suggestions on small slips of paper, eventually giving hundreds of recommendations to the architects. "To this day, people will point to a wall outlet and say, 'It used to be over there until I suggested they move it,'" Powanda adds.

Charmel, promoted to COO, clashed with the CEO, who thought the solution for Griffin was to focus on its wholly owned HMO. Charmel disagreed with the transfer of financial resources from Griffin Hospital to support growth of the HMO. This shift was thwarting patient service and damaging Griffin's ability to fulfill its mission. The fight resulted in Charmel's termination.

With the popular COO fired, a revolution began. An underground employee newsletter appeared, urging staff members to "Wear a Yellow Ribbon. Save Griffin and bring back Pat [Charmel]." After three months of turmoil, including petitions, votes of no confidence, and community meetings, the board, acting on advice from consultants and an investigation committee, asked the CEO and executive vice president to resign. The board asked Charmel to return.

On the day Charmel came back to Griffin, now as interim CEO, over four hundred staff members, volunteers, community leaders, and members of the press welcomed him back with a surprise reception at the hospital entrance filled with yellow balloons. It was an emotional "tribal moment" for Griffin.

The level of loyalty to Griffin and Charmel is stunning. It survived the layoffs that followed his return, difficult decisions including closing the money-losing HMO, and even a potential panic after the nation's fifth anthrax death at Griffin in 2001. As a result, so many people want to see the Griffin miracle that the hospital now charges visitors from other hospitals who want to use the Griffin's patient-centered care model within their organization. Teams representing almost six hundred hospitals have paid to see Griffin for themselves. The U.S. Secretary of Health and Human Services appointed Charmel to the National Advisory Council for Research and Quality in 2005. Charmel's office features seven years of *Fortune* magazine best employer covers. Charmel is blunt in his belief that it is the employees who have put Griffin on the *Fortune* list as a result of their pride in the organization and their dedication to those Griffin serves. Powanda's office features pictures of himself with Bill Clinton and Colin Powell, as well as a "Toga Man of the Year Award" from the Connecticut Senate for outstanding civic and community service. Both men turn the credit back to the tribe, which Powanda says includes not only the Griffin family but the community as well. When we asked Charmel about his greatest achievement, it took several seconds of thought before he answered. When he did, he said, "Seeing people live the philosophy. They are my inspiration."

Tribal Leadership Up Close

What did Charmel and Powanda do that was different from what most leaders do? First, they spent most of their efforts building strong relationships between Griffin's tribal members—its employees, volunteers, and patients. Second, instead of telling people what to do, they engineered experiences (such as the retreats) in which staff members would look at the same issues they were dealing with, so that strategy became *everyone's* problem. Third, they got out of the way and let people contribute in their own way to the emerging tribal goals.

Most important—and hardest to see—they unstuck Griffin's tribal culture and nudged it forward, stage by stage, until people charged after problems with the zeal of converts, not the indifference of hired guns.

In a sentence, this is what Charmel and Powanda did: they built the tribe, and as they did, people recognized them as leaders. The more Charmel and Powanda put the tribe first, the more people respected and identified them, giving their efforts more credibility and impact. This is Tribal Leadership in a nutshell, and this is what you'll be able to do after mastering the principles in this book.

A visitor who talks with Griffin leaders and staff hears what sounds like false modesty. Charmel and Powanda are adamant that the praise should go to the employees, while people at all levels credit these two (and many others) with the success. Who is right? Tribal Leadership says both. Without the leaders building the tribe, a culture of mediocrity will prevail. Without an inspired tribe, leaders are impotent.

Today, when patients come in, they aren't treated as customers but rather as members of the tribe. Doctors build relationships between patients and nurses. Volunteers talk up the quality of the physicians to patients. Administrators bring people together and allow the tribe to decide what's best. Years after the perfect storm passed, Griffin is a hospital with wall-to-wall leaders.

Every tribe has a dominant culture, which we can peg on a one-to-five scale, with Stage Five being most desirable. All things being equal, a Five culture will always outperform a Four culture, which will outperform a Three, and so on. People and groups move only one stage at a time, and the actions that advance people from Stage One to Stage Two are different from those that advance them from Two to Three. Since each stage has a unique set of leverage points that will nudge people forward, most of the "universal principles" from the "log cabin management books" work in only one stage. Try them in another stage and your efforts will fail. If tribes are the most powerful vehicles within companies, cultures are their engines.

Charmel and Powanda inherited a set of overlapping tribes (remember, a tribe is at most 150 people) with an engine in need of repair. In Tribal Leadership language, they had dominant Stage Two cultures. The leaders unstuck people and guided them to a Three. They used a different set of leverage points to bump people to a Four. On its best days—and Griffin has many best days—it operates at a Five.

Each culture has its own way of speaking, or "theme," that appears whenever people talk, e-mail, joke around, or just pass one another in the hallway. Griffin reveals its tribal cultures when the valet remembers people's names, and when the nurses introduce patients to doctors as if they were introducing dear friends.

After reading the first part of this book, you'll be able to hear these themes any time two people have even a single conversation. We now turn to the five tribal stages in detail.

Stage One

Fortunately, most professionals skip Stage One (only about 2 percent of American professionals operate here at any given point), which is the mind-set that creates street gangs and people who come to work with shotguns. If people at Stage One had T-shirts, they would read "life sucks," and what comes out of their mouths support this adage. People at this stage are despairingly hostile, and they band together to get ahead in a violent and unfair world. Although most people reading this book will not have been in Stage One, they've seen it on HBO's *Oz* or Fox's *Prison Break*. Most anthropologists say that human society started at Stage One, clans scratching out an existence while fighting with one another. We're not going in depth on this stage because organizations usually don't hire Stage One individuals, and when they do, they are quick to expel them. Chapter 4 goes into what you need to know about Stage One—how to spot it and how to assist people in it to move forward.

We've consulted to several organizations with Stage One tribes. One disappeared after a series of accounting scandals. Another had constant problems with employees stealing money—seemingly without remorse. A third was so stressed out that no one was surprised when an employee came to work with a shotgun.

Stage Two

In 25 percent of workplace tribes, the dominant culture is Stage Two, which is a quantum leap from Stage One. People operating at Stage Two use language centered on *"my* life sucks." People in this cultural stage are passively antagonistic; they cross their arms in judgment yet never really get interested enough to spark any passion. Their laughter is quietly sarcastic and resigned. The Stage Two talk is that they've seen it all before and watched it all fail. A person at Stage Two will often try to protect his or her people from the intrusion of management. The mood that results from Stage Two's theme, "my life sucks," is a cluster of apathetic victims.

If you've ever walked into a meeting and presented a new idea with passion, only to get back looks of passivity, you've probably walked into a Stage Two culture. Stage Two is what we see when we watch *The Office* or walk into the Department of Motor Vehicles. There is little to no innovation and almost no sense of urgency, and people almost never hold one another accountable for anything. During the "perfect storm" at Griffin, the company had a dominant Stage Two culture.

Most large companies have pockets of Stage Two, often divisions that don't have an impact on strategy or direction. Although Stage Two can appear in any discipline, we've seen it most often in human resources, procurement, and accounting. That said, we've also seen Stage Two in boards of directors, executive suites, sales, and operations.

Years ago, we consulted to an agency of the United States government. When we showed up, employees and managers would stand in their doors of their offices and entrances to their cubicles, looking out at a shared hallway. People looked as if they just woke up (and many had). They would hold coffee mugs flaunting messages like "I'd rather be fishing" and "I live for the weekends." No amount of team building, motivational speeches, discussions of core values, or new strategic plans would make any difference with this tribe. It was solidly locked in Stage Two. As a result, very little got done. The tribe produced few new ideas and almost never followed them up.

The focus of Tribal Leadership is to move Stage Two to Three before asking anything new of the group. Chapter 5 gives the leverage points.

Stage Three

The theme of Stage Three, the dominant culture in 49 percent of workplace tribes in the United States, is "I'm great." Or, more fully, "I'm great, and you're not." Normally, doctors operate at this level on their best days, as do professors, attorneys, and salespeople. Within the Stage Three culture, knowledge is power, so people hoard it, from client contacts to gossip about the company. People at Stage Three have to win, and for them winning is personal. They'll outwork and outthink their competitors on an individual basis. The mood that results is a collection of "lone warriors," wanting help and support and being continually disappointed that others don't have their ambition or skill. Because they have to do the tough work (remembering that others just aren't as savvy), their complaint is that they don't have enough time or competent support.

> **TECHNICAL NOTE:** *At each cultural stage, there is a specific "fingerprint" made up of language that people use and observable behavior toward others in the tribe. These two almost always correlate perfectly. As a result of lots of people operating together at this cultural stage, a certain mood results. People trained in Tribal Leadership—and you are on your way to being one of them—can detect this mood within a few minutes of walking into a work group.*

The gravity that holds people at Stage Three is the addictive "hit" they get from winning, besting others, being the smartest and most successful. Before we judge people at this stage as having big egos, we have to remember that society made them—us—this way. From the time we enter school, the one who knows "2+2 is 4" gets a gold star; then it's our ABCs and a smiley face, an algebra test and an A+, SATs and admission into Stanford, letters of recommendation and an MBA, a great interview and a job offer, and an almost postcoital glow of success. If thirty years of reinforcement aren't enough, go to Barnes and Noble and look over the books in the business section. From Machiavelli to Robert Greene's *The 48 Laws of Power* to anything with Donald Trump's picture on it, helping people get to and maintain Stage Three is a multi-billion-dollar industry. Once Griffin moved people to the point where they took individual responsibility for crafting a patient experience, they had moved to Stage Three.

Like most professionals, our careers have been spent in and among Stage Three. It's most common in pockets of companies where success is measured on an individual basis: in sales and among executives. We've seen it in architecture, real estate, health-care, law, and a place we know very well—the university.

A typical faculty meeting shows the limitation of Stage Three. One professor after another gives his opinion and says what he thinks should be done. The result is that most educational pro-grams look as if they had been designed by a committee—because they were. Students often ask if faculty ever speak to one another, and the answer is "not often"—at least about important topics. People show up, do their individual research, teach their classes in a manner described by IDEO's David Kelley as a "sage on stage," and then leave. Staff members often gripe that professors see only their little corner of the world, and in many cases the criticism is legitimate. Organizations run by Stage Three behavior feel dehu-manizing. As one former aerospace manager told us, "I thought I was loved until I left. Now I don't even get a Christmas card from anyone."

As with Stage Two, no amount of team building will turn this group of self-described star players into a team. Give it a new strat-egy, and tribal members will show either that they embrace it more than others or that they don't need it. Again, the focus of Tribal Leadership is to upgrade the tribal culture first. Chapters 6 and 7 give the leverage points for Stage Three.

Stage Four

The gulf between "I'm great" (Stage Three) and "we're great" (Stage Four) is huge, Grand Canyon huge. This level represents 22 percent of workplace tribal cultures, where the theme of people's communi-cation is "we're great."

Although Griffin spikes into Stage Five, it is mostly a Stage Four company. When two people at the hospital meet in the hallways, they're excited about being with another member of the tribe. Take the tribe away, and the person's sense of self suffers a loss. As we watch, Bill Powanda is fully himself, and people are fully themselves. No corporate cult here. Everyone seems happy, inspired, and genuine. You see it on people's faces as Charmel works the room, and it's equally true that the room works Charmel. Leading a tribe with a dominant Stage Four culture, the leader feels pulled by the group. At times, Tribal Leadership at this stage is effortless. A most impressive characteristic and display of confidence as we toured Griffin was that everybody—staff, volunteers, doctors—made eye contact with us, which is highly unusual in medicine.

As we watch a Griffin meeting from a distance, the overall vibe of the room is "tribal pride," which is the mood that results from the Stage Four culture. A "we're great" tribe always has an adversary— the need for it is hardwired into the DNA of this cultural stage. In fact, the full expression of the theme is "we're great, and they're not." For USC football, the "you're not" is usually UCLA (and in good years, whichever team is contending for the national championship). For Apple's operating systems engineers, it's Microsoft (although this is changing as Apple has moved to using Intel processors). Often, it's another group within the company. A tribe will seek its own competitor, and the only one who has influence over the target is the Tribal Leader. Powanda has argued that Griffin's only worthy competitor is the entire way of doing business in healthcare. The rule for Stage Four is this: the bigger the foe, the more powerful the tribe. Griffin would not be the success it is if it were to target a single hospital as its rival.

People often ask Charmel and Powanda how they can lead the way they do. The real answer is, lead by building a Stage Four critical mass culture in the tribe, and then they'll recognize you as a leader. The other part of the answer is to remember that these are consecutive stages, so attempt to build a Griffin-style culture only with people who are already at Stage Three. Charmel and Powanda had to move the tribe from Stage Two to Three before instilling the "we're great" hallmarks of Four. We will show how this is done in later chapters.

Chapter 8 is the realm of Tribal Leadership. When groups get to this point, they see themselves as a tribe, with a common purpose. They commit to shared core values and hold one another accountable. They will not tolerate *The Office*–style performance or the personal agenda of Stage Three. Fully three-quarters of tribes operate below Stage Four, and those in the zone of Tribal Leadership haven't stabilized at this level. As a result, they oscillate in and out of "I'm great" (Stage Three). The purpose of this book is to build great companies, and this means getting you and your tribe to Stage Four. Since tribes move only one stage a time, only those at Four can make leaps into the most advanced stage, described below.

TECHNICAL NOTE: *In the West, the word "tribe" is increasingly being used to represent a social unit, bigger than a group but smaller than a society. That is how we're using the word. Many people who have done work in Africa, including* Spiral Dynamics *author, Don Beck, cautioned us against the use of the word "tribal." Having been to Africa, we understand the concern. "Tribalism" (in a different sense than we mean the term) has been responsible for torture, war, and genocide. To be clear, Tribal Leadership for us means Stage Four, a culture based on a "we're great" language screen emphasizing shared core values and interdependent strategies. Tribalism, as the word is often used in parts of the developing world, refers to the violence and despairing hostility of Stage One. Ethnic cleansing and other horrors are inconceivable in a Stage Four tribe.*

Stage Five

Stage Four is a launching pad for Stage Five. When we explain this last stage, which reflects less than 2 percent of workplace tribal cultures, we see skeptical looks coming back at us. Stage Five's T-shirt would read "life is great," and they haven't been doing illicit substances. Their language revolves around infinite potential and how the group is going to make history—not to beat a competitor, but because doing so will make a global impact. This group's mood is "innocent wonderment," with people in competition with what's possible, not with another tribe.

Teams at Stage Five have produced miraculous innovations. The team that produced the first Macintosh was at Stage Five, and we've seen this mood at Amgen. This stage is pure leadership, vision, and inspiration. After a short burst of activity, Stage Five teams recede to Stage Four to regroup and attend to infrastructure issues before possibly returning to Five. In sports, these bursts win Olympic gold and Super Bowl rings. In business, these explosions of leadership

Stage	Mood	Theme
5	Innocent Wonderment	"Life is great"
4	Tribal Pride	"We're great (and they're not)"
3	Lone Warrior	"I'm great (and you're not)"
2	Apathetic Victim	"My life sucks"
1	Despairing Hostility	"Life sucks"

TABLE 1

make history. Griffin is a model for the best organizations in the world as its culture oscillates between Stage Four and Stage Five.

Table 1 summarizes the five cultures.

You Can Take the Person Out of the Tribe . . .

In the Austin Powers movies, Mini Me was always a loyal follower—but you had to keep up with who had his loyalty. When backing Dr. Evil, Mini Me would stop at nothing to kill or harass Austin Powers. When his allegiance switched to Austin, our little hero then attempted to take out his old master's influence. It might be said that we are all Mini Me's for the cultures that dominate our tribes.

When a person soaks long enough in a Stage Three tribe, she becomes an ambassador for that culture, even when moved to other environments. At the same time, the culture the person soaked in was shaped by her influence. People's default stage, and the cultures around them, mold each other. Over time, the language the person speaks and that of the tribal stage sync up. You might say that Mini Me and his boss shape each other.

We can predict the performance of the tribe by counting the number of people who speak the language of each stage, and noticing who is in positions of leadership. The one factor that makes Griffin extraordinary (after its turnaround) is the high number of Stage Four people who talk Stage Four language. If someone at Griffin were to talk the language of Stage One or Two, the tribe would reject that person. When the old CEO fired Charmel, the tribe refused to accept the decision. That's the power of tribes: they accept who we are, or they mold us. If we reject their advice, they ostracize us. Very few people have the ability to change a tribe's dominant stage. Those people are Tribal Leaders.

Most companies we've seen have tribes that are mixtures of

Stages Two, Three, and Four, with most people hovering around the dividing line between "my life sucks" (Stage Two) and "I'm great" (Stage Three). Here's what results:

A battle ensues between the personal agenda-driven people at Stage Three and the vision-driven people who talk Stage Four, with those at Stage Two largely sitting back to see who wins. Executives get frustrated that change is so hard to implement. Senior managers read Jack Welch's books and fire the bottom 10 percent of performers. Amazingly, people just redistribute to the stages as other people leave. The company buys hundreds of copies of *Who Moved My Cheese?* or sends its people to time management training. On top of this tribal chatter, the CEO fights to make quarterly earnings, and the head of human resources wonders why trust and communication are always the weak points on the climate survey. People complain about "all the politics around here," but despite money spent on training and time spent away from work, things never seem to change.

So far, we've seen that people always form tribes and that the dominant cultural stage determines effectiveness. The way to move the entire tribe's performance to the next level is to move the critical mass to the next stage. This process involves moving many people forward, individually, by facilitating them to use a different language, and to shift their behavior accordingly. As that happens, the tribe itself will produce a new, self-sustaining culture. When it gets to Stage Four—like Griffin—it won't tolerate people who talk Stage Three or below.

Each person in this tribe is on a journey through the stages, and the tribe makes that journey long or short. The job of you as Tribal Leader is to expedite this journey for each person, so that a new critical mass forms at Stage Four. When that happens, the tribe will see itself as a tribe, just as Griffin does, and embrace you as the leader. This is Tribal Leadership in a nutshell.

When we refer to working with individuals in this book, we do not mean changing their beliefs, attitudes, motivation, or ideas—or anything else that isn't directly observable. Tribal Leadership focuses on two things, and only two things: the words people use and the types of relationships they form. (We'll warn you now: there is one exception to this rule, which is in Stage Five.) Moving a person from one stage to the next means intervening in a certain way to help this person change her language and set up different types of relationships. As that happens to one person and then another, the entire tribe goes through a change as a new cultural stage becomes dominant. We call these ways of intervening leverage points, and they are summarized in Appendix A for all five cultural stages.

> **TECHNICAL NOTE:** *Unlike most researchers, we weren't interested in where people came from—what psychologists call their socioeconomic status. We ignored their age, gender, income, and ethnicity. As our research base expanded to include people in Asia, Europe, and Africa we even ignored people's native language. We didn't profile their personality type, measure their IQ, or ask about their education level. Rather, our research stems from an ancient way of understanding people: that they—we—create our reality with language. Appendix B gives the full version of this story, including the scholars we're indebted to, but for now it's enough to say this: when a person looks out at the world, he sees it filtered through a screen of his words, and this process is as invisible to him as water is to fish. We see the world and our words in one impression, as if we're looking at a forest through a green filter. We can't see what's really green and what's not. If we were to walk around with the filter in our eye long enough, we'd forget it was there, and life would just be green.*

A Journey through the Stages

People come to this book at various stages, and that's natural. The point is to learn the language and customs of each stage, to inspire others along as they help you along, graduating everyone up to the "we're great" language of Stage Four, which is the launching pad for Stage Five. You literally cannot make this journey alone—your tribe will either help you or prevent your forward movement. In fact, you can move forward only by bringing others with you. Tribes are more influential than individuals, no matter how smart or talented they are. As you move forward either you will become a Tribal Leader—upgrading your tribe with you—or you will stall. The only exception to that rule is that there are people who have changed themselves by switching to a new tribe.

Without any external coaching, people advance through stages very slowly. Children usually start school at Stage Two on that first day of kindergarten—disconnected, trapped, and wanting to go home. In short, their lives suck, and that's what they say. As they make friends, paint with those huge brushes, and learn the ABCs, they feel accomplished and rise to Stage Three, saying that they're pretty great. Most formal education, by design, keeps people at Stage Three all the way through graduate school, with each course showing them what they don't know (often bumping them back to Stage Two for a time), imparting knowledge, and allowing them to prove they have learned it through exams and papers. Depending on their grade and how much they care, they graduate somewhere in the Two to Three range.

When people take their first job, they talk about their achievements but also miss their friends, and again they are in the range of Stage Two to Three. People often feel stuck for a while, or they have a setback when they start saying the boss is an ass (and that their lives therefore suck). People regress to the ineffectiveness of Stage Two; perhaps they spend the weekends talking about how true *Dilbert* is and that they can't do anything about it. Then they find their groove and some success, and they move up early to mid-Stage Three, again exuding "I'm great" language. Many people live their entire lives in Stage Three, eventually mentoring people at Stage Two as their way to "give back." This mentoring often sounds a lot like Donald Trump ("here's what I would do"), only nicer.

Professionals usually cap out at Stage Three. Attorneys, accountants, physicians, brokers, salespeople, professors, and even the clergy are evaluated by what they know and do, and these measuring points are the hallmarks of Stage Three. "Teams" at this point mean a star and a supporting cast—surgeon and nurses, senior attorney and associates, minister and deacons, professor and TAs.

People start the climb to Stage Four in one of two ways. The first is that they have an epiphany that Stage Three won't get them the success they crave, and then they seek out a stronger community. The second, common in high technology and the sciences, is that they join a technical project that is bigger than one person can take on. The group that forms is much closer to a real team—more than the "star and support cast" of Stage Three. As people see the results of this collaboration they adapt and become full contributors. Until the mid-1980s, such groups were the exception. As the complexity of tasks and their technological requirements have soared, people have been pushed into Stage Four. Today, business schools believe their mission is to turn out team players—although the evidence suggests they are really turning out Stage Three people who can act like Stage Four individuals.

Chapter 7 delves into the set of insights that people need to make the leap to Stage Four. These epiphanies hit at many levels: intellectual, emotional, even spiritual. In that chapter, we get serious about the divide that keeps most American professionals speaking "I'm great" on their best days. That chapter explores nuisances that will send some of you reaching for Tylenol to soothe your headache—the same headache we had in interpreting data and making sense of what makes truly great leaders.

The Promise of Moving to the Next Stage

The tribal cultures form a bell curve with its peak at Stage Three. Shifting the center of this distribution from Stage Three to Four makes the tribe visible to itself, and others, as was the case in Griffin and in the young American colonies in the time of George Washington. We've whispered in the ears of dozens of Tribal Leaders as they have created stable Stage Four cultures, resulting in the following benefits:

◆ People collaborate and work toward a noble cause, propelled from their values.

◆ Fear and stress go down as the "interpersonal friction" of working together decreases.

◆ The entire tribe shifts from resisting leadership to seeking it out.

◆ People seek employment in the company and stay, taking the company a long way toward winning the war for talent.

◆ People's engagement in work increases, and they go from "quit on the job but still on the payroll" to fully participating.

◆ Organizational learning becomes effortless, with the tribe actively teaching its members the latest thinking and practices.

◆ People's overall health statistics improve. Injury rates and sick days go down.

◆ Setting and implementing a successful competitive strategy becomes stunningly easy as people's aspirations, knowledge of the market, and creativity are unlocked and shared.

◆ Most exciting for us is that people report feeling more alive and having more fun.

In short, companies with tribes at the later stages earn more, employ better performers (and upgrade the performers they have), serve their markets, and have a blast doing it. Everyone wins—except those individuals unwilling or unable to adapt from Stages Two and Three.

The next chapter is your navigation guide to this book. Most corporate tribes are mostly at Stage Three or below. Where's yours? The next chapter will help you find out, give you a few rules of the Tribal road, and then direct you to the chapter that will give you the tools to nudge your group to the next level.

Key Points from This Chapter

◆ What makes some tribes more effective than others is culture. Each time people speak, their words exhibit the characteristics of one of five tribal stages. Stage Five outperforms Four, which accomplishes more than Three, which gets more done than Two, which is more effective than One.

◆ A medium to large tribe (50 to 150 people) usually has several cultural stages operating at the same time.

◆ Tribal Leadership focuses on language and behavior within a culture.

◆ This book does not address cognitions, beliefs, attitudes, or other factors we cannot directly observe.

CHAPTER 3

The Tribal Leadership Navigation System

About three-quarters of workplace tribes have a cultural Stage Three or below. The goal of this book is for you to upgrade your tribes to Stage Four. This chapter is your navigation system, showing you which chapter to jump to find the leverage points to nudge it forward faster, and how to emerge as a Tribal Leader.

Tribal Locator System

The key in locating your tribes is to listen for how *most people* talk, to notice how *most people* structure their work relationships. You'll see elements of many cultural stages in your tribes, so look for what is most common.

Signs of Stage One. Most people talk as though they are alienated from organizational concerns. When they cluster together, they form isolated gangs that operate by their own rules, often based on absolute loyalty to the group. Many people are socially alienated, never talking to anyone. The theme of their words is that life has given them a bad deal, so it's ok to do whatever it takes to survive. There may be acts of violence, such as fistfights or extreme verbal abuse. Minor acts of theft or vandalism are a problem. If this description represents your work groups, they are stuck in Stage One. **Go to Chapter 4 and read through the end of the book.**

Signs of Stage Two. People talk as though they are disconnected from organizational concerns, seeming to not care about what's going on. They do the minimum to get by, showing almost no initiative or passion. They cluster together in groups that encourage passive-aggressive behavior (talking about how to get out of work, or how to shine the boss on) while telling people in charge that they are on board with organizational initiatives. The theme of their communication is that no amount of trying or effort will change their circumstances, and giving up is the only enlightened thing to do. From a managerial perspective, nothing seems to work—team building, training, even selective terminations appear to do nothing to change the prevailing mood. The culture is an endless well of unmet needs, gripes, disappointments, and repressed anger. **Go to Chapter 5 and continue reading to the end of the book.**

Signs of Stage Three. People engage in anything that's going on, with energy and commitment, but when you listen closely, they talk mostly about themselves and focus on appearing smarter and better than others. They think they're focused on team concerns, but their actions show their interest is personal. People tend to form two-person relationships, so if they manage a group of ten, they have ten relationships. They rarely bring people together, they resist sharing information except when it's necessary, and they pride themselves on being better informed than others. Winning is all that matters, and winning is personal. People at this stage complain that they don't have enough time or support and that the people around them aren't as competent or as committed as they are. **Stage Three has a symbiotic relationship with Stage Two, so it's important to start there. Go to Chapter 5 and continue reading to the end of the book.**

Signs of Stage Four. Teams are the norm, focused around shared values and a common purpose. Information moves freely throughout the group. People's relationships are built on shared values. They tend to ask, "what's the next right thing to do?" and to build ad hoc partnerships to accomplish what's important at the moment. Their language focuses on "we," not "me." If two people get in a squabble, a third will step in and repair the relationship rather than create a personal following for himself. Unlike Stage Two, the group is composed of people who have played the Stage Three game and won—and are ready for genuine partnerships. **Your first job is to make sure each person is stable at Stage Four, as most groups at this level crash down to Stage Three when under stress. Go to Chapter 7 and read to the end of the book.**

Signs of Stage Five. Your tribes hardly ever refer to the competition, except to note how remarkable their own culture is by comparison, and how far their results outstrip industry norms. The theme of communication is limitless potential, bounded only by imagination and group commitment. People in this culture can find a way to work with almost anyone, provided their commitment to values is at the same intensity as their own. (Unlike Stage Four, the focus isn't on "our values" but on resonant values.) There is almost no fear, stress, or workplace conflict. People talk as though the world is watching them, which may well be the case, as their results are making history. **Your job is to make sure the infrastructure to maintain these leaps to Stage Five is in place. Go to Chapter 9 and read to the end of the book.**

How to Become a Tribal Leader

The people who use the stage-specific leverage points to upgrade the tribal culture emerge as Tribal Leaders. Such individuals, we've found in our research, do a lot of work on themselves as they make changes in the tribe. This "Tribal Leader prep work" includes

◆ Learning the language and customs of all five cultural stages. Look at the next six chapters as a travel guide for all five lands.

◆ Listening for which tribal members speak which language—in essence, who is at what stage?

◆ Moving yourself forward, so that your own "center of gravity" is at least Stage Four. You can do this only by talking a different language and shifting the structure of relationships around you. Chapter 7 is the most important in the book—if you let it, it will nudge you into seeing the value of Stage Four and the hollowness of Stage Three. We suggest you spend some time thinking about the content of that chapter and discussing it with important people in your life. Remember that Tribal Leadership is not about changing ideas or gaining knowledge; it is about changing language and relationships. It's not about intellectualizations; it's about actions.

◆ Build a support network around you so that you are stable at Stage Four. Chapters 9 and 10 are the keys here.

◆ Take these actions as you upgrade the tribe around you. Remember that as a person builds the tribe to Stage Four she is recognized as the Tribal Leader, which gives her the ability to bring the group to higher levels of success.

Once you have completed the "prep work" on yourself and have gotten a core group of people in your tribe to Stage Four, there are shortcuts that stabilize them *very* quickly so that they don't fall back to Stage Three. Chapters 9 through 11 explain these techniques. Pay special attention to triads, values, developing a noble cause, and building a tribal strategy. Leaders can upgrade most tribes one full level within ninety days, boosting everything from revenue to employee satisfaction.

In the next five chapters, we will go through each stage and show *exactly* how Tribal Leaders advance individuals within the tribe to the next level of effectiveness. We now turn to the language and customs of each culture, and the next chapter takes us to Stage One.

Key Points from This Chapter

◆ Each cultural stage has its own way of speaking, types of behavior, and structures of relationships.

◆ Tribal Leaders do two things: (1) listen for which cultures exist in their tribes and (2) upgrade those tribes using specific leverage points. (The chapters that follow detail each cultural stage and present the leverage points to move to the next stage.)

PART II

Your Journey as a Leader: Leading Others Through the Stages

CHAPTER 4

Stage One: On the Verge of a Meltdown

F rank Jordan's childhood was spent on the brink. His mother died in 1945, when he was ten years old. In a time before foster homes, he was sent to live with a series of relatives and then with families of friends he made in school. He lived in eight different San Francisco neighborhoods in five years, until he was fifteen. "I had a lot of time on my hands, and that's dangerous," he told us, "but when I turned about twelve, I ran into a Boys & Girls Club, and if it hadn't been for that, who knows where I would have ended up." As it turns out, Jordan ended up in some amazing places—as chief of police and then mayor of San Francisco. Now at age seventy-one, he is a Tribal Leader in the Gordon and Betty Moore Foundation (Moore was the founder of Intel), which invests in projects that will benefit future generations.

Many parts of Jordan's story are exceptional, and we'll get to know him more in later chapters. Perhaps the feature that stands out the most is that he never gives up on anyone, especially on the people many of us pretend don't exist: those at Stage One.

Although Stage One accounts for fewer than 2 percent of American professionals (employed people in our studies), the percentage of those people in society is much larger. If you ask people in it what they think about life (as we did), you'll hear "It's not fair," "I can't cut a break," and "You do what you have to do to survive." In this chapter, we'll look into Stage One—what it looks like from the inside, how it works, and what you can do to nudge people out of it.

Stage One

Each stage has a beginning, a middle, and an end. At the earliest point of Stage One, we find a cluster of people who all buy into the same view—that "life sucks"—and they act accordingly. For many readers of this book, early Stage One is as foreign as life on Mars, but it is a reality for millions of Americans, many of whom end up employed at some point. Companies need to know what to do about Stage One, and our society has to address it.

As a former police officer, Jordan sometimes receives cold welcomes at San Francisco community events. "You're the problem," people sometimes tell him. "Why?" is his question. As though Jordan were the entire police force, he hears "You arrested my brother" and "You broke down my door."

"You have to see it from their side," he told us. "There's a resentment because they feel life is upside down, and they don't know who else to take it out on. So you listen, and listen, and listen." Once he hears all the reasons why people distrust police, he'll say, "I have been there. I don't know how difficult your situation is, but I've had some difficult situations, too."

As he describes his life to community groups and to children one-on-one, he tells about many of his childhood friends who ended up in violence and prison. He told us, "Some of my friends were stealing cars, and money out of their mothers' and fathers' wallets. Some started to shoplift. It starts so easily. We'd find someone coming out of a side door at a theater, and we'd slip in and see movies for free. If you continue down that road, it's how you end up in the wrong crowd." We would change the end of his sentence to "a Stage One tribe."

"If I talk to a group of forty-five people, I might reach five," he says, a note of desperation in his voice. "And then another five, but what else can you do?" When he's successful, he often gets them involved in the Boys & Girls Clubs, where, as he says, "They have mentors and teachers for everything." Jordan is right—the best way to jump out of early Stage One—the zone of prisons and gangs—is to become involved in tribes with a later dominant stage.

In another city thousands of miles away, Tom Mahoney, Charise Valente, and Brian Sexton have the job of keeping the rest of us safe from early Stage One. They are prosecutors in the gang unit of the Illinois state's attorney's office in Chicago. Tom dresses like a banker and always has a joke at the ready; Charise looks like Mariska Hargitay (who plays a female detective on *Law & Order: Special Victims Unit*), complete with jeans and a large belt buckle. Brian, a tall aging athlete with the boyish air of a choirboy, is the supervisor of the group. Tom and Charise are deputy supervisors, and their group totals seventeen prosecutors.

The usual pattern is that a kid is born into a family with a gang history—the uncle, father, even grandfather, is a gang member. There's nothing to do in the neighborhood, and because the kid often lacks a father figure, the gang becomes a surrogate family. They get busted for property crimes and spend some time in juvenile hall. When they get out, they have earned "rank" in the gangs. Brian notes, "At some point, the value system gets all screwed up. They can make minimum wage at McDonalds or thousand dollars a day doing drug sales."

The prosecutors know Stage One well. According to Tom and Charise, Stage One is not based on lack of intelligence, as many people outside it may think. In fact, while most gang members lack education, some are brilliant, such as one gang that developed an elaborate strategy to commit mortgage fraud. Some of their members pirated a Christian radio station, played uncut obscene rap music, and inserted code words to warn their members if the police were coming or send word out that there would be a shooting later in the day.

Every once in a while, the gang would try to intimidate a witness, as in one case when sixty people showed up at the court wearing white T-shirts and jeans instead of gang colors. They were trying to scare witnesses and the jury, many of whom lived in the same neighborhood.

The three prosecutors are passionate about their work; yet, when they talk about the lifestyle of the many people in gangs, their faces change to looks of concern, empathy, and sadness. "These kids are usually neglected or abused," Charise said, "and they really don't feel they have a choice."

"The cost of this lifestyle is prison or death," Brian said, his two deputies agreeing. "It's tragic."

Exploring Stage One

We asked people in Stage One to tell us about "life," and we listened to what words they associated with it. We heard "not fair," "shit," "pointless," and "f----- up." The most common word we heard was "sucks." People at Stage One don't *believe* life sucks because for them it *does* suck. They think they are reporting the way it is. In fact, their view of life is a direct consequence of the language they use.

Early in our research, we were doing a consulting project for a youth center that helps to get kids out of gangs. Dave sat with someone new—"fresh off the streets," as the staff described him. As often happens when people with different language systems sit down, they couldn't communicate at all. Dave tried to give him a pep talk, and the boy shifted his weight, leaned on an elbow, and said, "Man, you just don't get it at all." He was right. In fact, neither of them got it.

It was like shining a red light into a green filter. No matter how much a person says it's really red, it still looks green to the person on the other side of the lens. No matter how much Dave said life doesn't suck, for that young man, it *did* suck, and from his perspective, Dave was just stupid for not seeing it.

Stage One: A View from the Inside

So what is it like to live inside Stage One? From our research, it goes something like this. Life sucks, so there's no point to values, vision, or morality. In fact, these seem like con games designed to make us miss the obvious truth of life, which is that it isn't fair, it's a vile place, and we all die. Sure, life would be better if everyone followed the game, but at its core, life sucks, so it's both better and easier to give in to the reality of the situation. As the prosecutors told us, people at Stage One don't feel that they've chosen this way of living; rather, they have recognized life as it really is.

COACHING TIP: Emphasize choice. *Frank Jordan told us: "I tell people they have a choice, and at first they don't believe me. But I say, 'I'm like you; I grew up with one parent and not much to do, and I chose a life of service, and so can you.'" There are two aspects of his pitch that are noteworthy. First, he doesn't look down on people, no matter their cultural stage, and as a result he slowly builds rapport. Second, he emphasizes*

> *the one thing that Stage One doesn't see: choice. As he told us:*
> *"If people can see that they have a choice, they sometimes*
> *choose a life better than gangs and drugs."*

Stage One is a place where people feel that they are cut off from others. It's as though life is happening "over there," and they aren't invited. At its deepest level, it takes the attitude that the only really enlightened people are the ones over here who know that what's going on over there is a sham, so it's actually *better* to be over here, away from the hypocrisy. After all, life is going to end badly, so what's the point of pretending otherwise? This is the viewpoint people express through their words.

All of this leads to a mood of despairing hostility. People give in to their desires. They act against their values, and everything is permissible: violence, suicide, drugs, any kind of sex. If indulged long enough, these appetites turn into addictions, reinforcing the person's view that life sucks.

One of the addictions people surrender to is that *they're special.* Many of the people we interviewed in doing our research said, with anger in their voices, that their teachers didn't recognize their gifts, so they left school. Their friends don't see their uniqueness, so they aren't really friends. Stage One is where people embrace this feeling of being different to the point where their functional tribes (with a dominant Stage Two and beyond) disown them. They are alienated, adrift, but also free to act on any impulse.

As we've seen in our empirical research, Stage One can only lead to one of three places: a Stage One tribe (e.g., a gang), death, or Stage Two. Prisons, we learned in our research, are mostly Stage One cultures. (There are obvious exceptions—Nelson Mandela was clearly at Stage Four, if not Five, when he was in prison in South Africa, spending his time teaching fellow inmates to read, raising his fellow prisoners to at least Stage Two.) Sadly, most people at early Stage One leave it only by dying.

Early Stage One

Early Stage One is a place where people's tribes are exclusively Stage One. They arrive at Stage One in two different ways. First, they descend into this stage, and their tribe (made up of people at later stages) disowns them. They are lost, alienated, and alone, and a Stage One tribe adopts them. Since for all of us our tribe tells us who we are, the Stage One tribe grinds into them that "life sucks." As the prosecutors told us, one of the few rules of gangs is loyalty, so they find they can't leave even if they wanted to.

The second way they enter early Stage One is that they feel their tribe doesn't really "get" them; it doesn't see how special they are. Another tribe—at Stage One—does see their talents, and they switch.

Early Stage One calls our prison system into question. People enter prison at all stages, but most dominant prison cultures are at Stage One. As people do their time, their new tribe tells them how life works and who they are. They leave prison, now disowned by the people who used to be in their tribe (including their families), and they drift to dominant Stage One tribes. Our prison system literally drives people to the bottom of Stage One. This situation becomes a problem for the organizations that employ them.

Middle Stage One

People at the middle of the stage usually descend from Stage Two in an addictive binge. As they give in to their appetites their tribe disowns them (at least for a time), and they are lost. Those who wander for long without a tribe often end up in early Stage One.

One man we got to know in our research is an artist named Joseph. He describes his work and his method of creation in this way: "There's a technique I do that people call painting, but professionals call it sculpting. Mind-altering substances are involved. A lot of controlling of the mind is involved." He takes cocaine for several days, then shuts the world away for a forty-eight-hour stretch of making art. When he emerges from this drug high and from the crash, he finds that his wife, daughter, and mother have kicked him out for a month, in what they call the thirty-day penalty. He crawls his way out of Stage One to Two, where, as we'll see in the next chapter, *his* life sucks (as opposed to *life* sucks).

We interviewed a member of Joseph's tribe, William, a designer and general contractor in Chicago, who often employs him as a subcontractor when he's sober. He describes his reaction to Joseph this way: "It's like the movie *The Horse Whisperer*. If one of the younger horses misbehaves, the head horse will push it away, but not totally out of sight. After a while, she'll let the horse back in and try again. Hate the sin; love the sinner. That's what I do." As they are pushed out, the offender falls to the middle of Stage One.

Another member of the William-Joseph tribe is Rick, who has eighteen misdemeanors for theft. His friends describe him as a kleptomaniac. When he gets caught, he descends to the middle of Stage One—cut off, unemployed, and alienated.

While the person at the middle of Stage One feels alienated, the truth is often that others are waiting, watching, and hoping they recover. When they do, tribes with a dominant Stage Two or higher welcome them back—but also put them on probation. Some remain in the middle of Stage One for months—in fact, many famous artists and writers have done astonishing work in this zone—but most either descend to early Stage One or, in the case of drug use, die.

> **COACHING TIP: Set the boundaries, but never give up.** *William's advice is consistent with our research. A surprising number of managers we interviewed had dealt with employees who abused drugs, who were alcoholic, and who even committed rape and murder. While your response to such behavior should be governed by your human resources department, we found that many managers never gave up on employees, even when they were terminated. Many would phone, go see the ex-employee, and keep in touch—sometimes visiting them in prison. Many ex-employees who were treated this way eventually returned to the working world, often in the same company, crawling their way out of Stage One and inspiring many others along the way.*

Late Stage One

Many readers don't identify with demons like kleptomania or cocaine, but everyone fights something. Many seemingly successful people (at Stage Three and beyond) visit Stage One from time to time. Doctors self-medicate. Professors claim their research assistants' work as their own. "Morally upright" employees steal computer equipment when the company doesn't pay bonuses. No matter how educated, intelligent, or "together" people may seem, each of us is capable of descending into this stage. In the moment we do, "life sucks," and anything is permissible. Helping those at Stage One starts with seeing that we're all capable of it.

If the demon is let out of the cage for long, people at Stage One go into the middle of the stage: often alienated from their tribe, and alone. For many, the secret remains tucked away—they drink themselves into oblivion every night and wake up sober and go to work. Others enlist support for their addiction, and create codependent relationships. When their tribe has had enough, they perform an intervention, and people are forced to make a choice: give up the addiction and move up to Stage Two, or remain addicted and find themselves alone, in the middle of Stage One.

Moving Others Up

As we'll see again and again in this book, the essence of advancing stages is giving up the language and behavior of one zone and adopting the practices of the next.

People can skip substages, but they cannot skip whole stages. That is, a person cannot go from One to Three. Like "passing Go" in Monopoly, they have to visit Stage Two first. Sometimes this process means switching tribes.

There are two ways to move from Stage One to Stage Two. First, the person has to substitute "life sucks" with "*my* life sucks"—the mantra of Stage Two. The difference in these stages is huge, and moving forward means dropping language that the nature of life is flawed, and saying instead that life works for some people but not for you. When we interviewed Joseph, he talked as someone who had made the transition: "I had to give up my art, because the cost is my family." He sounded like a victim of circumstance: that others can do art, but not him. *His* life sucked—he's made it to Stage Two.

Second, the person can move to a tribe where the offending behavior is not tolerated. The mother of a former gang member, whose son began attending a church-run youth center, told us, "I'm worried; he used to be so alive, but now it's like the cord got pulled." From a tribal perspective, her son went from the fire of despairing hostility (Stage One) to the passivity of being an apathetic victim (Stage Two). This was progress. When we interviewed him, he looked sad and said, "This place sucks—I don't know anyone here." He had gone from the alienation of Stage One to the disconnection of Stage Two. If people in his situation follow the advice in later chapters, they will continue their forward progress into Stage Three and beyond.

We conclude with the principle that runs throughout this book: give everyone a choice, and then work with the living; don't try to raise the dead. There are people in all three parts of Stage One who want life to be different, and our advice to employers is to give them a chance. William, part of Joseph's tribe, has made doing so a part of his design and general contracting business, Design For You, in Chicago. He employs former gang members, convicts, and people who have fallen into (and out of) heavy drug use. He believes that helping people out of Stage One is the responsibility of every person in society. At the same time, if people aren't willing to leave the allure of Stage One, he doesn't pursue them. If they relapse into despairing hostility, he invokes the "horse whisperer" protocol and pushes them out, but watches for when they're ready to try again. In the next chapter, we look at what happens when he's successful and people move to Stage Two.

Summary of Stage One

◆ The person at Stage One is alienated from others, expressing the view that "life sucks."

◆ When people at this stage cluster together, their behavior expresses despairing hostility, such as formation of a gang.

Leverage Points for a Person
at Stage One:

◆ If the person is willing to move forward, encourage him to go where the action is. This means having lunch with coworkers, attending social functions, and going to meetings.

◆ Further, encourage him to notice ways in which life itself works. For example, a person can notice that your life is pretty good, so it's possible that his may improve.

◆ Encourage him to cut ties with people who share the "life sucks" language.

Success indicators:

◆ He will use *"my* life sucks" language, as opposed to "life sucks." In other words, his concern has shifted from a generalized gripe to a specific set of reasons why *his* life doesn't function as it should. In particular, he will compare himself to others' abilities, social advantages, and, most of all, interpersonal connections.

◆ He will exhibit the passive apathy of Stage Two, as opposed to the despairing hostility of Stage One. This shift may appear as a setback to people who aren't familiar with Tribal Leadership; in fact, it is a major step forward.

◆ He will cut his social ties to people who are in Stage One.

CHAPTER 5

Stage Two: Disconnected and Disengaged

The essence of Stage Two is *"my* life sucks," and it accounts for 25 percent of workplace cultures. People at this stage feel they are victims of circumstance and that there's no way to get traction for their ideas or ambition. When they are presented with new visions, their reaction is "We tried that before, and it didn't work then and won't work now." They tend to be passive, doing the minimum amount of work necessary to get by.

It's easy to spot Stage Two from the outside—to see it, we only have to look at the organizations most people love to hate. The Department of Motor Vehicles, doctors' offices that make us wait forty-five minutes reading magazines older than we are while the receptionist moves so slowly we wonder if she may have died. Travelers all scratch their heads as security screeners sit around talking while the line stretches out the terminal door, the workers apparently oblivious that people are about to miss their flights.

From an outsider's perspective, the two questions people ask, often with anger in their voice, are these: "Why doesn't anyone do something about this situation?" and "How can people be so stupid?" As one person asked Dave on a recent plane flight, as the flight attendants "forgot" to offer beverages, "How can they be that stupid and still live? I mean, their brain at least remembers to make their heart beat, right?"

Doing something about Stage Two is difficult. Most managers are trained to utilize techniques that not only don't advance people but hold them at this zone of apathy. As a result, Stage Two is the second most common we find in organizations, after Stage Three. We've seen Stage Two in the highest levels of government in Washington, DC; among bank executives in Asia; on boards of directors of Fortune 500 companies; in Italian cathedrals; and in the halls of companies praised as "America's Best Places to Work." Overall, about 25 percent of workplace tribes are dominant Stage Two, and the percentage goes up when organizations hit major obstacles, like a recession, falling reimbursement rates in healthcare, tight competition among the airlines, or increasing competition for manufacturers based in the United States. We see Stage Two mostly when people believe they cannot act creatively, where jobs are so mechanized that they feel like part of a machine. We've seen vibrant organizations (Stages Four and Five) devolve into canyons of bureaucracy; as a result, tribes drop from Stage Four to Three to Two.

As we saw with Stage One, the insider's view as a member of Stage Two is different—it holds together, is consistent, it deflects advice from any other stage. Our goal in this chapter is to see how it works, what holds people in its grasp, and how to get ourselves and others to advance, so that tribes can leave Stage Two behind.

Stage Two: A View from the Inside

Stage Two and Stage Three need each other. Roger's story shows the dynamic.

It was early Friday when Roger boarded a plane from Chicago to the West Coast, where he worked as a manager for a major high-technology company. He was tired from running focus groups the night before, gauging the likely reaction to his company's upcoming product launch. When he landed and got to his car, he checked his voice mail. "Five messages—odd for a Friday morning," he thought.

The first was from one of the company's attorneys, who said that there was a potential lawsuit alleging that one of Roger's products violated a copyright of a competitor. The second and third messages were panicked calls from one of Roger's team members, ending with "This is getting big fast—get here now!"

The fourth message was from the attorney again, this time on a speakerphone. "The general counsel of the company is waiting to see you," he said. His tone was different, "like we had never met before," Roger told us months later. He added, "It was clear to me that the general counsel, known as the Tiger in the office, was standing over his shoulder. This is someone I had never seen in the office, and the lore was that if the Tiger ever wants to see you, it's really, really bad for you."

The last message was from Roger's boss, Todd (only the names have been changed—every other detail is exactly as it happened), yelling: "The Tiger wants to see you! What's going on here, and where are you?" As with the attorney, Todd's tone was as though they never met.

Finally, Todd arrived. Roger tells us the story: "I show up at the office, and I'm tired, dirty from travel. I round the corner, and I see Todd's assistant waiting outside my office. 'Wait out in the hall; I need to go get Todd,' she says. I had just enough time to peek in my office, and everything I had was in boxes. Even the pictures were off the walls and wrapped up. I said, 'Oh my God!'

Todd marches in and says, 'They're waiting for you downstairs in Legal.' I asked if I could put my stuff down, and he said, 'No—let's go now.' I pointed to my office and said, 'Really?' I couldn't believe it. 'Todd, three years and it comes down to this? Really?' By now a crowd is gathering. Members of my team look scared. Todd has already turned and is ten steps ahead of me walking down the hall. 'Are you sure?' I couldn't believe it. His assistant grabs my arm and escorts me behind Todd. It was like security leading me from my office.

"We get about fifteen steps, and Todd turns to me and says, 'Ahhh! Gotcha!' He high-fives his assistant, who looks apologetic, and then shouts 'That was money!'" People in Roger's team were looking away.

"So the whole thing was a joke?" Roger asked. Todd answered, "That you're being fired? Yes; well, at least for now. But Legal really does want to see you, and this copyright issue is getting ugly fast. Come on; they're waiting for us."

Todd led Roger to the Tiger's office. After a two-hour meeting, which Roger describes as an interrogation, he unpacked his office and went home, took a nap, and spent the afternoon working out his rage on the tennis court.

The effects of bosses like Roger's are devastating to a culture. Their actions have the same effect as an earthquake or a bomb going off. People scatter. They dive under their desks. Some leave the building and don't come back. After the emergency is over, they check on one another, treat the wounded, mourn the dead, and go on, living with the knowledge that it will happen again.

Not surprisingly, a lot of energy is spent in quiet protest of the boss and the company that permits—even seems to encourage (from the perspective of the employees)—random acts of ruthlessness. The culture that forms as a result is the essence of Stage Two. People's words express that they are victims, powerless. Their life sucks, they say—not life itself (which is Stage One)—but *their* life. They can see the boss's life is good. They see their bosses as Teflon characters, for whom no misdeed is punished. Roger's VP in this story drove a Porsche, made a lot of money, was respected in his industry, and often took calls from headhunters.

Someone who works for a boss like Todd, who is typical of Stage Three ("I'm great and you're not"), has a choice: fight the boss or give in. The person who fights it moves to Stage Three, and the battle for supremacy begins, like dogs fighting for alpha status. For Roger, this move would have cost him what he wanted most: his first big promotion after getting his MBA from Kellogg (at Northwestern). If he left before getting the "brand manager" title, he would lose career momentum.

The choice Roger made, as he told us, was to "suck it up." Although still intelligent and ambitious, he temporarily became a lap-dog (his words) to get what he wanted. In the meantime, he disconnected from his passion and put up with the nonsense.

Many people in Roger's situation do put up with it until they're promoted, and then they find themselves the victim of another set of circumstances: the next boss. This pattern can continue for an entire career, and we've seen some CEOs (happily, not most) firmly planted at Stage Two, complaining that they couldn't implement the right directives because the board of directors wouldn't let them.

As long as people are in Stage Two, they believe their destiny is not their own. As a result they avoid accountability. People tend to use phrases like "I'll try," "I can't promise," "I'm not sure what my boss will say about that," "That's not possible," "We can't do that," "It's against policy," and "I can't make someone else do their job." Physicists define power as the time-rate of work. In that sense, the

Stage Two language screen nets out to "my words are not powerful" because even though I gripe all day, nothing changes.

Sometimes the cause of Stage Two is not a person but a system. We worked with one company that had a Stage Five culture in its early days. As the company hired more people, many were bureaucrats who implemented "best practice" systems. Ten years later, one person told us: "It used to be about the mission; now it's about the paperwork." She went on to say, "I'm paid too well [mostly in options] to leave, so I just put up with it." In this way, her life sucks, and the dominant tribal stage in this company is a Two. Even golden handcuffs can become a trap to keep people in Stage Two.

The language system of Stage Two also deflects core values. When we asked people at this stage what principles guide their lives, we heard a sort of pseudo-wisdom. In the words of one manager at a public utility, "I thought values were important once, too, but I came to see that sort of talk just disappoints you in the end." Stage Two has an ineffective relationship with values that comes across as cynicism, sarcasm, or resignation.

Most, like Roger, eventually advance to Stage Three, where they become the same sort of manager they hated. (As we'll see in the next two chapters, they don't need to stay at this stage for long.) In the meantime, they tend to join forces with others who feel disconnected, and a Stage Two culture forms. If it's early Stage Two, the group is in danger of lapsing into hostile behavior (one of the hallmarks of Stage One). Most Stage Two cultures are in the middle, and they represent what our colleague Scott Weiner, a CFO in healthcare, calls the entrenched mediocrity. Late Stage Two is where Roger went: a group of people all vying for promotion, putting up with the nonsense until they can get themselves out.

Early Stage Two

People in early Stage Two are on the edge between Stage One and Two, so they are always in danger of regressing. We consulted to a large manufacturing company that was in the process of offshoring its operations to Asia, and during the waves of layoffs the tribe descended to early Stage Two. Although the end of the U.S. plant came without incident, the managers organized a betting pool about which division would be the first to have an employee show up and "go postal."

When people advance from Stage One, they usually end up in early Stage Two. Joseph, from the last chapter, is in early Stage Two. In this zone, he's always in danger of relapsing into "life sucks" language and the accompanying behavior of despairing hostility linked with out-of-control drug use. As long as he stays sober, though, he believes that he's gotten the short end of life's stick but that life can work for some people. People in early Stage Two are often on probation in their tribes, either for past lapses or for what people perceive as likely future behavior.

> **COACHING TIP: Have zero tolerance for Stage One behavior.** *The key to stabilizing people at Stage Two is to stay in the midst of others who don't tolerate Stage One behavior. If they withdraw, people should go after them, attempting to bring them back into the tribe. If it becomes clear they have decided to lapse and won't listen to anyone, the tribe should give them clear rules about how to come back, such as Joseph's thirty-day penalty for drug use.*

When people cluster into Stage Two, their discussions often focus on how they're being "screwed" by management or the system.

Unlike the people we met in the previous chapter, their beef is with *their* life—and with the people they see are to blame for their lot—not with life in general. They can see that their lives could work out, while Stage One sees only continued despair.

People at early Stage Two concern those at later stages. Since early Stage Two is unstable, it's at risk for descending into the abyss of Stage One. Managers, like those in the manufacturing company, fear—and rightly so—workplace violence or self-destructive behavior, including suicide. We noted several suicides in dot-com companies that went out of business in the crash. People had descended from Stage Five ("we can do anything—we're reinventing retailing") to Four ("we're greater than our rival because we have more cash than they do") to Three ("you're losing your job—that's too bad; I still have mine") to Two ("I'm out of work, there are no prospects, and my Porsche just got repossessed") to One (drugs and suicide). This is the fear people have of early Stage Two behavior: that the person will go all the way to Stage One—especially if the person has fallen quickly from the later stages. "It seems like he's melting down. When will he hit bottom?" is how one manager expressed fear about an ex-employee to us.

People in early Stage Two take one of three paths: (1) they find a tribe that is mostly early Stage Two, and they stay there; (2) they leave behind the edge of their anger and move upward; or (3) they descend to Stage One, like Joseph.

Middle Stage Two

People at the middle of Stage Two tend to cluster together in tight bands that from the outside resemble Stage Four ("we're great"). Unlike these later-stage tribes, however, middle Stage Twos are united in their belief that someone or something is holding them down, standing in their way. It might be the boss, the system, their lack of education, or their belief that mom or dad didn't raise them to be competitive. The key is that they accept this obstacle as the way it is and the way it always will be. They give up, and they band together in a sort of support group for the oppressed.

The most usual suspect is the boss, and one of the hallmarks of middle Stage Two is *Dilbert* cartoons on cubicle walls, taped on the coffee machine, even hanging from the leaves of plastic office plants.

In a sense, *Dilbert* creator, Scott Adams, has become the spokesperson for people whose lives suck because, in their view, they work for an ass. *Dilbert,* a cartoonish parody, is uncomfortably accurate for what 25 percent of professionals in the United States experience in their everyday workplace.

Making fun of bad managers—"idiot bosses" in Dilbertese—is Adams's stock-in-trade and, from our research, constitutes a lot of how people in middle Stage Two spend their time. Because Stage Two discussions often resolve down to "my boss is making my life suck," we couldn't think of anyone better than Adams to help explain the mind-set from the inside.

We interviewed Adams about what why so many people are unhappy at work and feel they can't do anything about it. "[Idiot bosses] are built into the system," he said. "If you hire somebody who truly cared about the employees, they would be completely ineffective as a leader. You'd be saying stuff like 'Well, we couldn't get the profits because we didn't want to miss our kids' little league games. Why don't we push the deadline out a little bit?'

"As soon as the employees smelled weakness, everybody would have a dead relative they'd have to go to the funeral for. There's a level of toughness and coldness and evil . . . that is required. The system breaks down if you don't have that."

The word "evil" is carefully chosen, as Adams pointed out when we asked what kind of boss Dilbert would be. "He'd be a poor boss, because I've often said that leadership requires a deep and innate sense of evil. If you think about it, the whole point of leadership is to get people to do things they don't want to do on their own. So, for example, you don't need a leader to say, 'Eat this bowl of delicious cookies.'"

Adams continues: "But what about 'I'd like you to work on the weekend instead of seeing your family because I'll get a big bonus when you're done?' It's just pure evil. You're trying to get people to do things that aren't in their best interest, and they know on some level it's not in their best interest, but using your 'leaderly' skills and your Rasputin-like ability to get people to do what you want, they do it anyway. The essence of leadership is getting people to do things that they know isn't in their self-interest."

Adams has created a perfect parody of Stage Three, and he's made it seem obvious why Stage Two cultures form as a reaction to "I'm great (and you're not)" (the mantra of Stage Three) bosses. He also helps answer a question that people at later stages often ask about those who work for Stage Three bosses: "If your boss is such an idiot, why don't you go somewhere else?"

He answered the question this way: "I worked at Crocker Bank in San Francisco, and I thought that things happening at that big company couldn't be happening in other big companies. It must be something deeply defective about the one place I chose to work. Then I changed jobs, and the acronyms changed, and the buildings changed, but all the stuff that bothered me was eerily similar.

"A lot of people wrote to me when Dilbert first started," he added, "saying that I had cut down on their desire to change jobs because they could see it must be the same everywhere."

Adams contends that this growing awareness that "evil bosses" are everywhere led to an acceptance that organizations are just ineffective and that "evil bosses" are part of corporate DNA. (We should note that we don't use words like "evil" to describe any aspects of any stage. In fairness, we believe Adams was using this word for dramatic effect. The problem with words like "bad," "evil," and "wrong" is that when they are used as labels, the person can't escape from them.)

The Trap of Middle Stage Two

While Stage Two often forms in response to evil bosses, it forms for lots of other reasons as well. In our research, people blamed lack of education, poor social networks, lack of political skill, an inability to think strategically, or an unsupportive spouse who wouldn't let them work the extra hours required for success.

At this point, guru Adams and Tribal Leadership part ways, although we hope on friendly terms. (We tried to get Adams's assurance that we wouldn't become the newest villains in *Dilbert,* but he merely e-mailed back a smiley face.)

For many people in middle Stage Two, their residence at "my life sucks" seems immune to getting rid of the subject of their complaints—if managers fix what they snarl about, they go out and get more reasons to be unhappy. People in our studies did complain about "idiot bosses" but also about the name of the company (it took too long to type out on e-mails), the temperature at 72 degrees (just too hot), the printer took "forever" (actually, ten seconds) from the time they hit control-P until they had hard copy.

Even though we just gathered data, we found that our own mood fell to "my life sucks" when we spent time hearing about why people's lives suck. We felt we were being pulled into Stage Two right along with the complainers. "My coworker has BO," we heard.

"Then tell him to get Right Guard," we thought. "My boss is mean to my friend," people said, making us wonder, "and this is your problem . . . because?" "The floor is too slippery," we heard. "That's why they call it wax," we thought. The more we heard gripes, the more our lives sucked for having to hear them. The truth is that no one is immune to the sirens' song of Stage Two, not even people collecting data on it.

What's going on here? we wondered. Not only do some people appear complaint-addicted, but also they seem miserable about it. As we fell down the Stage Two well, one manager asked what he could do, and we suggested putting Prozac in the water cooler. (We later apologized, even though the manager thought it was funny.)

The fact is that Stage Two wants to avoid accountability at all costs and will invent reasons to remain disconnected and disengaged. In our public seminars, we've developed a method to show people how quickly Stage Two can form. "I'll tell you why my life sucks, and then you have to do the same," we'll say, often to groups of a hundred or more. We start, "My life sucks because I have to be here with all of you."

At first, stunned silence fills the room. People look around, reach for their water glasses, or try to look distracted by noticing the design of the carpet—that same flower design that haunts the dreams of people on the speaking circuit.

"My life sucks because I have to listen to you!" someone will say. Nervous giggles bubble up, followed by the awkward silence.

"Who said that?" we'll ask. No one volunteers—except, on occasion, people around him pointing the finger in the guilty person's direction.

We'll then ask, "Whose life sucks more than his?"

"My life sucks because I drove three hours to get here, and I have to listen to this drivel!" someone will say, usually laughing. Laughter floats up again, this time lasting longer.

"My life sucks because my mom lives with us!"

"My life sucks because my boss is here so I can't say how much he sucks!"

"My life sucks because I have three kids in private school!"

"My life sucks because my company just changed its health plan again."

The comments come faster and faster. The laughter gets louder and louder. Finally the whole room gets going. Depending on the type of group (doctors are polite; salespeople aren't), the room will become so boisterous that we have to unclip our lapel mikes, move them an inch from our faces, and yell, "OK! Come back!"

Before order resumes, the bitching continues. "My life sucks because I have to do eighty hours a year of training." "My life sucks because I have two hundred unread e-mails."

Almost every time, as if scripted, someone will end the gripefest by saying, "My life sucks because this discussion is what my job is like every day!"

We've never found a workshop where Stage Two fails to form, and we've tried it with some unlikely people: church leaders (where we substitute the word "stinks" for "sucks"), state senators, judges, deans of college schools, accountants, executive coaches, and lots and lots of doctors.

COACHING TIP: Upgrade the culture; don't attack conspiracy theories. *At early and middle Stage Two, conspiracy theories tend to form. They result from our desire for cognitive consistency—that everything needs to make sense—and the psychological drive to have some control. As people at Stage Two told us, "If I see it coming, I can prepare." As a result,* *conspiracies are hardwired into Stage Two cultures. Conspiracy theories we heard included these: "They're going to close our operation," "The company is about to be sold," and "They're going to cut our pay by ten percent." Managers often try to attack these conspiracies by denying them, putting their personal credibility on the line. This approach almost never works, as people remember Ken Lay (former Enron CEO) giving his assurance that his company would recover. We often remind people that Stage Two thinks of the boss as evil (in Scott Adams's language), so personal credibility is meaningless. In fact, denial of the conspiracy becomes proof of the vastness of the cover-up. A better approach is to work on upgrading the culture, which we discuss at the end of the chapter. As the culture moves from Two to Three the conspiracies disappear on their own.*

That's the point. No matter how educated, successful, talented, ambitious, or enlightened you are—we are—Stage Two is like a trap waiting to snap shut. It starts with one gripe, then another. Soon everyone says only negative comments. The cycle amplifies as the entire group joins in. In our sessions, people's laughter is a positive reinforcement that keeps it running. In work tribes, the discussion is often somber, the mood like a movie when the hero has discovered a conspiracy so vast it is unstoppable. We heard comments like "They're reducing our benefits" and "They're cutting the subsidies at the cafeteria." Those were followed with "It won't be long until they start to move our jobs to India" and "I heard the board decided to close us down."

We hold out the hope that the Dalai Lama or the Pope may be so enlightened that they wouldn't play along. Deep down, though, we think they'd fall in line, too, or at least tacitly encourage their followers to play. As people who use language, Stage Two is lurking in the shadows for all of us.

> **COACHING TIP: Tell people they're valued.** *The language system of Stage Two nets out to "I'm not valued." As a result, people feel disconnected and disengaged, and their culture acts as a support group for others who are disengaged, as well. Managers can start to break up this culture by taking a personal interest in the lives of their employees, in a way that doesn't seem to be part of a formula. (Remembering everyone's birthday, for example, is interpreted by Stage Two as nothing more than a computerized scheduling system and an administrative assistant ordered to buy a cake.) Bosses who know the names and ages of employees' children, their hobbies and interests, do better than those who offer programs such as "employee of the month."*

One of the best ways to attack the "I'm not valued" view is to say, "I value you. What can I do to encourage you to stay?" Beverly Kaye and Sharon Jordan-Evans offer great tips in their book *Love 'Em or Lose 'Em*. Such tips work best when they are combined with the steps to advancing culture at the end of this chapter.

Dominant Stage Two cultures all seem to have "wise" people appointed by the culture (never by management). One of our clients calls them "keepers of the sacred flame of 'no accountability.'" In a large nonprofit organization where one of us worked, we overhead a seasoned employee giving advice to a young recruit. "Don't try too hard; it only raises expectations," the older man said. "The key word is 'pretend.' Pretend you're overworked, and no one will bother you. Pretend it's someone else's fault, and you get to do what you want. Pretend you're waiting on another department, and you'll get praised at raise time."

Middle Stage Two soaks in this cycle of accountability avoidance and complaint generation. As a result, managers who attempt to earn trust by fixing what bothers people feel that their energy is being drained by a cultural vampire. The needs are endless, the complaints inexhaustible, and in the end most managers give in to the inevitable and assume this is all people are capable of doing.

TECHNICAL NOTE: *In our research, people are accurate in identifying the cultural stage of others. In fact, they are almost as accurate as trained observers using surveys, focused interview questions, and sociograms (methods of graphing relationships). There is one exception: people give themselves a two-stage bonus. People at Stage One think they're at Three. People at Two think they're at Four. How can you tell if you're in Stage Two or Four? Look for power: do your words create change in the organization? Are your relationships connected by core values? What bonds you to your tribe—a common enemy or a common view that "we can't win?"*

Late Stage Two

At the time of Roger's story, he wasn't a member of middle Stage Two. He didn't hang *Dilbert* cartoons on the wall, and he wasn't part of the entrenched mediocrity. He represented a band of employees who were putting in their time, waiting for the promotion out of what one person in our study called the ghetto of corporate despair.

This last part of Stage Two doesn't want to continue in "my life sucks" but rather get to "I'm great" (Stage Three). They often feel their careers are temporarily set back because of "idiot bosses" like

Todd, but with one more promotion, some political maneuvering, or one vocal executive, they will succeed. What holds them in Stage Two is the belief that "I'll be great soon." Ironically, if the person were just to shift "soon" to "now," he would be in Stage Three, since language creates the stage.

While our studies focused on language use and the structure of relationships rather than age or education level, we noticed late Stage Two mostly among people who expressed the view that their careers were in their early stages. We also noticed late Stage Two among people who had achieved success but were knocked back by a temporary setback—a missed promotion, an extended illness, divorce, or a bad business quarter. These individuals are looking for a way to get in the game, or get back in the game.

Over time, people at late Stage Two either ascend (or re-ascend) to Stage Three or give up, and slide into entrenched mediocrity. If they regress, they often become the "elders" of middle Stage Two—the ones who counsel young people looking for their first break that, in the words of Scott Adams, "evil is engineered into the system." It's better to give up than to try and get disappointed.

> **COACHING TIP: Work one-on-one rather than addressing culture-wide concerns.** *There's standard advice in management: if you take people's concerns seriously, they will feel empowered. This advice is reliable only for late Stage Two and above. Early Stage Two lacks the stability of tribal support, and middle Stage Two is an endless fountain of griping. If you try the technique of listening to and resolving issues, and it fails, it means you're dealing with low to middle Stage Two. Instead, try working one-on-one with those who want things to be different. Upgrade the culture, and people will take care of their own issues.*

We believe that companies need to focus more attention on late Stage Two. Generally, this group receives few resources, as companies are mostly run by people at Stage Three. Late Stage Two are the ones who are "paying their dues" in the minds of bosses, or people who have been given chances but have never "stepped up." Many executives we talked with actually believed that late Stage Two is a Darwinian test, and only the fittest escape.

Roger, whom we met earlier in the chapter, did escape. He got the promotion he sought and almost immediately left the company. Now busy with his own start-up venture, he's building a company with, in his words, "no idiot bosses anywhere." Companies need to focus attention on late Two and on the cause of their malaise, Stage Three. The alternative is to lose good people like Roger.

Coaching Advancement

There are three keys to nudging people out of Stage Two. First, communicate only *one* stage above. This principle holds for all five stages (except for Five, which we'll discuss in Chapter 12). In the case of a Stage Two tribe, leaders should talk the language of Stage Three—"I'm great."

COACHING TIP: Build amplitude. *Many managers in our study said with pride that they don't speak Stage Two. This is a problem, as all of us go there from time to time. If you can't speak Stage Two, you won't be able to really listen to people, which is the most potent of the Tribal Leadership skills. We call the ability to speak cultural languages "amplitude," so if a person speaks only Three and Four, we say the person has a two-stage amplitude. Tribal Leaders, almost without exception, speak all five languages. Remember, this book is about language and* *relationships, so it's not enough to understand Stage Two or form opinions about it. As a Tribal Leader you need to speak the language as an insider. Only then can you build trust with a tribe at this stage and use leverage points to advance it.*

Second, spot and work with the few members of Stage Two who want things to be different—those people at late Stage Two—and work with them one-on-one. Start by explaining to each one that you see potential in him, that you want to assist him in developing leadership. Depending on how long he's been in Stage Two, he may have developed an immunity to praise, believing it to be a technique of manipulation. Your goal is to build both trust in your intentions and confidence in his abilities.

As you start this process you will become the person's lifeline into Stage Three—that is, he is great because you are mentoring him. If you cut the lifeline too early by stopping the personal attention, he's in danger of regressing to Stage Two—and this time, lapsing into deep cynicism. Spend your time pointing out things he does well and directing him with specific action, all in the context of developing his abilities.

COACHING TIP: Use the power of three. *"Bank shot" people at Stage Two to Stage Three by finding a person they trust who is at Stage Three, and set up a three-person meeting. If the trusted person is seen to "have the back" of the person at Two, the meeting will have a stronger degree of trust from the outset.*

The third leverage point is to encourage him to form dyadic (two-person) relationships. In our research, we often asked people to draw out the network of their relationships at work, using thick lines to strong personal ties, thin lines for what we called minor friendships, and dotted lines to represent information exchange. People at Stage Two tended to have mostly thin and dotted-line relationships, and not many of either. People at Stage Three, however, formed "hub-and-spoke" networks, with themselves at the center. Jordan, part of the William-Joseph tribe from the previous chapter, shows the power of dyadic relationships.

Jordan had such a major drug problem that when he was a teenager, his parents had the police arrest him and take him in handcuffs from his bed at 2 a.m. to a detox center. At age nineteen, he woke up literally in the gutter and realized no one was going to put a roof over his head unless he did. As William said, "He just got it." This was the realization that he was at Stage One. Almost immediately, he cleaned himself up and went to work at Starbucks, where he didn't know anyone. He was in the midst of people but was disconnected. He had moved to early Stage Two. A natural talker, Jordan chatted with people individually as he made their coffee drinks. He would learn about odd jobs they had, and he began doing work on the side. Each job came through a dyadic (two-person) relationship. He transitioned to late Stage Two and decided it was time to leave Starbucks, where he had an "idiot boss." He describes being in Stage Two this way: "I did everything I could, and I just got shat on. At the end of the day, the boss would just say how you f-----up. You forgot to sign for the deposits—do that again and you're fired. You wore your apron to the restroom—do that again and you're fired. I'd just had enough." There wasn't any anger in his voice, but rather optimism, as though he were looking forward to his next adventure. He leveraged off his dyadic relationships to move into different lines of work, including working with William. He had moved into early Stage Three.

One of the biggest insights we had in collecting our data is that people's language always correlates to the specific stage, nature, and structure of their relationships. As Jordan formed these dyadic relationships he was at the center of a network of people and part of several dynamic tribes. His language expresses the can-do attitude of Stage Three: "You put out your financial goals for the week," he says with a confidence that makes most of Dave's MBA students look insecure. "I'm going to make three hundred dollars this week just because I have to. Next week, I have to make six hundred dollars. Every night you come home and if you see something you didn't do—I could have made one hundred and fifty dollars today but I didn't, so tomorrow I really have to make it. I don't know, you f--- with yourself like that you get things done. I just don't want to have the average. I'm not far along in this process. I have enough money to live in a good neighborhood and have some fun and have a little backup, so I don't feel like I'm sweating all the time. Money stress is a bitch, and everyone has the ability to keep it away."

Jordan had transitioned to Stage Three, the most populated stage and the subject of the next chapter. It is both the biggest problem and the largest opportunity in organizations, as it is often the cause of Stage Two, and also the launching pad to Stage Four: Tribal Leadership.

Summary of Stage Two

◆ The person at Stage Two is separate from others, although unlike those at Stage One, they are surrounded by people who seem to have some power that they lack. As a result, their language expresses "*my* life sucks." Unlike Stage One, a person at Stage Two communicates the view that others' lives seem to be working.

◆   When people at this stage cluster together, their behavior shows characteristics of being apathetic victims.

Leverage Points for a Person
at Stage Two:

◆   Encourage her to make a friend. Then another friend.
Then another friend. In other words, encourage her to
establish dyadic (two-person) relationships.

◆   Encourage her to establish relationships with people
who are at *late* Stage Three. Such individuals can be identified by their eagerness to mentor others into becoming
mini-versions of themselves. (However, the same individuals will not tolerate another becoming greater than they
are.)

◆   In one-on-one sessions, show her how her work *does*
make an impact. In particular, show her areas where she
is competent and where her strengths are. In the same
meeting, point out abilities she has that she has not yet
developed, but be careful to make the tone of these discussions positive.

◆   Assign her projects that she can do well in a short time.
These assignments should not require excessive follow-up
or nagging, as this behavior may reinforce her "my life
sucks" language.

Success Indicators

◆   She will use "I'm great" language, as opposed to "my
life sucks." She may name-drop, point to her own accom-

plishments, and brag. Many of her sentences will start with "I."

◆ She will exhibit the lone warrior spirit of Stage Three, often comparing herself with her coworkers and using disparaging language like "What's wrong with them?" and "If they tried, they'd succeed."

CHAPTER 6

Stage Three: The Wild, Wild West

By any measure, Martin Koyle is living the American dream. So why is he so frustrated?

Dr. Koyle, described by his colleagues as a world-class surgeon, is chairman of his department at Children's Hospital in Denver. After doing his residency at Harvard, he pioneered new surgical procedures that are now used around the world. He's been president of two associations in his field. He is financially successful, has loving children, and has a tribe of medical students who love and respect him for conveying his passion for medicine. He's written articles in all the leading medical journals in his field and has lectured in Egypt, Africa, Canada, Israel, and England. Almost every year, he volunteers in third-world countries, both performing operations and mentoring local doctors with the understanding that they will spread his teaching to benefit others. Koyle is regarded as one of the top surgeons in the world in his specialty.

With all that success behind him, here's what he had to say in a recent meeting with us: "I'm a victim of a system that is broken . . . I get zero support." He continues: "I was recruited to this institution by a series of broken verbal and written commitments. Perhaps I was naïve, but unkept promises are very disheartening! I'm just another commodity here, a replaceable faceless item. It makes no difference to anyone in the system that I've been a successful leader and mentor to so many others. The unspoken mantra is really 'What have you done for me lately?' "

Along with 48 percent of American professionals, Koyle is operating at Stage Three in a Stage Three culture, the zone of personal accomplishment. Like almost everyone in this group, he feels that he is putting more in than he's getting out, and we've met people like him in investment banking, sales, the humanities (including bestselling novelists and artists with galleries around the world), real estate, entrepreneurship, the clergy, high tech, government, and the law. His story, like that of so many people interviewed, shows a string of successes, where in each case he was recognized as the best and the brightest, and yet he has become frustrated with the system in which he excels.

The essence of Stage Three is "I'm great." Unstated and lurking in the background is "and you're not." Ask people at this stage how they see work, and you hear: "I'm good at my job," "I try harder than most," "I'm more able than most," and "Most people can't match my work ethic." The key words are "I," "me," and "my."

Many of the world's great companies are dominated by people at Stage Three. It's not a place for the mild. As Dr. Koyle described the business of medicine, where he practices, one of us commented that it sounds like the wild, wild west. He laughed. "That's what they should put above the sign at my hospital," he said. In fact, that sign should be displayed at about half the companies in the United States and most around the world.

Early Stage Three

A person enters Stage Three when he finds his groove, acquires confidence, and is recognized for his gifts. People told us about an awakening of personal ambition that turned to a drive for career success, coupled with recognition that they had work to do. We heard: "I have to prove myself," "I'm just beginning to come into my own," and "I have to win people over."

Koyle found Stage Three early, doing well in college and then in medical school in Canada, where he grew up. Like many people who accomplish great things, he felt a desire to learn and to see the world. He started his residency at County USC in Los Angeles, training to be a trauma surgeon. Although recognized as both talented and hard-working, Koyle quit the program, telling us that "The people I was helping frustrated me, although many patients were innocents. Many were victims of their own life, and I felt like, 'Why am I doing this?'" Koyle reflected a common theme from our interviews: a desire to work with people like themselves—gifted, hard-working people.

People entering Stage Three express insecurity with their positions, their gifts, and their colleagues, which is a leftover from Stage Two. For people at "I'm great," this fear fuels their drive to perform. At a training program in Cancun, after several days of getting to know one another, we ran an experiment that Abraham Maslow suggested in his writings. We asked people to write their greatest fear on a piece of paper, fold it up, and toss it in a basket. Of the thirty or so successful executives, most with MBAs from top schools, *every* person said some variant of "I'm afraid they're going to find out I'm not as good as they think." This experiment marks the difference between Stages Two and Three. At "my life sucks," this same insecurity freezes people into inaction and comes out as "I'm only as good as my performance, and I don't put in my best." For this group of highly accomplished individuals in Cancun, fear came out as an "I'll show everyone I can do it" spunk.

COACHING TIP: Don't call someone Stage Three. *When we teach Tribal Leadership, one of the most common reactions is for someone to point out a specific name and then say, "He's a Stage Three." Doing so puts a person in a box from which it is hard to escape. Stage Three is a set of language and a pattern of behavior; it is not a permanent state like "tall" or "short." We asked Don Beck, author of* Spiral Dynamics, *what he'd do. He said, "Well first, I'd go have a talk with the person who called the person orange (very similar to our Stage Three). It's not an orange person; it's a person who is exhibiting the characteristics of orange." Likewise, it's important to not use "Stage Three" as a label, but rather as a description of language and action.*

TECHNICAL NOTE: *The essence of moving up stages is taking everything from the previous level and reconfiguring it. Stage Three, especially at the early point, shares many of the characteristics of Stage Two. The key difference is an emerging passion for personal success, which overcomes the person's feeling of powerlessness. An increased sense of self-reliance forms, which becomes the center of the person's language screen. As a teaser for the next chapter, moving to Stage Four means taking all the conviction, ambition, drive, and discipline from "I'm great" and shifting it around. Moving up doesn't mean giving up any of the fire of Stage Three. Once a person has graduated from Stage Three behavior, she never becomes weak or passive but, after the epiphany of Chapter 7, becomes much more powerful and effective.*

COACHING TIP: Ask, "Does it fit?" *We asked Steve Sample, president of the University of Southern California, about his view of Stage Three. He said, "In a university, it can be very helpful to have people focused on their accomplishment. The individual genius can go a long way." Reflecting on his other role as an accomplished engineer with several patents, he added, "It [Stage Three] is that way in engineering, too." People operating at Stage Three win Nobel Prizes and major awards or become best-selling novelists, he added. Some environments are set up for people at Stage Three, and this behavior leads to organizational success.* Spiral Dynamics *author, Don Beck, echoed this theme when he said, "The first question to ask is, 'Does the job require [Stage Three]?' " Coaching people to drop behavior that is required by the system is harmful to everyone. "If he's doing what the job requires," Beck added, "don't bother him." The question to ask is, would you be more successful in Stage Three or Stage Four? Increasingly, the needs of business require a level of collaboration impossible at the "I'm great" level. Ken Wilber, the most translated American academic and head of the Integral Institute, added, "The center of gravity is moving away from Stage Three in business." We agree.*

Many people enter Stage Three with the best of intentions. It often starts with a desire, maybe even a vow, that they are going to be a different type of professional, treating people with respect and dignity. "I'll empower them," they often told themselves (repeating the vow to us later) instead of just telling people what to do. But as they tried—like Dr. Koyle—they learned that the system around them doesn't support empowerment, in spite of the rhetoric that "people are our most important asset." People operating at Stage Three told us that when they started mentoring and investing in people's development, their bosses asked them, "Why are you doing that?" or said, "It's time to get your ship in order!" They often realized, like Koyle, that despite preaching empowerment, their company operates by giving and taking orders.

Scott Adams (*Dilbert* creator) became a new boss when he and a partner opened Stacey's Café in 1998 and, later, Scott Adams Foods. He said, "What I learned . . . is that I don't really like being a boss because I'm not good at it. I'm a little too generous. My personality is more along the lines of 'you want a company car, take two!' I removed myself from that because I need people who are capable of doing the tough stuff. I try not to make any decisions."

Adams took a rare path and gave up managing. Since you're reading this book, you probably took a different path. Most people in our research, as we heard several times, "sucked it up and got in line," and as they did they saw their disappointment in the system (and the company) deepen. "I worked harder and harder," Dr. Koyle told us, "and have done very well for myself, the patients I serve, and the other physicians I lead."

> **COACHING TIP: Don't wait.** *Several CEOs in our study said that they learned they had to operate by command-and-control (giving orders and taking orders) rules, but they vowed that, in the words of one, "I'll set a different standard when I get to the top." The same person went on to say, "But between the board, Wall Street, and my own reputation for being a certain type of manager, I guess that was unrealistic." He reported feeling stuck in managing the way he had been managed. By contrast, the people we will meet in the second half of this book decided to do things differently now, before they had all the resources they thought they needed. If you feel your business would be better served by migrating your corporate tribe's*

dominant culture to Stage Four, we suggest you begin that effort right away.

While Stage Three is the zone of personal accomplishment, it's an area where people tend to feel let down by others. "I'm going to be the kind of boss who promotes hard work," one new manager in a large New York company told us." Six months later, the same person said, "I learned that most people aren't interested in putting in the effort like I am."

Since you're reading this book, there's a good chance that you, too, have been disappointed in other people, because high achievers almost always report this feeling. A senior physician (not Koyle) told us, "As a resident I learned that nurses are nurses for a reason—they don't want to work hard enough, or aren't bright enough, to be doctors." A lawyer said, "I treat the support staff as nice people, because they are, but they aren't motivated like I am, otherwise they'd be lawyers, too." One new sales manager said, speaking for hundreds of others, "It's tough to say, but most of my guys don't want to work as hard as I do." Inherent in Stage Three is the view that people are where they are because they worked for it, and others aren't there because they gave up.

Koyle fought the lack of support and became one of the top doctors in his field. Even when faced with adversity, people at Stage Three will put in the time, effort, study, and political savvy to thrive. Ironically, at this point—when they succeed without the perception of support—they feel the most alone, because everywhere they look, they see people who tried to hold them back and who gave up, and so can't understand how their success feels.

COACHING TIP: Encourage mutual contribution. *People at Stage Three rely on themselves. The issue that they need to address,* *especially later in the stage, is that their effectiveness is capped by their time, which is a limited resource. The more the person can accept help from others, the more he will see that help from others is not only helpful but necessary to his becoming a fully developed leader. Once he begins to form strategies that rely on others, and in which others rely on him, he will have taken a big step into Stage Four.*

The Building of a Stage Three Economy

For most professionals in the United States, Stage Three is the top of the mountain. How did it get to be that way? Between 1890 and 1920, along with the huge influx of immigrants, 80 percent of the rural population moved to the city to take millions of new factory jobs, and they brought their children with them. On the farm, many children meant many helpers, but in the factory, many children meant many accidents and acts of exploitation. Children's welfare and child labor practices became the issue of the age, and most people felt that something had to be done to protect and train the children while mom and dad worked in the factory.

The solution was to train a new generation of workers by teaching them inside a system that looked a lot like a factory. In school, bell rings, go to class; bell rings, recess; bell rings, go back to class; bell rings, eat lunch; bell rings, go home. At school, children with the "right" answer get a gold star, then an A. A star pupil is one who does the homework and has the right answers. This new system undid the classic liberal education, which said that the value was in the well-designed question, and this shift in focus made the worker exploitable, often consigning him to a Stage Two or Three career. (Stage Four, discussed in the next five chapters, starts with well-designed questions.) In between bell rings, children learned what they needed to become effective workers, and that amounted to reading, writing, and math. The system didn't emphasize creative thinking, strategizing, leadership, or innovation. Stars were smart conformists, and people who stuck to the pattern became model students. That approach also bred the "I'm great (and you're not)" mentality, based on homework, grades, and knowing the right answer. It does not emphasize empowerment, creativity, or individual satisfaction.

When children come of age, they find a familiar model. Whistle blows, go to work; whistle blows, take a break; whistle blows, go back to work; whistle blows, eat lunch; whistle blows, go home. A star employee is one who knows the right answer to a factory problem, obeys the rules, and doesn't make waves. People are encouraged to repeat this pattern until they retire.

While the system of education is changing, critics (including us) believe it's happening too slowly and that the new approach needs to build Stage Four thinking, not Stage Three addiction to personal success.

People tend to have compassion for those going through the transition of early Stage Three. Employees often said (behind closed doors, without the person in the room), "She's under a lot of pressure to prove herself, and I feel for her." A sales manager, talking about a new salesperson who had done well, said, "He had a good month, but this is a tough business, and next month may be rough for him." A nurse reported, referring to a new resident, "He's a nice guy who isn't used to giving orders, so we're trying to help."

Because people at early Stage Three aren't stable in the "I'm great" language, they tend to oscillate in and out of late Stage Two. On good days, they are great. On bad days, their lives suck. One manager expressed the flip-flop this way: "When my boss is happy, I'm happy. When he's angry, it really sucks to be me."

The transition to the middle of Stage Three happens when people find a group that accepts them for their gifts. In professions requiring significant education, it's often a mentor who encourages the person to finish training and get serious about a career. For many managers, it is their title. In Dr. Koyle's case, he had left County USC without finishing his residency, so his options were limited. At the time, the laws in Texas allowed a physician in his situation to work as an emergency room (ER) doctor. He again rose to the top, running one of the ER departments, but was, in his words, "bored to tears." During this time he met a world-famous surgeon who convinced him to complete his residency, this time at Harvard. With his training behind him, he moved to the middle of Stage Three.

Middle Stage Three

In time, people make friends whom they believe are at their level, and this tribal support stabilizes them at Stage Three. In a statement characteristic of this part of the stage, a Silicon Valley engineer said, "I never got along with people and then realized I was brilliant, so I went to Stanford and built a network based on my vision, and we all get along very well."

COACHING TIP: Point out that gifts are different. *A by-product of the "I'm great" language system is that any measurement of the person becomes a standard for others. For example, we've met many people at Stage Three who have gone through personality, leadership, and temperament assessments, resulting in one person saying, "ENTJ [one of sixteen personalities according to the Myers-Briggs Type Indicator] is the best personality. I'm going to make sure I hire only that type from now* *on." Another said: "I'm a high D (a classification from the DISC Profile system), so I need to work only with people who are like me." Others said, "I'm smart, so I'll hire only smart people" and "I want only people around here who are good with people, like me." A good coach will point out that such views foretell problems. Companies that are run by people who all have the same background, temperament, personality, IQ, and learning style become easy targets for competitors because the leaders all share the same blind spots, no matter how smart or accomplished they are.*

Many of the people at middle Stage Three we interviewed work in knowledge-based organizations—medicine, the law, education, even politics. In universities, we heard statements like these: "My work in the business school is more important than public policy because business runs the world," "Philosophy is the most important subject in the university because it's the only one that gets at the nature of things," and "The real challenge is getting people to work together, and that's what I do as chairman of this department." In each case, the person shows mild respect for others while promoting himself or herself as better.

Others at middle Stage Three see these minor put-downs as good-natured debate. In a law firm, people were aware that others thought less of them because of factors like where their degree was awarded or the type of law they practiced. However, these barbs were seen as evidence of the *listener's* superiority, in lines such as this: "Yes, Bill thinks I'm not a good lawyer, but that's just because he doesn't even understand the kind of work I do." If we examine the language of this sentence, though, it isn't a debate at all—it's a blatant put-down of the other person rather than a comparison of specialization. It's no more substantive than a presidential debate, each making himself great by showing that the other is less great—a common characteristic of Stage Three.

The middle of Stage Three, then, is when people find others like themselves—people with similar gifts, or different gifts but at the same level. A clarifying Stage Three moment for us came in a large hospital, when Dave was riding in a staff elevator. Three male doctors, all in white coats, walked in. One said, "Did you see my article in the *New England Journal of Medicine?*" The next one said, "Yes, impressive, but while you were doing your research [with a tone of sarcasm in his voice], I was performing more surgeries than anyone on my floor." They laughed, reminding Dave of fraternity brothers. The third said, "While you were doing your research, and you were doing your meatball surgery, I was teaching the new leaders of medicine by supervising more residents than anyone at this hospital." They laughed again, patted each other on the back, and, as the doors opened, walked out. It was a perfect Stage Three moment: all were members of the same tribe, and they showed respect to others with the same gift, but in the end, the message of each was "I'm great and you're not, and I have the statistics to prove it."

COACHING TIP: Point out the superior results of Stage Four tribes. *Since results are paramount to Stage Three, such examples are compelling. The next several chapters are filled with such cases.*

When he finished his residency at Harvard, Dr. Koyle assumed— as did so many in our study—that his hard work, natural talent, and dedication would result in greater and greater levels of success. "I assumed at the time that I would be catapulted to the position of chairman of surgery." Instead, he's chairman of a smaller department. What went wrong?

"The system rewards the wrong things," he told us, echoing the views of literally thousands of people in our studies. While people in the stories we collected all hit different obstacles, the net result was the same: no matter how talented they were, or how hard they worked, their efforts were thwarted by decisions that appeared unilateral and narrow-minded. In Koyle's case, he told us that he works for three masters: the hospital, the billing organization, and the university. "To accomplish anything requires I get them to agree, and they never agree," he said. Although he's become skilled at knowing how to work the system, as he told us, each "master" is run by people looking out for their own niche, not the interests of the whole. As a result, projects that Koyle has initiated have gone nowhere. Looking back over his career, Koyle laments, "I'm just a commodity. It makes no difference how much I've given to medical students, or how much pioneering work I've done. If I left today, they'd just find someone else, and that would be that."

This commodization of people is what's so discouraging to people at the middle of Stage Three. Many told us variations of this line from a lawyer: "No matter how hard I work, I'm valued for my results, not for who I am." Dr. Koyle went further than most when he said, "Many of us who view ourselves as successful are really survivors within our systems."

As a result, people like Koyle are seldom given the resources they want to take their success to the next level. Given their spirited nature, they work harder and look for a solution, and many get amazing amounts of work done despite a low level of support. Among real estate brokers, we often heard, "I could bring in another [large amount of revenue] if the company invested in another support person, and I just can't figure out why they don't." One government scientist said, "I could achieve a world-changing breakthrough if they'd give me one post-doc[toral student]. But they [the decision makers] don't think that way."

People at the middle of Stage Three notice that rising stars in the organization aren't treated well. Koyle said, "There's just too much insecurity and ego in doctors around me. When people see someone who can be more successful than they are, the whole point is to snuff them out." He adds with a laugh, "Or get them sent to a lesser institution or something."

As a result of frustrations like those reported by Koyle, many people at the middle of Stage Three develop almost psychic abilities to read situations and people. In a large accounting firm, one partner commented, "With the politics around the firm, I've learned to see through steel." At a large manufacturing company in the Midwest, an executive said, "I keep tabs on what's happening by chatting people up . . . administrative assistants, if they banded together, would run the world." Both the partner and the executive used Stage Three tenacity and talent to always be a step ahead of politics.

Many people stay at the middle of Stage Three for their entire careers. Increasingly, though, as middle age hits, because of the demands of the newest generation of workers, and as companies become more complex, people are moving to the last part of this stage.

Late Stage Three

Many people at the middle of Stage Three become so good at fighting and winning that it's no longer a challenge, and their interests naturally drift to another outlet. Some seek outside stimulation. Dr. Koyle has looked at ways to use his intelligence and hard work to become successful outside of the system he thinks is broken. In Denver, he tried to get franchises for three California staples: In-N-Out Burger, Trader Joe's, and California Pizza Kitchen. The first doesn't franchise; the second said that Colorado's laws prevent chain stores from selling alcohol in all their locations; and the third wrote back what Koyle describes as a "snotty note" saying that the Colorado palate wasn't sophisticated enough for their product. (He adds that his letter had suggested four locations, three of which now have California Pizza Kitchens.) Although none of these worked out, it's likely he'll find another outlet for his ambition and talent.

A move to late Stage Three often comes as people hit age forty or experience a personal loss. Sadly, Dr. Koyle's middle son died of cancer. "Despite having been a doctor for a quarter of a century, and having experienced death and dying and other traumatic experiences, it made me realize the fragility of life," he said, "and that time with my family was more important than anything else." Whether the move to late Stage Three comes through tragedy or maturity, it often manifests itself by a desire to give back. Koyle has always spent time in places around the world teaching others, and his passion when in Denver is his students and patients. "I'm lucky," he said at the end of our interview. "I really enjoy what I do, despite having to do so much unappreciated extraneous work in order to get the most minute leadership tasks accomplished. I still have fun doing what I do every day, and maybe the bruising is just less visible or I feel it less." That comment captures the end of Stage Three. The person has arrived, but the fire in his nature never goes away. He looks for his next challenge while he gives back to the next generation.

COACHING TIP: In tribes with a dominant Stage Three culture, gain credibility in areas that matter. The key here is to know what counts in that group. *Dave was introduced to an executive committee of a major public utility in the southern part of*

the United States as "a professor from the University of South-
ern California, a PhD, whose academic study and intellect we
should respect." The CEO of the company, a large man in his
late fifties, leaned back in his chair, stuck a thumb under each
suspender, and said in a southern drawl, "Son, what we don't
need around here is an academic flake from California telling
us what to do." Around the table, the other men laughed. In
that tribe, what mattered was real-world experience, not aca-
demic credentials.

The Cost

In many ways, Stage Three is the focus of this book. People at Stage
Two aspire to it, and only those at Three can make the leap to Four,
which is the zone of Tribal Leadership.

While we don't want to take anything away from the success of
people at this stage, it's important that they see its cost, which is
often invisible while they are moving up through the substages of
early, middle, and late. Often, outside observers can see the downside more easily than those in this turbulent stage.

When we interviewed people about Stage Three bosses, the
name we heard the most was that of Bill Lumbergh, the boss from
the movie *Office Space*. In the movie, Bill Lumbergh strolled around
his company, Initech (a software firm), in suspenders and a tie, coffee cup in hand, never making eye contact. He drove a Porsche (the
same car Roger's boss drove in the firing story of the last chapter).
Specifically, in our study, we heard "My boss is Bill Lumbergh,"
"I work for a guy just like that guy from *Office Space*," and (after
people heard the Tribal Leadership terminology), "My life sucks because I work for Lumbergh." Roger ended his story by saying, "Todd
[his boss] *is* Bill Lumbergh."

The Tribal Leaders we met had *all* gone through Stage Three, including learning how to outmaneuver others and win at political games. People who present themselves as Stage Four, but who have not owned Stage Three, come across as weak, often backing down from a fight the tribe needed to win. Tribal Leadership can never emerge out of weakness. Before moving out of Stage Three, it's important to own it, to the point where you're done playing the game this way—not because it's hard but because you're ready for what's next.

Gary Cole, the actor who brought Bill Lumbergh to life, has a knack for playing Stage Three characters who exude the "I'm great (and you're not)" vibe. His roles include Bob Russell, the Stage Three vice president on *The West Wing,* and the main character's father in *Talladega Nights: The Ballad of Ricky Bobby,* who tells his son in elementary school, "If you ain't first, you're last." Since good actors have to become their roles, we asked Cole about how he had to view the world, and himself, to pull off these performances.

As an aside, why would we interview an actor? While 48 percent of American professionals are operating at Stage Three, when they see the *Tribal Leadership* system, they often think they're at Stage Four or Five. Later on we'll get to why this stage inflation happens at Stage Three. A good actor, like Cole, becomes the role, and when in character he saw the world as a person at Stage Three sees it while still being able to comment on it from the outside, so to speak.

Cole told us, speaking of Mike Judge, the writer/director of *Office Space:* "Mike's inspiration for Lumbergh was a guy he used to work for. This guy sat in a cubicle, and it was like the old joke on *Home Improvement* where you could only see half the person. You'd see his coffee cup rise, but that's it. Lumbergh works because he's recognizable, and I just became that boss we all know."

As Cole played the role he avoided all human contact, looking others in the eye "only when necessary . . . emphasizing that [Lumbergh] couldn't be more passive-aggressive." This reflection gets to the heart of early Stage Three: it is a sense of insecurity mixed with a passion to win. From the inside, it feels as if one is working harder than others and gaining the trappings of success as a result of the effort. From the outside, this mix gives the appearance that the person is looking down at others.

Although people at Stage Three often feel treated as a commodity, the truth is that they treat others that way, as well. Cole told us, "All day long, Lumbergh has to tell people what he wants them to do. Short of being someone who argues, he comes across as someone talking to children. Lumbergh's key phrase was 'Wouldn't it be great if' instead of saying 'Do this and do it now.' " His goal is to get compliance by using his badge of authority, rather than what he knows deep down he doesn't have: people's loyalty. The tribe, at Stage Two, now makes him the cause of why their lives suck. People in this situation often immerse themselves in the trappings of their role, and as they do, the people around them feel treated as objects.

Likewise, those at Stage Three tend to hire employees who are at Stage Two. The moment a job candidate looks more intelligent, ambitious, or promotion-worthy than the boss, they are nixed from consideration. When hired, the people at Stage Two feel like the supporting cast, or as one person in Silicon Valley said, "If this were *Star Trek*, [the boss] is Captain Kirk and I'm wearing a red shirt, and you know what happens to the people in the red shirts." (They're the nameless security personnel who always die on alien planets while Kirk gets the girl.)

Some companies we've consulted cut off the Stage Two tail (by firing people), but it always grew back (through new hires). Why? People at Stage Three like to hire those at Stage Two, or others at Three who aren't as accomplished as they are, so they can dominate the Stage Two position. Stage Three, to be successful, needs people at Stage Two to do the work, but this lower cultural stage will never produce the passion or initiative necessary to provide full support. As a result, people at Stage Three often say, "I don't get enough support."

COACHING TIP: Allow the person back to move back to Stage Two to deal with the underlying issue. *In an earlier book (*The Coaching Revolution, *2000), we detailed that all development progresses through a J curve, with things getting worse before they get better. This pattern is especially important for early Stage Three. The person needs to retreat to Stage Two and use the coaching tips in that chapter to see what's behind their feeling that their life sucks. The key is for them to notice ways in which they are powerless and to dissociate from those. As they do they will be able to progress to Stage Three, this time owning it, getting to the point where they are done with it, and advancing to Stage Four.*

In our research, we heard several people say, "My boss treats me like Milton, the guy from *Office Space.*" In the movie, Milton had been fired years ago, but no one ever told him, and rather than level with him, the boss decided to just let him figure it out on his own. Over time, Milton was moved to a series of smaller cubicles, eventually going to the basement, where Lumbergh told him to do his best to control the rat population. Cole says, "Mike [Judge] told me that when you're dealing with Milton, he's not even worth looking at. You're more interested in his space, and where he needs *to get out of.* You're talking to him but not acknowledging that he's there." (As Tribal Leadership would predict, Lumbergh's actions drove Milton deeper into Stage Two, and as he worked alone in the basement, all his social ties broke, regressing him to the despairing hostility of Stage One, which he acted out by burning down the office building.)

Although they often don't hear it, people at Stage Three use language that is "I" focused. In their grammatical structure, they are the mover, the actor, the dominant one, and others are the recipients of action or the provider of services. As Appendix B makes clear, a premise of our study is that language forms reality, so by dropping "I," "me," and "my" into almost every sentence, their reality becomes *"me."* One person in our study said, "So enough about your meetings; let's talk more about me," as naturally as if he were asking for more coffee. When we pointed out what he had said, he responded, "I did?" We had to play back the digital recorder before he believed us. Other hallmarks of early Stage Three language are nonstop references to personal accomplishments (for example, "I went to Harvard" and "I have my PhD") and perks ("I got to ride on the corporate jet" and "I had a meeting with the governor").

Another of Cole's roles, *The West Wing*'s Bob Russell, captures the middle of the stage. "He's clear that he's in a battle for preeminence [seeking the job as president]," Cole said, "and until the very end [when the nomination for president went to another candidate], losing was unimaginable." It's that Stage Three instinct to fight that gives rise to the cost, and the reason why many professionals around the world are putting down their "wild wild west" revolvers and entering Stage Four.

Stage Three Fingerprints

There are seven distinct fingerprints of Stage Three, each with a cost. We've seen these again and again in people, and in ourselves. If these patterns are familiar, perhaps it's time to question whether there might be a different way. To make the point that these costs are personal, we've phrased them in "you" language. We're not assuming you are operating at Stage Three, but the tone of this section, we've learned from experience, needs to be personal. See if they fit. If they don't, notice the people in your organization whom these describe.

First, you form a series of dyadic (two-person) relationships, so that if we were to graph your network, it would look like a hub with spokes. You can get what you want from each person by using some combination of personal appeals, charm, manipulating the truth, distorting information, trading favors, and selectively disclosing facts. As Dr. Koyle mentioned to us, "A big part of how to play the game is how you phrase things." He uses one set of communication when he works with people in the hospital, and another set when he works with the university. The downside of so many dyadic relationships is that they take an enormous amount of time to maintain, and keeping everything straight requires a high cognitive load. People with many dyadic relationships report feeling mentally fatigued.

COACHING TIP: If a person is stuck at Stage Three, find what's holding her there. *If it's an unresolved insecurity, deal with it by focusing on the Stage Two issue (e.g., "my life sucks because people don't like me"). It may be an addiction to dominating and belittling others, and if that's the case, the coaching tips later in this chapter will be helpful. The most important*

*part of this tip is get the person to own why she's at Stage
Three. At first, it will probably seem like good news—"Wow, I
am addicted to achievement!"—but over time, she'll see the
limitations of behaving this way.*

While people operating at Stage Three often preach the need for
teams, their behavior shows that they discourage teaming—unless it
is a situation where they can be the star. A team meeting is another
opportunity for a series of two-person conversations, but unlike
one-on-one meetings, these people have to be very careful what they
say. The exception is that people at Stage Three like meetings if they
see them as a chance to be the star. In any case, people at Stage
Three do more talking than most.

Second, you hoard information. At Stage Three, knowledge is
power, so the way to remain on the top is to know more, and dis-
close less, than others. You might remember times when it wouldn't
have done any harm to reveal information, but you stopped yourself,
thinking, "Is it my place to say this?" Maybe, deeper down (as
people told us), your motivation was "Is it in my best interest to say
this?"

By keeping secrets, you push even more of the burden to perform onto yourself. Hoarding also prevents effective networking,
thereby missing the sale, the next great opportunity, or the innovation that could make millions.

Third, you try to keep your "spokes" (the other person in your
dyadic relationships) from forming relationships with one another.
Many people at middle Stage Three will, for example, tell their
direct reports to "cc" them on all e-mails going outside their department, or to check before having meetings at all. People treated this
way often fall to Stage Two, and they form silos with very little information exchanged between groups for fear of upsetting you. You

may think you're sharing information, keeping everyone informed, and encouraging teaming. Again, look at what people actually do as a result of your leadership efforts, and you might find they are not as informed as you thought, and hence are not as effective. The difficulty in seeing reality on this point is that people tend to tell you (if you're in early or middle Stage Three, especially) what they think you want to hear. Many people at Stage Three believed they were at Stage Four because people around them said they felt like family. In this situation you need to bring in unbiased people to perform a study, or find people who will level with you.

As an aside, if you take these behavior patterns together, you'll see that in the long run, a person using them will almost always be unsuccessful. People you rely on as loyal feel commoditized. Addiction to information—a tool of controlling the situation—often results in your being labeled a gossip. More important, by focusing on "me," you may not see what really matters to others: tribal success, not personal success. Ironically, many people in our study thought personal success mattered, only to be denied a promotion because they were seen as selfish. The only way the Stage Three system can maintain itself is by creating blind spots, which is why so many people at this stage react so angrily to the accusation that this reflects them.

Fourth, you rely on gossip and spies for political information. This behavior happened less often in organizations where people don't care about politics, but it is almost universal whenever people feel their position is insecure. One person at a dominant Stage Three high-tech company said, "People are loyal to me and tell me things before they're common knowledge. I've used this information to thwart several attempts to fire me." Your spies may be others at Stage Three who do information swapping, cold war style. Other spies are simply gossips—people who love to repeat scandals.

(In our studies, the truthfulness of the gossip was less important than the fact that people were saying it. One manager took great pride—and assumed the tone of a concerned friend—by asking another, "Do you know what they're saying about you and your administrative assistant?") Your spies might also be those at late Stage Two who hope to leverage themselves out of the "corporate ghetto" with a quid pro quo: information for a helping hand. The test for whether they get your help is the same test as in spy novels: the value of the information, and your evaluation of the person's loyalty. The cost of using spies is twofold: (1) that you get a reputation as a gossip and (2) that the time requirement to always stay one step ahead is huge.

As you read the costs of these behaviors we hope you will take an introspective look at your career thus far. When we did, as we collected data, we both noticed two things: (1) our language was "I" focused, and (2) our identity was our accomplishments. John had coached tens of thousands of people and studied with some of the gurus in the coaching world. Before that, projects he worked on in Hollywood had won Emmy awards. Dave talked about his doctorate, his early academic successes, and his teaching evaluations. It's only when we saw our own behavior that we realized its costs and became willing to consider advancing to Stage Four.

Fifth, you might (especially if you're male and working in a macho culture) talk using military or mafia language. We heard comments like these: "I'm going to the mattresses" (a reference to an expected mob hit), "I'm calling in an air strike," and "I'm going medieval." All three phrases referred to either expecting a political challenge or launching one. Notice also the "I" language in all three. In our studies, people often reported that users of such language were "immature," "still developing," and "not a candidate for promotion."

The blind spots of Stage Three make it impossible for most of its residents to admit "I commoditize others." Instead, they will say, "I give people a chance," or "I'm always friendly." This fact has been one reason behind the success of 360-degree feedback instruments: when properly conducted, they show people what others really think. Often, the feedback comes as a shock. It's also common for people to reject the 360-degree report as flawed. From our experience, it is even more common to give the person the benefit of the doubt (or fear that the subject will know who said what), resulting in data that don't reflect what people actually think.

Sixth, you are hungry for tips, tools, and techniques that will make you more efficient. What surprised us, and may surprise you now that you see it, is the amount of effort you spend protecting your "I'm great" turf. In part because of this time expenditure, but mostly to make you better than others, you're looking for anything that will give you an edge. You may have been an early adopter of the cell phone, and have the latest gadgets. You went through the Covey time management phase, and you probably had a Day-Timer before that. Today, your life is run on Outlook. You can cram a sixty-minute workout into a half hour—while reading *The Wall Street Journal* and sending e-mails on your Blackberry.

People at the middle of Stage Three have an intense focus on time management, since they believe that they can rely only on themselves. Most time management books cater to this addiction on results and obsession with self. The vast majority of business, management, and self-help books, by contrast, are Stage Three messages written in Stage Three language, effectively telling people, "Here's how to be greater than other people." These books, in our view, may hold people and tribes back. If you want a shock, go to the business section of your local bookstore and mentally categorize books at Stage Two, Three, or

Four. You'll see what we did: "owning" Stage Three is a multi-million-dollar business in publishing alone. Add in training programs, education, and Stage Three coaching, and it becomes, in our estimation, a ten-billion-dollar field in the United States alone.

Seventh, unlike people at Stages One and Two, you talk about values. However, your focus is "my values," "what I've come to see," and "the principles I hold dear." In essence, your view of values is that they give you an edge in ethics and time management. We have yet to meet anyone at Stage Three who believed he or she wasn't fighting for good. The downside of this behavior is that values, like so much at Stage Three, are personal—and not empowering to anyone but you. We met many people at Stage Three who said that others were "galvanized" by "my values," but when we asked people around them, we never heard a single mention of values at all. People who thought they were values-based leaders were seen as doing their own thing.

● ● ●

The net of these seven signs is that people at Stage Three report, almost universally, that they don't have enough time, don't get enough support, and are surrounded by people less able and dedicated than they are. No matter how hard they work, they can't punch through the barrier of a day that has only twenty-four hours. They've hit the point of diminishing returns, so the harder they work, the less effective they are, and the less their efforts seem to matter. Simply put, they want to get to the next level but don't know how to get there, or even what the next level looks like. One-time labor union president Bob Tobias, whom we'll meet in the next chapter, said this: "What I realized is that I have a need to be judged on merit, which I defined [before his epiphany and rise to Stage Four] as working harder, better, getting up earlier. What I realized is that I would give speeches, and I would describe a vision for how things could be different. I thought that people would feel empowered, and so things would change. People were all too pleased to applaud my hard work, but when I left, nothing happened."

● ● ●

So what do we do about this situation? There's much more in the next chapters about how to break out of the Stage Three barrier that keeps nearly half of American professionals from full achievement, but here a few suggestions:

Break the illusion of "we're great." When many people fill out 360-degree surveys, they give the person the benefit of the doubt to such an extent that the data are often reassuring to someone who shouldn't be reassured. We agree with Don Beck, who told us that getting around this problem requires trusted advisors and tools that use "forced rankings" rather than simple statements that the respondent agrees with or not. If you're motivated to see what people really think, make sure the process will give you the truth.

Learn business—but without the "me" focus in most university degree programs. Unless people are focused and intentional, they may graduate from a professional program (such as law, business, or medicine) as Stage Three performers who use a few Stage Four words, such as "vision" and "values." This is true for two reasons. First, professors (like most professionals) tend to operate at Stage Three, with research and teaching done as individuals; promotion decisions are made mostly on the basis of individual performance, so people who adopt the single perfomer mentality do well. Second, one of the core limitations of Stage Three is that knowledge is equated with power, so giving someone at Stage

Three an MBA, JD, PhD, or MD is like giving an executioner a sharper sword—a way to be better and to cut down others' success as less than theirs. What moves people from Stage Three is the set of epiphanies in the next chapter. When combined with the knowledge from a top degree program, the results can be world changing. The best Tribal Leaders we met are highly educated individuals whose identity is not the letters after their name or a license hanging on the wall. Many around them were surprised to learn that they had advanced degrees, because they never brought it up.

Telling people you think they're at Stage Three can be career-threatening. Many readers of this book will recognize Stage Three in someone around them. Herein lies the danger. If you point out that he is Stage Three, especially if he is in the early or middle portions, he may deny the charge and become angry, seemingly out of proportion to the charge. (As we'll see in Chapter 7, many people at Stage Three think they're at Stage Five.) So what do you do? One approach is to give him a copy of this book with a note to read this and the next chapter. A less direct approach (and one that may work better) is to go to our Web site (www.triballeadership.net) and follow the links to send a copy to him, anonymously, with a prewritten note that someone who cares about him believes she would benefit from an introspective reading of Chapters 6 and 7. The anonymity of the process, and the fact that you invest a few dollars to help the person, may be enough to at least get him to read this chapter.

Find a mentor at Stage Four. One of our readers recently wrote to us, "The [Stage Four mentors] I have been blessed to know over the years have really made a difference in my life. They've certainly helped me to move beyond some of my Stage Three tendencies."

You might come to the same conclusion as many people in our studies: that you are operating at Stage Three, and while it's important to take pride in your accomplishments, maybe the costs of staying at "I'm great" are outweighing the benefit. When people see that their behavior tends to peg others as Stage Two, they look around with a new pair of eyes. One manager in South Asia told us, "I'm surprised to see that people around me are more gifted and special than I thought." A New York financial executive said, with a smile, "People aren't the idiots I thought they were." An ex-union president, whom we'll meet in the next chapter, said, "I saw that I wasn't making an impact and that the people I thought were my enemies should have been my partners."

Make the person aware that she's using management, rather than leadership. People at Stage Three approach leadership as though it were a set of tasks they could check off their to-do list (e.g., "set the vision," "get alignment," and "listen with intention"). The moment leadership becomes cookie-cutter, it isn't leadership at all—it's management. By making the person aware that he's behaving in a Stage Three fashion toward leadership, you might help him see that he isn't a leader at all. This realization may propel him into the set of epiphanies of the next chapter.

When you begin to see other people's insightful nature and unique gifts, they look like people worth developing, learning from, and leading. This perspective is your launching pad for the epiphanies that will bring you to Stage Four, the zone of Tribal Leadership.

Summary of Stage Three

◆   The person at Stage Three is connected to others in a series of dyadic (two-person) relationships. The language of this stage expresses "I'm great," and in the background— unstated—is "and you're not."

◆ When people at Stage Three cluster together, they attempt to outperform each other (on an individual basis) and put each other down. Although this is often done under the veil of humor, the effect is the same: each is striving for dominance. Individuals' behavior expresses a "lone warrior" ethos, and collectively the culture becomes the "wild, wild west."

Leverage Points for a Person at Stage Three:

◆ Encourage him to work on projects that are bigger than anything he can do alone. In short, assign him work that requires partnership.

◆ Point out that his success has come through his own efforts, but that the next level of success is going to require a totally different style. In other words, show him that what's brought him to this point will not be enough to move him forward.

◆ Describe role models (ideally in the company) that are exhibiting Stage Four behavior. You'll know these individuals by (1) their focus on "we," (2) the number of triads (three-person relationships, explained in Chapter 10) in their networks, and (3) success that comes from groups.

◆ When the person complains that he doesn't have time and that others aren't as good (the two chief gripes at

Stage Three), show that he has crafted his work life so that no one can really contribute to him.

◆ Tell stories about the time you made the transition from Stage Three to Stage Four.

◆ Coach him that real power comes not from knowledge but from networks, and that there is more leverage in wisdom than in information. Compliment his successes—and they are likely numerous—and emphasize that you're on his side. Also help him to notice that his goals require getting more done than he is able to do alone, no matter how smart and talented he is.

◆ Encourage him to manage using transparency, as much as is possible under corporate policy. Coach him to not follow the Stage Three tendency to tell them only what they need to know. Rather, encourage him to over-communicate.

◆ Encourage him to form triads.

Success Indicators

◆ He will substitute "we" language for "I." When people ask about the secret of his success, he will point to his team, not to himself.

◆ He will actively form triads, and his network will expand from a few dozen to several hundred.

◆ He will work less and yet get more done.

◆ His complaint about "there's not enough time" and "no one is as good" will cease.

◆ The results for which he is accountable will increase by at least 30 percent.

◆ He will communicate with transparency.

◆ He will communicate more information, and more often.

CHAPTER 7

The Tribal
Leadership Epiphany

In the years when Richard Nixon was president, Bob Tobias was living the wild world of Stage Three and loving it. Then a reporter asked him a simple question that led to a cascade of insights we term the epiphany. After this process, he emerged as a Tribal Leader.

He came to Washington in 1966 to go to law school and never left. While working at the Internal Revenue Service, he learned how labor unions worked, and that became his passion for the next thirty years. He went to work for what is now the National Treasury Employees Union (NTEU), becoming general counsel in 1970. In a Stage Three moment of glory, he filed a lawsuit against Richard Nixon for freezing federal employee pay. The suit was dismissed under the case law that a sitting president cannot be sued. Tobias appealed, expecting to lose, and then the famous Nixon tapes surfaced. In a separate case (in which NTEU collaborated), the U.S. Supreme Court ruled that no one, not even a sitting president, is above the law, and thus can be sued. With that precedent behind him, he eventually won a $533-million judgment against Nixon, on behalf of every federal employee.

"It was an ego hit of the highest order," Tobias told us, and his journey through Stage Three was just getting started.

Today, Tobias is deceptively quiet. He has a small build, bright eyes, and a wide smile, with an appearance that conveys the meticulous nature of an attorney who believes that details matter. We met with him on a muggy Saturday in Washington, when most people were in T-shirts and shorts. Tobias wore a sport coat and never broke a sweat.

The image of a soft-spoken, thoughtful man didn't match his words. "I told people that the way to make an impact as a union lawyer is to 'kick the s---out of them so that they never want to see you again.'" He referred to himself in the 1970s as a "badass" who would use any management slip as an excuse to arbitrate a grievance, file an unfair labor practice charge, or begin a lawsuit. By 1975, he managed his thirteen employees by directly talking with each person—creating dyads, as described in the last chapter.

When the staff doubled in size to twenty-six, Tobias hit the barrier of having only twenty-four hours in a day, so he appointed regional supervisors in Atlanta, San Francisco, Austin, and Washington. To the frustration of the new managers, he continued to reach out directly to each person. As Tobias told us, "They finally confronted me, asking why the hell I had appointed them." He went on: "It was painful for me. I had to give up something I loved, touching each person, but I had no choice." Tobias was working up the management ladder as many people at Stage Three do—by turning lessons into new ways to win.

From 1970 to 1983, Tobias would fly into a city, arbitrate a grievance or unfair labor practice charge on behalf of one or more union members, usually win, and then leave with the union applause still ringing in his ears. In 1983, the president of the union retired, and Tobias was voted in. Now running one of the most powerful unions in the federal government, he sat at the "big desk." On his first day, he took a call from a reporter, and he still remembers the question: "Now that you've been elected, what are you going to do?" Tobias had no idea. He told us, "I knew what I wanted others to not do—mistreat our members—but what was I going to do? That was a slap in the face. I couldn't answer the question." Tobias's epiphany was about to begin.

The Epiphany in a Nutshell

Having interviewed thousands of people who have made it into Stage Four, the zone of Tribal Leadership, we discovered that every person had an awakening. Some called it a major business insight. One said, "In the shower this morning, I realized there's a better way to do business that will mean much higher profitability." Some called it corporate karma. Others described it as a need to live their values. Some came to it after years of psychotherapy, or doing a self-help program. Some came to it through what Warren Bennis and Robert Thomas (in *Geeks and Geezers*) call a crucible experience: an event that causes people to reflect—at both an intellectual and an emotional level—on their core assumptions. For some people, 9/11 kick started the epiphany. For most people, the epiphany was actually a series of epiphanies, each presenting a deeper insight about what wasn't working in Stage Three.

While the epiphany happens to all Tribal Leaders, it may not happen in adulthood. Gordon Binder, former CEO of Amgen, apparently had it growing up in New Mexico, and finished it in the Navy. Mike Eruzione, the captain of the 1980 United States Olympic Hockey team, had something like the epiphany playing hockey early in his life. Frank Jordan became a Tribal Leader through the Boys & Girls Clubs. They all described the epiphany as *the* turning point in their lives, both personally and professionally, regardless of how they came to it or went through it.

Although it often took months or years for the epiphany to burble through their minds, once the moment of awareness happened, there was no turning back. They often described it in sound bites. We heard statements like these:

♦ Nothing that matters is personal.

♦ Stage Three has no legacy.

♦ To win at Stage Three is to win small.

♦ I now see I have been a manipulator, not a leader.

♦ I'm tired; isn't there some other game to play?

♦ I see myself through others' eyes, and I don't like what I see.

Many became evangelists for the epiphany but discovered that others weren't swept into life-changing insights with these taglines. What might be going through your mind is what others said in response: "I know that," "That's not a big deal," and "So what?"

People who've had this epiphany read books differently, often highlighting sections for others, hoping to spread the insights that changed their lives. To them, leadership books that once seemed simple and flat were now richly textured, filled with life-changing words. Books of tips and tools and techniques—once the staple of their reading diet—now strike them as drivel. To people still in Stage Three, the book of tips is still better, and highlighting sections of a book of platitudes is odd and unhelpful.

Our goal in this chapter is for you to be able to lead others through the epiphany the way it happened to several people in our studies. The sequence that Bob Tobias went through is typical, so we'll use it as the backbone of this chapter. Bob emerged as a Stage Four Tribal Leader, having far more success than he could have imagined at Stage Three.

Note that throughout, our focus is language, not psychology or spirituality. We didn't map why the people in our study changed their concepts and experienced an epiphany or had a shift in their awareness. We didn't measure anything about their spiritual beliefs or practices. Ken Wilber, a world expert on developmental stages in society, author of two dozen books, and founder of the Integral Institute, told us that these two parts of a human being—her psychology/worldview/spirituality and her conversations—tend to advance in stages together. Our focus is on what people said, and their resulting behavior changes in the tribe.

Epiphany Part One: What Have I Achieved?

The question the reporter asked Tobias sparked reflection and soul-searching, especially about how he had spent his time in the union up to that point. A memory that was fresh in his mind was a bitter fight in Chicago, where three hundred people picketed the IRS in the middle of winter. As a protest march got under way, he looked at the temperature on a bank thermometer, and it read minus 15. He sent out for coffee, and by the time he had distributed it, waiting for the press to arrive, a sheet of ice had covered the pot of coffee. That fight seemed to capture his time with the union: one bitter battle after another.

In thinking about the Chicago fight, and many others like it, Tobias says, "It occurred to me that we hadn't done a single thing that would affect how individual supervisors treated people, not a damn thing. We would go in, win a court victory, and leave. It was an institutional victory, but nothing changed in people's daily lives.

"I learned to name the thing I was doing that was holding me back," he continued. "Once I could name it, I could do something about it. It was 'working for' versus 'working with.'" He realized that his career had been spent working for the union members, which required that he work against the government and its managers. Tobias had always seen the first part of that sentence—that he was an advocate—but he had never before realized that his way of operating *required* an enemy. He assumed the fight, so he created it wherever he went.

It's worth noting that both Stages Three and Four *require* an adversary. When we work with people and groups, people in Stage Three groups will say, "I'm great because I sold more last quarter than anyone" or "I just bought a huge house." They begin to notice that these statements are all comparative, netting out to "I'm better than others." At Stage Four, people will say, "We're great because our team is winning" or "We have the best people." Again, this language system implies "We're better than them." At Three, the enemy is other individuals. At Four, it's another group, or a company, or even an industry. Only at Stage Five does the need for an enemy go away, as we'll see in Chapter 12.

There was another part to the epiphany for Tobias, and this was a realization about his own blindness. He said, "I loved winning. I loved being the lone ranger. I loved coming into town and slaying the dragon, with everyone saying, 'great job, we needed you!' It was a complete ego hit, so I couldn't see that I wasn't making an impact."

Bingo. The epiphany, part one. "When I got it, I got it," Tobias said, "and then I was relentless."

Many people told us, in exactly these words: "My impact is far less than I thought," "I thought I was winning, but it was all about me," and "I didn't do a thing that mattered!" Almost as the words are forming in their mouths, they begin to say what the solution is, still in Stage Three language: "I will find a way to fix this problem, just as I've handled every other problem in my life—with hard work, talent, and guts."

Epiphany Part Two: How Can I Fix This?

Tobias began preaching collaboration, "working with" rather than "working for." He learned about interest-based bargaining, working with a professor from the University of Michigan.

The more he preached, the more people ignored him. "I asked my staff why they weren't doing anything differently, and then it became clear: because I wasn't doing anything differently. I was still the lone ranger."

As Tobias examined his own behavior, he saw it was similar to what people all around him were doing, including many of the local union presidents. "I realized that they were elected as badasses, and that it would be hard to get them to do anything different." Again and again in our studies, people going through the epiphany became aware that Stage Three wasn't working for anyone. In some cases, they see others' shortcomings first. For other people, like Tobias, their own lack of impact came into view first. In every case, they saw that the general system of "I'm great" language and behavior was not achieving success.

Although we didn't know Tobias when his epiphany started in 1983, it's likely (in fact, almost certain) that he was saying the Stage Four words: "vision," "partnership," and "collaboration" but that his sentences were focused on "I," "me," and "my." His recollections in

2006 support what we heard from so many in our study: "I was talking facilitation, but my approach was still adversarial."

The Integral Institute's Ken Wilber told us that people's awareness (which he terms the cognitive line) always comes before feelings or actions. "All developmentalists agree on that," he said. In that case, we're in good company, as our research came to the same conclusion: that people start the move into the epiphany with an awareness of a different way to operate but without any idea how to make it real. Since we were measuring their language, not their psychological state, we noticed that people's discussion of Stage Four came before their actions. "Awareness comes first, and it has always been this way," Wilber commented. Mahatma Gandhi started out with the idea of a free India long before he took the first step to make it free. Jack Welch became aware that the lack of executive collaboration at General Electric was a problem before he had a strategy to deal with it. If this chapter first hits you as a set of ideas, that's exactly how it should start. The coaching is to let the idea create an awareness of how things can be different, for you and for others.

We described the threshold of Stage Three and Four to former Amgen CEO Gordon Binder. "There's a tremendous irony here," he said. "When [people] operate in the 'I' system, they can't have a legacy. When they operate in the 'we' [Stage Four] system, they can have an individual legacy. If you told them that, they probably wouldn't believe it." He's right, and that's what people at this point in the epiphany realize. The challenge for the coach is to nudge the person to see that the system of Stage Three develops no true followers; hence, no legacy. It's not that the person isn't capable of leaving a legacy—she is—it's that the stage in which she is operating isn't designed to do that.

The first part of the epiphany is that the person isn't making the impact he thought he was. The second part is that the "I," "me," "my" system isn't capable of fixing the problem. The person sees himself as others see him, and they don't like what they see. One of the most remarkable moments in our interviews came with actor Gary Cole, who portrayed *Office Space* boss, Bob Lumbergh. Since he is a great actor, he often answered our questions within character his voice reflecting the passivity of Lumbergh, or the spunk of one of his other famous roles, Bob Russell, the vice president on *The West Wing*. (Both characters took criticism for being narrow-minded and blind to their foibles.) During one of these moments, when his voice sounded like Russell, we asked what that character's pitfall was. Without a second of hesitation, he said, "I don't know that I see an Achilles' heel, or any weakness." Then he came out of character and a second later said, "If they have a weakness, it's that they don't recognize that they have any weaknesses. They don't acknowledge them. Humility isn't high on their chart." He added, "Lumburgh and Russell have blinders on, and they can only go forward. They have no reverse gear. They have no reflective genes in their body."

This moment captures the problem: when in character, when viewing the world through the eyes of someone at Stage Three, Cole reported no mistakes, no major weaknesses. The moment he took on the language system of Stage Four (which is how Cole speaks when he's talking about his own life), the pitfalls of his characters were as obvious as Bob Lumbergh's trademark coffee mug. Stage Three cannot see the effects of its behavior, just as without a mirror you can't see your own eyeballs.

As the second part of the epiphany was drawing to a close, Tobias saw the real problem with Stage Three: it cannot be fixed; it can only be abandoned. Saying "I will fix this situation" is another form of Stage Three, like saying "I'm great because I see myself the way others see me and am working on my legacy." Trying to do so merely creates new blind spots and repeats the Stage Three cycle.

Furthermore: the costs of Stage Three become increasingly clear: people are, in fact, accomplishing the *opposite* of what they want. "I was fighting for dignity and respect for federal employees," Tobias said, and yet his "badass" behavior wasn't in line with these values at all. He was removing dignity and respect from the system, not adding them.

Epiphany Part Three: What's the Real Goal?

The first two parts of the epiphany allow the person to ask a question: "What am I really trying to accomplish?" Other versions of the question we heard were "What's the point of all this?" and "How do we know if we're successful?"

In the midst of this epiphany, people we interviewed had many different goals that are surprisingly similar. David Kelley, the founder and CEO of IDEO (whom we'll get to know in the next chapter), said "The goal is to hang with friends and do things greater than any one of us could do alone." George Zimmer, the CEO of Men's Wearhouse (made famous on his television commercials saying, "I guarantee it!"), told us "The goal of business is that we have fun, and we are dead serious about it; it's even in our corporate bylaws." All of these goals boil down to wanting to make an impact on a large group of people.

At this stage of the epiphany, physicians remember that they went to medical school to help people. Lawyers, that they studied law to protect people's rights. Professors became professors to do for others what someone had done for them: kindle a love of learning. In a sense, this third phase of the epiphany brings people back to a simpler time in their lives. They're moving not back but forward—integrating and expanding their original goal with what they learned while moving through Stage Three.

As the person sees into her blind spots she realizes that the ego hit of accomplishment isn't the same as success itself. Her attention shifts to what's really important to her, and almost always, the goal is tribal. David Kelley of IDEO said his goal became "Hanging out with great people and creating stuff that makes a difference." George Zimmer, CEO of Men's Wearhouse, said, "We need to keep thinking about the people in our stores and how to make their lives better."

Frank Jordan, the former mayor of San Francisco (whom we met in Chapter 4), is one of the most self-effacing people we met. He now works as special assistant to the president of the Gordon and Betty Moore Foundation. Gordon Moore is the cofounder of Intel and founder of the foundation. Jordan said of Moore: "So many people are saying 'me, me, me,' and [Moore] is so unassuming, so humble. He says, 'We don't need publicity, we're not looking for publicity, we're looking for projects to fund.' It's so different from the people I knew in politics." Jordan revealed himself as someone who had the epiphany in saying this about his boss. People still at Stage Three might have said, "It's great to work with someone who can keep up with me."

As the seesaw tilts toward Stage Four, the person's language and behavior shift away from "I" and dyadic relationships and toward "we" and networked systems of people.

This is the part of the epiphany that is most remarkable to us: its work is automatic. Tobias said, "It was so obvious I couldn't believe I didn't see it before. The more the group succeeds, the more I succeed." As transformational expert Werner Erhard told us, "Let it use you; don't try to use it."

One of the most moving descriptions of this larger goal came from actor Gary Cole, this time talking about his life, not about his roles. Cole has a daughter with autism, and when he and his wife first heard the diagnosis, they went in search of a tribe to help them. As they talked with parents, medical experts, and people with autism they became tribal authorities on the subject, using Cole's celebrity to increase awareness and provide support to other families. When we asked him what drove this effort, he answered as if he were saying what everyone knows: "If you had to categorize any purpose in the world, it would be to help someone else. What is the reason anyone is here? You can point to having an experience and then someone down the road is in trouble, and they're going through what you've survived, and you stick your hand out. If you had to shortly define humanity, that would be it."

Once Cole saw the goal—having an impact on people—his behavior was automatic, like getting out of bed in the morning. He was "used by it," in Erhard's words. Also notice that his language is not focused on "I," "me," or "my." He is speaking for a tribe of people. Ironically, his epiphany is exactly what the characters he plays (such as Lumbergh) need to experience to move to "we're great." They would have to see the goal as clearly as the actor who brought them to life. First, though, they would have to see the effect of their behavior and that they cannot succeed alone.

With the goal in place, Tobias's actions fell in line with Stage Four. He no longer tried to beat up the local union presidents to get their compliance. His staff's complaint that "you haven't changed one bit" vanished as he spoke with people in the union and in government to look for common ground. He noticed that everyone around him valued dignity and respect, and he began talking about a union that would bring those values to life for everyone in the federal system. Now speaking for thousands of people, not just for himself, Tobias's words carried the weight of a Tribal Leader. He met with local union presidents and said, "It's not enough to be reactive, to sit behind your desk and wait for management to screw up, which they will, and beat the s---out of them. You have to be more than an insurance policy. You have to represent the ninety-five percent who never use any union services." Notice that Tobias now spoke for the people, and his language dropped the Stage Three focus on "I." He also found that when he spoke for the tribe, his words carried real weight. Ironically, by dropping the focus on himself, he became stronger.

Note that people don't lose ambition, drive, or work ethic by moving to Stage Four. After the epiphany, Tobias had more personal power, not less. Don Beck, author of *Spiral Dynamics,* told us, "The old system [Stage Three] doesn't disappear; the new system [Stage Four] transcends and subsumes it." In the same way that a glass of water is much more than the individual H_2O molecules that make it up, nothing is lost when people move to the next stage. Stage Four takes everything that works about Stage Three and reorganizes it, so that the person becomes more powerful. From our experience, people going through the epiphany found that fact reassuring, giving them a stronger vision for what was to come. Ironically, if people attempt to force the epiphany in order to become stronger, it doesn't work. They have to see—and feel and know and believe—that Stage Three will not get them to where they want to go.

Epiphany Part Four: How Does a Tribal Leader Use Power?

Niccolò di Bernardo dei Machiavelli's life would make a great story line for a daytime soap opera. He was expelled from his political office when the Medici family came to rule in Florence, Italy, in 1494. Desperate to return to politics, he wrote a book many of us should have read in high school (and didn't): *The Prince*. As the *Cliff's Notes* made clear to us, the authors of this book, when we were in college (we were both too busy living the Stage Three lifestyle to read the actual book), Machiavelli advocated cruelty and deception as the means to winning and keeping power. He is best known for his single admonition, "It is better to be feared than loved."

As often happens in history, public perception had more weight than the truth. Alone but with a cunning mind, he wrote *The Prince* as a treatise on power. Many assume that his intent was to prove his value as a mafia-style consigliere (like the Robert Duvall character in *The Godfather* movies). Although historians disagree on exactly how much of the book represents his thinking, one thing is certain: *The Prince* cemented the author's reputation as a cunning and treacherous political strategist. The public reaction against the book was so sharp that Machiavelli never gained the political office he sought, and he died alone in 1527. Seventy-five years later, Shakespeare wrote about a "Machiavel" in *Richard III*, essentially meaning "son of a bitch." His reputation is much the same today: someone who advocated any means necessary to win.

Why then does Steven Sample, president of the University of Southern California, think so highly of him? His admiration of Machiavelli is higher than that shown by any scholar of the writer we've met. Sample, whose doctorate is in engineering, is speaking with more authority than a layperson. He has studied Machiavelli for years, both as a subject he teaches in a leadership course with leadership guru Warren Bennis, and as a tool for leading one of the world's largest universities. His ideas about leadership, including his positive read on *The Prince,* became the subject of his book *The Contrarian's Guide to Leadership.*

Sample's view of Machiavelli is that, in the hands of a wise person, the techniques he advocated are critical to keeping the state (we would say "the tribe") strong by repelling enemies from without and from within. Here's one quote from *The Prince:* "Well committed atrocities are committed once so one may establish oneself. Poorly committed atrocities are done at first sparingly, then more and more. Therefore, one taking a state must commit all the atrocities at the beginning." It reminds us of Jack Welch's early days at the helm of General Electric, when he fired so many people he was nick-named "Neutron Jack," but the company emerged stronger and healthier because of his actions.

The critical question to ask about "atrocities"—or, in a business context, tough decisions—is, "in service of what?" We've met hundreds of managers who put this passage from *The Prince* into service for their own promotion—the Stage Three system. They fired the people who threatened their power, destroyed Stage Four cultures that preached a different way of operating, and purged their departments of anyone who didn't seem loyal to them. Sample admits that Machiavelli's techniques, in the hands of someone out for personal gain, can be disastrous. We've seen companies destroyed by people at Stage Three using *The Prince* as their bible.

Sample sees a higher purpose in Machiavelli's techniques because he's looking from the other side of the epiphany, from the perspective of Stage Four. As evidence of his Tribal Leader status, Sample has led arguably the most impressive academic turnaround in the history of American higher education, raising USC from a "jock school" to an institution where incoming test scores are among the highest in the nation—all in ten years. In the process, he has made many tough decisions, most of which net out to the institution coming first. He leads from a clear set of values, has taken on some large egos in the university, and, although respected, has made his share of enemies. Talking about university governance, Sample said, "You can get deans, provosts, even presidents, who are all about themselves, and not the institution as a whole, and they lead to a rotting, a corrupting, of the institution." How does he identify the people who are out for themselves? "You have to listen to all the feedback, including complaints. You learn to smell it out." Sample's view that Stage Three leads to institutional decay shows that he sees Stage Three for what it is: blinding to the person and damaging to the tribe.

Sample's view of Macchiavelli is that *in service of the institution, The Prince* is filled with principles that help ground the leader in a good understanding of human nature. It never occurs to this university president that people might use the techniques in service of their own egos, hence his positive view of the ancient scholar.

That's not to say Sample has a naïve view of people. Like most Tribal Leaders, Sample does see value in individual Stage Three performers. In the university setting, such individuals can bring success to the institution by winning grants and awards, even Nobel Prizes. "The same is true in companies," he told us, reflecting on his service on fourteen corporate boards. But Sample fumes over specific faculty (mostly in the arts) who have been nurtured by the university for years, and as soon as they make it big, "It's like they're owned by the cosmos, and have always been owned by the cosmos, and when asked about USC, they'll say 'Isn't that in Los Angeles? I remember being on the campus a time or two.'" As is true with people who have gone through the epiphany, Sample's anger is based not on personal offense but on a perceived act of disloyalty toward the tribes he leads.

We met a Tribal Leader in medicine, Dr. Mark Rumans of the Billings Clinic in Montana, who has taken Sample's advice and put "atrocities" into a Stage Four context. His wall has a plaque, visible from the chairs in his administrative office, which reads, "The first clean kill awakens the whole herd." This sign is stunning to people who know him as a man with a soft voice and a warm demeanor, and as a person famous for his self-deprecating humor. His tone and manners convey a Tribal Leader's set of concerns: a love for people, empathy for their problems, and putting the institution before ego. This Tribal Leader makes it clear that violating rules has consequences and that he will enforce them—and we've seen him follow the adage on his wall with such unwavering conviction and resolution that it has shocked people around him. Sample has done the same, as have hundreds of other Tribal Leaders we've met. Glen Esnard, a Tribal Leader whom we'll meet in Chapter 8, told us, "You have to publicly execute people who disobey the rules, otherwise everyone thinks you don't mean what you say, and then there's no leadership, only bulls---." What Machiavelli refers to as atrocities, Sample calls "decisions you have to make for the good of the institution." Glen, raised in the "wild, wild west" of Stage Three commercial real estate, calls it "doing the work of the sheriff"—but notice he's on the side of tribal values, not out for his own advancement. After the epiphany, old rules are repurposed for the advancement of the tribe.

Sample argues that great leaders, from time to time, need to use shocking methods to strengthen the tribe. In his book *The Contrarian's Guide to Leadership* and in his conversation with us, he repeats the story (which he admits may be apocryphal) that after World War II, Douglas Macarthur ordered the execution of many American soldiers who had raped Japanese women. The general went so far as to invite Japanese leaders to attend the event. "It was incomprehensible to them that an invading leader would execute his own soldiers for doing what soldiers had always done," he said. The action had the effect of strengthening the tribe of American soldiers and demonstrating the army's values to Japanese leaders.

While Steve Sample, Mark Rumans, Glen Esnard, and Bob Tobias haven't executed anyone (literally), each has demonstrated that Tribal Leaders don't back down from difficult decisions. Their approach isn't touchy-feely and they aren't pushovers. Their focus, however, is purely on the tribe. By drawing on the tribe's convictions and values, they become more powerful than they were at Stage Three.

End of the Epiphany: "I Am Because We Are"

Once the three phases of the epiphany have done their work, a leader's entire language system realigns. She still has an ego, but it's focused on the tribe, not on herself. "I" language is out, and "we" language is in. Dyads are being replaced by triads, which we'll examine in Chapter 10. Instead of speaking for herself and assuming that others will see the logic in her point of view, she begins to listen, to learn about the tribe, and to speak for it. As all this happens, a subtle but rapid change begins: she accrues respect, loyalty, followers, and an expectation of great things.

While amassing this following, she doesn't think it has anything to do with her. Several of the Tribal Leaders we interviewed, including Gordon Binder, first turned us down, saying that they hadn't done anything. Binder went further: "I just got out of the way and let the managers at Amgen do the right thing." We finally persuaded him to talk by pointing out that, at a minimum, he didn't stop the effort. (In fact, he was an active player, but his focus on "we" gives the credit to others.)

Tobias had spent years working collaboratively with the Internal

Revenue Service, rather than only filing grievances or unfair labor practice charges. His reputation as a collaborator spread throughout the government, including to then Senator Al Gore. With a change in the administration in 1992 (and the election of Clinton and Gore), there was an opportunity to change the labor–management relationships in the federal government. Looking back Tobias, said, "The whole idea for why we have a union changed. In 1992, I realized I could work with Clinton, which is ironic for a man who got started suing a president." He met with Gore, then vice president and chair of Clinton's "reinventing government" program. "The argument was compelling," Tobias said. "You can't change the workplace that's eighty percent organized without dealing with the organization [unions]." Tobias worked with the other federal sector union to send the vice president a proposal that he, together with the other union leaders, helped to implement as an executive order, stating that the government would work collaboratively with unions. Tobias said, "Then it wasn't me speaking, it was the federal labor movement and the executive branch managers, including the president of the United States." Tobias finally found leverage with union leaders who were still using the "badass" model.

Shortly after interviewing several people who had gone through this epiphany, we talked with Don Beck, who, after writing *Spiral Dynamics,* spent years in Africa. He said, after hearing about the three stages of the epiphany, "There's a word in the Bantu languages that [Archbishop Desmond] Tutu has used to help bring the entire country of South Africa together: *ubuntu,* meaning 'Today I share with you because tomorrow you share with me.'" The word can also be translated "I am because we are." The essence of tribal leadership is building the "we," and as a person does this his influence, respect, and power increase.

The Leap of Faith

Tobias describes his move through the phases of the epiphany as a journey in which he was pulled (rather than did the pulling), but he reflected that one element is required: a leap of faith. "I was committing to a system I couldn't picture," he said. "Somehow it just had to be better, and the allure of what I thought might be possible was enough to keep me moving."

When he finally stepped down from the National Treasury Employees Union after thirty-one years, the last sixteen as its president, it had grown from twenty thousand people, mostly IRS employees, to one hundred and fifty-five thousand, representing employees in twenty-six different federal agencies. As is common with Tribal Leaders, Tobias leveraged his experience and expertise, including the three phases of the epiphany, to grow into the final stage of leadership, what we call a Stage Five Tribal Elder. We'll meet up with him again in Chapter 12.

After meeting many people like Tobias, we met to summarize what we were learning. A metaphor popped up in our discussion that we've used ever since. It captures the courage required to take the leap of faith into Tribal Leadership. Here it is.

In school, when someone goes up a grade, say from third to fourth, the new grade isn't fun. There isn't as much art or painting. The old teacher is gone, as is our rapport with her. To make it worse, we see her at recess surrounded by children who aren't us, and it just feels unfair. A few months later, going back to the old grade seems unimaginably simple. We can barely believe we were challenged by the topics of third grade, now that we're on to tougher math and harder reading. The games seem juvenile and silly. When we're ready to leave the fourth grade, we have the same feelings as we did a year before.

Where this metaphor breaks down is that we don't ever have to leave Stage Three, so we get to choose to stay where it's comfortable, or to challenge ourselves and go for excellence. Whether to stay with Stage Three or advance to Four is the single most important question for individuals and corporations around the world.

As Tobias recounted the story of his epiphany, we asked what advice he would give to people still in the "wild, wild west" aspect of Stage Three. His answer summarized our research and was in line with that of other experts we interviewed: "I would ask what their goal is. If it's to win, keep on doing it. If it's to make a larger impact, how do you create relationships to get what it is you want them to do? You can't do it by yourself; you have to work with others." Transformational expert Werner Erhard told us that transformation begins with accepting things "exactly as they are, and exactly as they are not." When people see the effects of their behavior, they can make a decision: stay in Stage Three or engage the epiphany. The choice is up to each person.

Key Points from This Chapter

- The epiphany begins with noticing that people haven't achieved what they thought, that victories they thought were tribal are only personal.

- As the epiphany continues, people often try to achieve group victories using Stage Three behavior, which never works.

- People eventually see that the goal of Stage Three—winning on a personal basis—is self-defeating. Tribal successes, by contrast, are enduring and satisfying for everyone.

● Most people notice that power is a zero-sum game in Stage Three: the more you take from others, the more you have and the less others have. By contrast, power in Stage Four is abundant: the more you give to others, the more you get back.

◆ The last epiphany is seeing that the only real goal is the betterment of the tribe. Ironically, as people act to build the tribe they achieve everything they sought but couldn't achieve at Stage Three: esteem, respect, loyalty, legacy, and enduring success.

● ● ● ● ●

CHAPTER 8

Stage Four: Establishing Tribal Leadership

David Kelley looks like an unlikely corporate hero. With a mous-tache, glasses, and receding dark hair, he looks as if he'd be more at home in a university. And that's exactly where he spends some of his time, as a tenured professor at Stanford.

His passion is collaborative design, which he and a group of friends turned into IDEO twenty-five years ago. By most accounts, it is the most successful engineering design company in the world. As founder and CEO, Kelley has graced the cover of *Business Week,* and his firm of 450 employees (technically, a tribe of tribes) is credited with collaborating to create the first Apple mouse, stand-up squeeze toothpaste bottles, Steelcase's Leap chair (rated No. 1 by *The Wall Street Journal* in 2005), and the Palm V.

IDEO's physical space is built around its values of innovation, collaboration, communication, and fun. Housed in a modern build-ing of glass and steel that incorporates the brick remains of an old auto repair shop, it is not far from Stanford, where it recruits most of its employees. The lobby waiting area features a paper table with crayons, so that people waiting for meetings at the company can doodle and then rip off their work and take it with them. Lots of tall plants, bordering on trees, cover the inner landscape of the building. It looks like a scene of an inside park in some futuristic world, perhaps from *The Jetsons*.

David Kelley is a Tribal Leader, having seen the flaws of the Stage Three system while working in a large company. "This company [IDEO] is a reaction to big Fortune 100 companies," he told us in one of IDEO's signature conference rooms, which has brainstorming rules across the top of the walls: "Stay focused," "One conversation at a time," "Be visual," "Go for quantity," "Defer judgment," and "Encourage wild ideas."

As we talked with Kelley he followed every piece of the wall's advice except for one: "Stay focused." Our conversation ran from culture, to IDEO's recruitment system, to the problems in higher education, to why big companies often dehumanize their employees. One theme ran through all the topics: a company is only as strong as the culture of its tribe.

As is characteristic of many Tribal Leaders we met, Kelley ridicules many practices of corporations without ever seeming mean-tempered or judgmental. "Come sit next to Freda and Harry," he says, referring to a hypothetical employee's first day in a large company. "Well, I didn't pick Freda and Harry as my friends; how come I have to have them as friends?" He goes on: "You always get evaluated by what your boss's boss does. Who wants that?"

"I started the company because I wanted to work with my friends," he says. He describes his epiphany as coming from two sources: large companies—which he learned don't work very well—and a mentor, who encouraged him to write how he hoped someone would some day eulogize him. He describes what he scribbled for his mentor, written in the past tense as a description of one who had died: "I started a collaborative, and at Christmastime, we sold stuff out of the basement." The ideas were the genesis of IDEO: "We started with ten of my friends, and all but one are still here, thirty years later. It was more build a culture than do design. We focused on what we cared about. The feeling is we were—are—all in it together."

●　●　●

In our research, after a person has had the epiphany that takes him from Stage Three to Stage Four, he behaves differently than before. Our data show that people tend to take one of three paths. David Kelley took the first: he gets together a group of like-minded friends and asks how they might make money. The relationships come before the business model; the tribe before the profits. If the group is composed of people who are really operating at Stage Four (rather than dropouts from the system in the midst of Stage Two), the ventures tend to do very well, like IDEO. The key question is, "Have we all owned, and are we all done with, Stage Three?" If the answer is yes, a small group of people becomes what we call a tribal seed. As it grows it attracts resources, people, money, and ideas, and it flourishes into a tribe.

The second path is that the newly minted Stage Four person looks for people in a large organization (usually a corporation, nonprofit, or government) who are eager to play by a different set of rules. Often, these will be people in late Stage Three, or individuals in the process of going through the epiphany. The Tribal Leader collects and nurtures them and forms a tribe based on their values and aspirations. The group—often a new department or, in a matrix organization, a "project"—becomes unusually successful, often being labeled a "miracle." As the group succeeds, people at Stage Three notice the results, often trying to replicate the tribe's strategy within an "I'm great" culture. Such approaches fail, and the Tribal Leader's group moves further ahead, with people scratching their heads about how he does it.

The third path is that the person forges out on her own, developing what we call tribal antennae—an intuitive ability to find people who can contribute to success on a larger scale than one person working alone, and who value her help in return. From the outside, her actions look like networking gone wild—she's constantly reaching out to more and more people, with others around her saying that she needs to learn focus. In fact, her actions are systematic: she is shopping for tribal members. As she finds people who fit, she networks them into the group, and a tribe slowly takes shape. Unlike the first approach, where the tribal seed determines the nature of the business from the start, this third path produces rapidly changing tribes and business models. The key to this third path is that it's not "my tribe" but "our tribe." The person who cobbled it together is recognized as the Tribal Leader, not the single visionary who calls the shots. In this system, anyone is welcome to play—and tribal members all have a hand in recruiting, provided they have something to offer and obey the rules.

In this chapter, we will go through each of these three paths to see how a person becomes established as a Tribal Leader. We'll start with how David Kelley learned the rules of Stage Four and how the "group of friends" became the most successful business in its niche.

Stage Four at IDEO

Simply put, IDEO is a company built from the tribe up. It's more important to maintain its Stage Four culture than to win the next contract or hire the latest Stanford graduate. As we've seen throughout this book, the more it wins on the cultural front, the better its profit-and-loss statement looks.

"When you get a good culture going, it's hard to ruin it," Kelley said. "When you get a bad culture, it's hard to fix." IDEO's culture has been strong since its founding more than two decades ago.

IDEO not only reconceives shopping carts and reengineers toothpaste dispensers but also constantly refocuses how it functions as a business. Like most professional services firms, IDEO bills for its time, although Kelley adds, "We're trying to get away from that." In addition to paid gigs, the firm manufactures what it calls concept projects, which, Kelley says, "bring different kinds of people together." Concept projects have included reinventing flip-flop sandals, exploring new forms for chocolate, or rethinking the modern business card. These projects accomplish the job of bringing the tribe together and getting new members up to speed. Kelley summarizes: "It's like orientation, but it doesn't seem like bullsh--.

"We would never say we have a 'training program' or 'human resources' or any of that stuff," he says, with a wave that is both dismissive and good-natured. "We have an orientation program where people introduce themselves to the group in weird ways. First they have to send out an e-mail [introducing themselves]. Groups of new interns might be given a fun design challenge, and deliver their findings and proposed design solution by standing up and doing skits. In a program called IDEO 101, they do a revolving workshop around the country, and they do team-based things. In between, they learn about medical benefits and all that stuff. If it looks like a meeting, we don't want to have anything to do with it. But make funny hats to introduce ourselves—absolutely."

Debbie Stern, a consultant, who has worked with Kelley both at IDEO and at Stanford, adds, "It seems weird to pull people out of a business to orient them, so we don't do that. We orient them here, where they work." As is typical of Stage Four organizations, everyone seems an equal in IDEO discussions. New employees, seasoned veterans, and top people like Stern and Kelley mix together as though all play on the same soccer team.

> **TECHNICAL NOTE:** *Stage Four tribes pay almost no attention to organizational boundaries. Palo Alto is filled with small businesses run by people who are also Stanford faculty. Some of the most innovative people we met are "on loan" from other profit centers in the same company. Many Stage Four companies have contract or part-time workers, with people acting as free agents. What matters is contribution, not whether people are regular full-time employees.*

Kelley notes that the hardest part was getting started, even after the epiphany that a Stage Three company was not what he wanted. "If you look at any design firm, other than a few, it's named after a person. Their name was on the door, and I started out that way, too. I started out as David Kelley Design. I figured we could get to fifty [people]. We're now at [almost] five hundred. Even at fifty, I had to decide to give up or build the stage that others would perform on. I changed the name of the company, brought in new people, and that's how it all started."

Getting a job at IDEO means convincing the tribe that the candidate will make a contribution and fit within the culture. Candidates are taken to lunch—"lunched," in IDEO language—by ten employees. Kelley explains the thinking: "If ten people are emotionally committed to making that person being successful, he will be. I say that to my friends at Google, and they say, 'We have to grow faster than that,' but as a private company, it works for us." For a candidate to survive being lunched means that people have to think she will succeed culturally and technically—that she will be a contributing tribal member.

Note that for public companies, Wall Street's focus on short-term results can take a Stage Four tribe off purpose. If IDEO were looking to cut its costs in the short run, it might consider streamlining its hiring system or dropping concept projects. Both actions would harm the culture and, in the long run, its profitability. Tribal Leaders of publicly traded companies often act as a buffer against the short-term thinking of analysts and stock speculators. They do demand success, but they keep the focus on values, structure of relationships, and strategy—the topics of Part III of this book.

One of the big differences between IDEO and companies that are dominated by Stage Three thinking is that IDEO truly walks its values. Kelley says, "If we were going to measure what makes a leader here, it would be to measure how nurturing people are." Many leaders of Stage Three organizations said similar things, but the same companies had large offices for executives and cubicles for employees, and they rated people every year according to their impact on the bottom line. IDEO, on the other hand, has, in Kelley's words, "a crummy little space of your own where you have your shrine to your kids and all that," but nice furniture and "cool" technology in their teamwork spaces.

When the early buzz about Tribal Leadership began to form, many company leaders asked us to help them figure out why they couldn't get any traction on teamwork. One visit to their company showed at least part of the problem: their physical space didn't match the values of the Stage Four tribe they wanted to be. Manager's offices lined the walls, with *Dilbert*-style cubicles in the middle for the people who were doing the work. Many of these companies preached "open-door policies" and "'we' not 'me,'" yet their physical design sent a different message. We believe that the future of commercial architecture must hold hands with the future of collaborate cultures, producing workplaces like that at IDEO—where the culture, values, and physical space are consistent. Griffin Hospital, from Chapter 2, shows off the best practice of giving staff a voice in creating the space, not merely delegating the decision to executives who work with designers. "We drove the architects crazy, but they were committed to the same things we were," Griffin Hospital's Bill Powanda said. As is typical for a Stage Four organization, the architects had to handle input from hundreds of people.

Kelley has a system for working with clients, essentially turning them into partners on IDEO projects. When IDEO partnered with Kaiser Permanente in 2003, originally to help design new buildings, the IDEO staff asked the physicians, nurses, and Kaiser managers to role-play being a patient going through their system. Everyone involved in the process saw that that the problem was not a lack of facilities but a need to rethink the patient flow process. The partnership with IDEO allowed Kaiser to develop a new sensitivity to the patient and save several million dollars by not building new buildings. He says: "You can take the whole company and redesign it around 'we' spaces, but that's not enough . . . You have to measure for it, play little games, and see when it works. It's iterative, but it works."

We'll examine how IDEO works with clients in Chapter 10, but as you'd expect, it's not a typical business services approach. Because it's built from a Stage Four culture up, IDEO is successful by any measure. It makes money; its designs are used throughout the world; it attracts the best and brightest who want to collaborate; and it is an example of a company fashioned on core values. This company, built from a few Stage Four people up, is the first way to establish Tribal Leadership. We now turn to the second: carving a Stage Four niche within a Stage Three organization.

TECHNICAL NOTE: *In our research, we learned of several keys to see whether a person is operating at Stage Four, as opposed* *to late Stage Three using "we" language. When we met with Brian Sexton's team of gang prosecutors in Chicago, Sexton used both keys right away. First, he brought his team in for the meeting—Tribal Leaders opt for groups of at least three. Second, as we asked our questions, he mostly took blame for things that went wrong and passed the praise on to his team members: Tom Mahoney and Charise Valente. Third, we asked how new team members are trained. Sexton said, "In the old days, the new people got the cases from hell, and no support. Today, they get easy cases and lots of 'How you doing?' and 'Do you need anything?'" The three giveaways are a tendency toward meetings of at least three team members, giving credit and keeping blame, and support from the entire team (encouraged by the leader) during training. In short, Sexton's actions revealed that his interest is the tribe, not himself.*

Finding People Who Are Ready for Stage Four: The CB Richard Ellis Private Client Group

One of our favorite companies is CB Richard Ellis, the largest commercial real estate services provider in the world. It is a company with heart, passion, and commitment. Unlike most real estate companies that disappear when the market dips, CB Richard Ellis just celebrated its hundredth anniversary.

Part of what makes the company so remarkable is that it remembers its roots. It was founded in San Francisco right after the earthquake of 1906, and the founders pioneered a new model of obtaining leases. Rather than quoting the client a low price, leasing the property for a high amount, and pocketing the difference (common at the time), Colbert Coldwell, the company's cofounder, used the practice we know today: finding the best price and working off a commission. The revolution he started was putting the client first, and the firm holds to that value today.

Largely because the company has invested so heavily in employee learning, many individuals at CB Richard Ellis are now late Stage Three, asking, "what's next?" A few have moved through their own epiphany and are now emerging at the "we're great" stage.

In 2001, Glen Esnard, then a senior managing director with the company, learned to spot those emerging leaders who wanted to play at Stage Four and band them together in a new line of business he and other leaders were pioneering, the Private Client Group, a client-focused segment of its investment sales division. Unlike the rest of the division, which was mostly going after institutional money, Glen's group focused on smaller players, such as dentists who wanted in on the red-hot commercial real estate market. The magic of the Private Client Group (or PCG for short) is that hundreds of brokers are pooling their leads into a common database, giving PCG a competitive advantage that is "almost thermonuclear," in Glen's words. Recently, a PCG rep visited a man wanting to sell an apartment complex in Arizona. The rep was able to pull up hundreds of people who were ready to invest in that type of property in that state, many of them not even living in Arizona. Most PCG competitors have to go off their personal contacts, and that might amount to a handful of people. Simply put, in head-to-head competition, PCG almost always gets the business.

Most people in commercial real estate make their money from the people they know, so they hoard their contacts. With a grin on his face, Glen said that getting brokers to pool that information is like asking a vampire to give to the Red Cross.

Glen built the group by putting together a PowerPoint presentation on the size of the market, the opportunity, and the values that would drive PCG. He then asked local managing directors for CB Richard Ellis to set up broker meetings, and he flew in and gave his presentation. Glen recalls that a few people would linger, ask some questions, and seem interested.

When people agreed to join PCG, Glen had them sign a list of ten business principles, including No. 2, which says: "Our group is built on the concept of 'team'. . . . We have no room for those who put their personal interests ahead of the interests of the group and its clients." Glen then negotiated with the brokers on their "sandbox"—a limitation of geography, industry (retail, industrial, etc.), or both. Glen had done what *Spiral Dynamics* author, Don Beck, suggested to us: "Set the condition and then see who shows up at the party."

Glen had to pin on the sheriff's badge more than once and bust people for violating PCG values. Some joined the group and turned in "garbage leads" but got access to everyone else's real data. Others expanded their geographic territories without consulting anyone.

Slowly, as the database grew and PCG had a few victories, word of this new way of doing business caught on. Many brokers were attracted because it was unlike the "eat what you kill" approach for most of the industry.

Watching Glen work the crowd at early PCG national conferences (in 2002 and 2003) was like watching Bill Clinton running for office—with a twist. He does shake hands, give hugs, and ask how people's kids are. But if you froze a moment of his behavior, you'd see that he was almost always talking to two people at once. Somewhere in the conversation, he speaks to the relationship between them, either introducing them to each other or reinforcing why they should be the best of friends. It's so subtle that you might not see it if you didn't know what to look for. This subtle technique is part of "the triad," a technique Tribal Leaders almost always use, which is the topic of Chapter 10.

As Glen moves on, the people he has just introduced often spend a moment talking, usually about Glen. "He's a great guy," "He looked goofy in the hat at last year's party," and so on. Some say, with almost an "I've slept in the Lincoln Bedroom" tone, that they've been to Glen's house to watch football games on Saturday afternoons.

An entrepreneur at heart, Glen left CB Richard Ellis in 2005 to build up a smaller company in commercial real estate, but not before making an industry-wide impact with the Private Client Group. To this day, when two members of the group meet, they're excited about being with another member of the tribe. As we watched the Private Client Group mingle at the company's one hundred-year anniversary in San Francisco, people were fully themselves. No corporate cult here, and no copycat Glens running around. Everyone seems happy, inspired, genuine. The overall vibe of the room is "tribal pride," which is the mood of Stage Four.

Glen created a Stage Four tribe in a very systematic way. First, he built a presentation that spoke to people at Stage Four, or those ready to make the leap from Stage Three to Four. It spoke of collaboration, of the promise of an untapped market that cannot be captured by individuals working in isolation. It is a Stage Four message, and while people at Stage Three can hear it, they often scoff at the tone as unworkable. Those "with ears to hear," as Glen says—those done with their epiphany or still in its process—found the presentation energizing, engaging, and, in the words of several, "exactly what I'd been looking for."

Second, he had them sign agreements in which they promised to play by the rules. Every tribe needs its sheriff, and these statements gave Glen the badge he needed to keep order.

Third, Glen put in technology that specifically screens out those unwilling to play by Stage Four rules. If people don't add their data to the PCG infrastructure, they're sent packing. If you work in an organization dominated by Stage Two or Three behavior (which is most companies in the world), you don't need to upgrade the entire corporate culture first. Instead, you can, like Glen, craft a message that will reach those ready to join a new tribe-within-a-company, and build success around this new "center of excellence." People will notice the results, and as the insights of Stage Four spread, others who are ready will join the new emerging culture.

COACHING TIP: What if my CEO is at Stage Three? *This is one of the hardest questions we've been asked, as is its cousin: "My team wants to play at Stage Four but our boss is solidly at Stage Three—what do we do?" We recommend creating a pocket of excellence in whatever small ways are allowed by the boss, and then let the results speak for themselves. Harry Truman had to use this approach when he worked for the Tom Pendergast political machine in Missouri. Pendergast, who was at Stage Three to the bone, wouldn't allow Truman to run for Congress or for governor. In lesser roles, including county judge and then presiding judge, Truman built small Stage Four tribes. The results of his efforts were so impressive that he was eventually allowed to run for the Senate, and he won. He later become vice president and, when Franklin Roosevelt died in 1944, president of the United States. Chapter 10 will include additional tips for what to do if your CEO or your boss discourages Stage Four behavior.*

Note that although tribes always form, only Stage Four tribes have a sense of their own identity. People at Stage Two feel disconnected, and at Three, they report constantly battling it out with others in an ego war. At Stage Four, however, everything changes. People identify with the group and its values. In Stage Four organizations, it's common for employees not to list their job titles on cards. As David Kelley told us, "At Stanford, when I'm introduced, it's as a tenured professor, member of the National Academy of Engineering, blah, blah, blah. At IDEO, I'm David Kelley, a member of the team." We now turn to the third way of establishing Tribal Leadership: building a new tribe one person at a time.

Building a Tribe from the Leader Up: She Beads

Sandy Rueve was a stay-at-home mom with three part-time jobs, including working as an X-ray technician for the Chicago Bulls. To make ends meet, she also made and sold crafts. A natural talker, she told everyone about her bracelets and necklaces as she ran them through the X-ray process. In her words, "Next thing I know, Michael Jordan is asking me for some of my work." Day after day he asked, and Sandy kept putting him off, and game after game he asked.

"All I did was string other people's beads together," Rueve told us. "He thought I made the beads from scratch." As a woman of deep pride she couldn't give mere machine-made beads to His Airness. To not disappoint the basketball player, she spent months studying ancient techniques of bead making: designing, rolling, and baking. Four months later, on Jordan's birthday, she presented him with one of her first original designs, and he loved it. "Next thing," she said, "Scottie Pippen is calling and asking, 'Where's mine?'" Not to be outdone by Jordan and Pippen, Dennis Rodman asked for some, and then more and more. In fact, he wore several long necklaces of Sandy's beads, and rumors are that he wore them when he got married. Sandy laughed when she spoke about designing for Dennis. "They went all the way down to here," she said, gesturing below the table where we sat. "They all got in on it, even Phil Jackson," she said. "They were all wearing my beads."

Years later, Rueve has gone from razoring clay on her kitchen table to CEO of She Beads, with thirty-six employees in two locations. Her work went from "crafty crap" (her words) to grossing several million dollars a year. She dreams of opening her own high-end stores across the country. People can buy She Beads direct from the Web or through numerous boutiques and sales divas. She has agreements with Macy's in Chicago and has other deals in the works with boutiques and department stores. Each method of distribution has its own product line, each with its own characteristics, "so that we keep it all straight for the customer," she says.

We have to see two things about how Rueve made the leap from "I'm great" to starting a Stage Four tribe from scratch. First, she built the company around a set of values: vitality, quality, and passion. As we'll see in the next chapter, values are at the heart of every "we're great" tribe. Several of her beads feature subtle pink ribbons highlighting her company's commitment to beating breast cancer, as well as other strands that include red dresses (American Heart Association) or gold ribbons (National Childhood Cancer Foundation) or teal ribbon (Chicago Ovarian Cancer Alliance). Sandy, the walking embodiment of the tribe, is dedicated to improving these issues. "We keep donating more and more to charities, and that trend will continue," she said.

Second, Rueve has developed a common characteristic of Tribal Leaders who form a tribe from scratch: they have "tribal antennae"— the ability to identify contributions of people not yet in the tribe.

She draws them in and keeps them based on a commitment to values.

Rueve points out that if she didn't consider her contractors, sales divas, and employees part of her tribe, "we'd be nowhere." She treats her customers in the same way—constantly listening for suggestions and advice. Reid Hoffman, the CEO of LinkedIn, whom we'll meet in Chapter 10, went even further: "I tell Internet entrepreneurs that if you are not embarrassed by your first product release, then you have launched too late." By releasing a product and then creating dialogue with partners, a Stage Four tribe learns what it should change to become more successful. In essence, it creates partnerships with its clients, just as the corporate itself runs on partnership.

Rueve went from an X-ray technician to an entrepreneur by listening to hundreds of people tell her who she is—starting with Michael Jordan insisting that she was an artist. Her employees, originally working in her basement, suggested that natural light would brighten all their moods and thus enhance quality, so she rented an above-the-ground work space.

We see the effect of her tribal antennae when we look at her work space. Her customers liked to come by and watch the teamwork, even when it was a few people in a basement. Through a mutual friend, Rueve met William Brian Ross (mentioned in Chapter 4), who runs Design For You, a design and general contracting firm in Chicago. Design For You remade her workplace into an expression of She Bead's dedication to quality. The crowning achievement is a Ross design that She Beads calls the spaceship. Ross says: "The spaceship is an eight-sided table, where the stringers [those who string the jewelry together] sit and work. The center of it has a series of stacked, independently rotating lazy Susans. We designed it so stringers can sit on any side and be able to reach all the beads they need by spinning the lazy Susans." Rueve's customers *love* watching the stringers work the spaceship, and the company is considering a similar design for her stores as a way to attract visitors and customers, just as Krispy Kreme draws people who want to watch the donuts being made. By listening to people and engaging her tribal antennae, Rueve built a Stage Four tribe and a successful business in the process.

Stabilizing at Stage Four

IDEO, CB Richard Ellis's Private Client Group, and She Beads are three remarkable organizations in that they are stable at Stage Four and sometimes float into Stage Five.

Most of the corporate tribes we studied only had moments of Stage Four before falling back to Stage Three. Part II of this book gives the three keys we found to corporate tribes stabilizing at the "we're great" zone of Tribal Leadership. Only groups at Stage Four can move forward to the last and most effective stage.

Key Points from This Chapter

◆   After a person has the epiphany, there are three ways to establish a Stage Four culture. The first is to get a group of like-minded people together and ask how to create or expand a business. This is the model that David Kelley and others used to found IDEO.

◆   The second is to look for a group of people within a Stage Three organization who want to play a Stage Four game. This is the model Glen Esnard used to create CB Richard Ellis's Private Client Group.

◆   The third is to ignore organizational boundaries and to use tribal antennae to find people who want to create a Stage Four tribe, allowing them to guide the development of the group. This is the model Sandy Rueve used to create She Beads.

PART III
Owning Tribal Leadership: Stabilizing Stage Four

CHAPTER 9

Core Values
and a Noble Cause

When we first spoke with Gordon Binder, the former CEO of Amgen, he asked the same question almost every other Stage Four Tribal Leader asked: "Why do you want to talk with me?" He added, "I didn't do anything."

We asked him for a few hours of time to tell us the Amgen story from his perspective, so other leaders could learn from it. That was enough to convince him to talk with us to chronicle the story of how Amgen owned Stage Four—a story we had seen from inside as consultants to this historic company in the mid-1990s.

Early in Binder's tenure, many people realized that the Amgen culture, as he told us, was "really good, far better than other companies." He adds, "People said, 'It makes my life more fun, and it's effective. It's good for me, good for the company, good for everyone.'"

Most, though, expected its "specialness" to end as its size kept doubling. He continued: "People would sit around trying to figure out if it would change [as the company grew]. When we passed fifty, or a hundred, or a thousand employees, they worried that we would lose our special culture. It was a frequent topic of discussion."

Our memory of the early Amgen culture was high energy, dedi-cation to the cause of curing disease, and focus on collective suc-cess. We overhead custodians—right along with research scientists and marketing staff—saying that their work was helping to cure cancer. It is almost impossible for us to convey that their words rang of genuine passion for their affiliation with Amgen, but they did.

During this time, a middle manager decided, without any formal authority, to record the Amgen culture. Binder recalls: "We hadn't thought about the difference between values, principles, and so on. He wanted to write down what Amgen's values were. He started talking with a lot of people to see if he could figure it out. When I found out about his project, I decided that it was too great to let him do it alone. We should get the whole company involved and really do this right.

"By the time we were done, we had individual interviews with about four hundred people, focus groups, and so on. It literally turned out there were eight [core] values, absolutely not seven or nine. Along the way, I concluded everything grew out of the values; the culture was based on them. If we could start with the values, everything else would follow."

Identifying Values

A key point for companies that want to attain Stage Four is to go for values *now*. One of the most common misconceptions we heard in our research is that values is a topic for organizations that have a lot of money, and that struggling organizations should focus on the day-to-day tactics of survival instead. Almost without exception, we found that wildly successful organizations talked about values when it appeared they could least afford to do so. IDEO, Amgen, and CB Richard Ellis's Private Client Group all *started* with a common set of values, either by luck or by design. Amgen was fortunate to have started as a culture dominated by scientists eager to collaborate, so their culture reflected science-based inquiry, competition, teamwork, creating value, ensuring quality, collaboration, and communication, and being ethical—the eight values that continue to lead the company.

Binder and the team wanted to keep the resulting document short, but they knew every word would be important. "When we got down to the almost final draft, someone had the bright idea of getting the top management team in a room and having a whiz at a keyboard sit there, and put the first value up on the screen," Binder recalls. "Everyone made suggestions, and we rewrote it real-time on the screen. We spent hours on this thing, and every word was worthy of discussion and consideration. We ended up publishing it. Ten years later, there were some minor changes, hundred percent of which were for the purpose of clarity. These were the values, still are the values."

The effort to clarify Amgen's values, in Binder's words, "was the most important thing we ever did." Managers were expected to hire on the basis of values, promote people who lived them, and fire people who acted out of line with them. Binder recalls one day when he learned that a manager he had hired and interviewed had been fired by the head of human resources. He said, "I was annoyed that he had taken that action without talking with me first, until [the head of HR] said, 'He lied on his résumé. That's against our values.'" Binder laughed as he told us the story. "What could I say? He was right!"

Getting Binder to talk values isn't hard, and when on the subject, he's as passionate as any Tribal Leader we've met. "I remember many meetings when we just couldn't decide what to do, and then someone would ask, 'What do the values say?'" Binder told us that most such meetings ended within minutes, everyone happy with the decision that now seemed obvious.

In his view, the most important part of his schedule as CEO was his monthly evening meeting with all new Amgen employees. He would spend a few minutes on the history of the company, and then, in his words, "get right to values." He would talk through each one, saying what the company felt it meant and how it applied. "I would say to them, if these aren't your values, you should leave," Binder said. "It doesn't mean you're a bad person, but it does mean you're the wrong person for Amgen."

Although he laughs when we bring it up, Binder is considered one of the most successful CEOs of the twentieth century, in part because of the culture he helped build. One of the industry's favorite stories expresses the Amgen value of "compete intensely and win." In 1989, fifteen members of the staff lived and worked in a motel for over ninety days, working day and night on the U.S. Food and Drug Administration application for Epogen, which allowed the company to file its application in what may still be record time.

Perhaps most remarkable, he and the managers largely made up this focus on values. The only model they drew on was a decades-old initiative at Hewlett-Packard, which they learned about only after a draft of the Amgen values had been completed. We referred to several other famous examples from recent years, most of which he dismissed. "We looked into those," he said. "Mostly, they are written by the PR department, or by consultants. This [approach to values] is only real if the whole company does it and if the leaders take the most active role." We would add: it is by taking an active role that the tribe recognizes them as leaders.

Even considering that Amgen entered biotechnology at almost the perfect time, the company's success is nearly unprecedented. One share purchased at the 1983 IPO price of just under $17 would be worth, after splits are considered, $2,784 in the year 2000, the year Binder stepped down. In 1994, Amgen was awarded the National

Medal of Technology, which represents the highest presidential award for the use of technology. At that time only two other industrial organizations, Bell Labs and DuPont, had received the award. Mention of his name in the company he headed for twelve years elicits smiles and looks of respect. Truly, Binder's focus on values helped make him one of biotechnology's greatest Tribal Leaders.

The Foundation of Stage Four

The purpose of this chapter is to examine the two most important aspects of owning Stage Four: identifying and leveraging core values, and aligning on a noble cause. Everything else the tribe does should be sandwiched between these constructs. Projects, activities, initiatives, and processes—unless they are fueled by values and reach toward the tribal vision—should either be rethought until they are consistent with these guiding principles, or pruned.

By definition, core values and a noble cause can never be "checked off," in the same way that companies complete an upgrade to computer technology. A value such as "integrity" or "innovation" is timeless, and a noble cause is so far-reaching that even with all the technical breakthroughs Amgen had, it will never be fulfilled.

We found stable Stage Four tribes in all sorts of places: architecture, engineering, high technology, government, and education. In every case, "we're great" cultures rested on core values and reached toward a noble cause.

The Importance of Shared Values

Even if Tribal Leaders do nothing more than recognize people for their values, the effect is intense. Kathleen Calcidise, the former COO of Apple Retail, described one of her most moving days at the company: "I asked [people in my team] to write down what they really did like and admire about someone else in the group. We asked about their values . . . I had them written on parchment with calligraphy, and then I gave it out to the team members. A guy had tears in his eyes because he had never been appreciated like that before." Calcidise adds, "There was mutual respect within the team. Everyone was part of the team."

Finding values that cut across a group of people can take an entire tribe to this zone of appreciation and emotion, and lead to a level of performance that from the outside can seem miraculous. Mike Eruzione, captain of the U.S. Olympic hockey team that won the gold in 1980, said it all came down to shared values. Taking exception to the press about his team's history-making performance, Eruzione added, "When we won in 1980, it wasn't a miracle; we won because of a strong commitment and work ethic, not just for one game, two games, three games, but for six months, and for when we started to play as young kids. There are thousands of people they could have put on that Olympic team, but there were only twenty, and there had to be a reason for that." The reason, to him, was talent built on a foundation of "making a commitment . . . and pride . . . It all ties back to old-fashioned values." His statement made us think of the recent U.S. basketball "dream team," composed of superstars, most of them Stage Three overachievers. No team formed, and they were defeated by "lesser" players who gelled to Stage Four.

Most Tribal Leaders in our study knew the importance of hiring for values, but few could articulate it as well as Binder, who drew on his time in the military for insights. He said: "Get a group of [military] special forces people, separate them, ask each one the same questions, and you'll get roughly the same answers from each. Values uniformity goes a long way to building effective teams.

Bullets are flying; they don't have time to debate. They have to react in similar ways."

Bullets were flying during much of Binder's tenure at Amgen, and as they did, employees came together. His watch as CEO, from 1988 to 2000, saw the Congress seriously consider reducing the exclusivity period granted to innovative companies who developed drugs for medical problems affecting fewer than two hundred thousand people. A collation of non-U.S., noninnovative companies led the effort with help from the U.S. biotech licensors. This effort, ironically, was a reaction to how successfully Amgen had defended its rights to Epogen, one of its signature drugs. Despite a large amount of its revenue spent on research and development—up to 29 percent in some years—it was not easy to turn science into new products. The size of the workforce increased dramatically, as Amgen employees predicted in the mid-1980s, which strained the company's systems. However, by making as many decisions as possible stem from their eight values, Amgen was able to maintain its standards and focus, and retain its Stage Four culture of tribal pride.

Identifying Values

Once people hear how Stage Four companies are built on shared values, they almost all have the same question: How can I identify the values of team members and of potential employees?

Dilbert creator, Scott Adams, pointed out that this approach is very hard. "People aren't stupid," he said. "If I were going for a job, I'd say what I think the person wants to hear, and if that's the corporate values, that's what I'd talk about." He's right on both counts: people aren't stupid, and they often try to say the "right" thing. We put this question to Binder, who said, "It's amazing how many people—even accomplished scientists and business executives—didn't know our values at all." He added: "Even if they'd read about them, they didn't *feel* them, and a good interviewer can sniff that out." (Interestingly, "sniff out" is the same expression USC President Steve Sample used to describe how to spot Stage Three behavior among university administrators whose jobs require Stage Four behavior.)

We put the same concern to David Kelley of IDEO. He went back to the policy of the company to have ten employees "lunch" a candidate. "You might fool one or two, but you're not going to pull the wool over the eyes of ten."

Both Binder and Kelley added that for this tribal hiring approach to work, people have to know what the values and culture are, and what they mean. As Binder says, "It's not enough to just to know the words—you have to know what they *mean*. Some people try to use the right words, but if it's not in their heart, that's clear."

We'll offer two ways to detect values, both of which we've learned from people in our studies. The first—longest but most effective—is to tell a story about how you learned one of your core values. This is one of John King's stories:

> I was six years old and had made a good friend named Richie Todd. We played dodgeball every day, and after we played, he'd open up his Donald Duck lunch box, pull out a Snickers bar, break it in half, and let me choose which piece I wanted. About three weeks into it, I decided I wanted to be the one to bring the Snickers bar for a change, so I got really excited, saved up my allowance, and the next day, I jumped into my new jeans and red-hot tennis shoes, and Scout top. I left early so that I could stop by the dime store and pick up the candy.
>
> The owner of the store, Mr. Ridgely, said, "Hi, John!" I said "Hi" back, and since I was a little early, I went to my

favorite section of the store, which was school supplies. I stood there and looked at the protractors and pencils, and I saw something I just had to have: a blue notebook, the kind that folds open with "spiral" on the cover, and it was my thing. I had to have it. The problem was it cost a nickel, which is what a Snickers bar cost in those days. I solved the dilemma by putting the notebook down the front of my pants, and waddled up to the counter, put the Snickers bar on the counter along with my own nickel. I couldn't look up. He said, "Is that all, John?" I said, "Yes." I turned and was shuffling out and got almost to the door when he said, "What about that notebook down the front of your pants?"

By the time I turned around to face him, I was engulfed in tears, embarrassed, and afraid. I cried, "Please don't call my mom." He said, "We're going to have to call your mom." He calls my mom and she can hear me crying on the phone, and Mr. Ridgely said, "Mrs. King, John is here, and I need to talk to you right now." She was over to the store in a flash, bursting in the door and saying, "What have you done to my son?" He held up the notebook and said, "John tried to steal this." After a moment of silence, she walked over to me, and said, "I'm very disappointed in you," and then uttered the words that sends children of every generation into fear and despair: "You will have to speak with your father about this when he gets home."

She paid for the notebook and sent me to school with it, and told me to think about what had happened. When I got to school, I was late and in a coma. I don't remember much about what Sister Mary Elizabeth taught that day, but I do recall a lot about thieves and death and hell. After school, when I made it home, I had to talk to my dad—one of the most difficult conversations of my life. I learned something about honesty that day, which is that honesty is the *only* policy. It affected me for the rest of my life and, in that moment of realization at age six, became one of my core values. To this day, if I see someone do something dishonest, I have to say something or leave.

When people hear a story like this one, they often respond with a story of their own. In many instances, what they say will communicate the same value—in this case, honesty—but not as often as you might think. In an experiment with thousands of people, John has told this story and then, after hearing a story back, has asked a third party what value they heard in the second story. Most of the time it isn't honesty—it's family, integrity, creativity, or some other value.

One of our clients is the Sierra Health Foundation, which runs a leadership development program for leaders in the nonprofit sector, now in its sixth year. Once we noticed that Tribal Leaders tend to tell value-laden stories, we began starting this nine-month journey by telling one of ours and asking if our tale sparks any stories from the listeners. Although the program always starts as a roomful of strangers, a few hours later, every person has told his or her story, and people now know one another as their core values. Often, this part of the session stretches into the evening. Most remarkable is that nine months later, most people remember one another's stories, often in vivid detail.

The second way to get at someone's values is to ask a simple question and follow it up with three to five open-ended questions. A good question is "What are you proud of?" The person will usually start out with résumé-style accomplishments: a job, a degree, or making a tough sale. After a few open-ended questions, you'll find the reason that accomplishment gives the person pride is that it's helped people, supported the family, or made a difference for someone. In short, you'll find that the pride ties actions to values, and you'll learn what those values are.

We worked with a group of surgeons who claimed they didn't have values and weren't proud of anything—a sign of the powerless detachment of Stage Two. After many failed attempts to reach their values, we finally asked, "What ticks you off?" These accomplished surgeons mostly responded, "managed healthcare" or "hospital bureaucrats." When we asked why those factors angered them, we heard, "Because I'm the doctor!" When we asked why that's so important, we heard their values: "Because I'm in this business to save lives, so why is someone who doesn't know anything about medicine making life-and-death decisions?" Depending on the person, the value is "health," "vitality," or "making a difference." The doctors went from passive to passionate as their answers shifted from chatter about the industry to their core values. When people talk about "a principle without which life wouldn't be worth living" (which is our definition of a core value), they become excited and vibrant.

Even scientific organizations, which often claim to be dispassionate and value free, share core values: "enriching human knowledge" and "advancing science" are as much values as "integrity," "collegiality," and "accuracy"—all hallmarks of good scholarship.

We asked comedian Carol Burnett what she is most proud of, and after a few open-ended questions, she said, "The deal is that we are big kids in bigger bodies—here to play, entertain, and feed ourselves with the joy of what happens when we get out of our own way. Because we [the people who worked on the *Carol Burnett Show*] were a family, there was very little fear of making a joke, but we didn't allow cutting humor." In one sentence, she conveyed her guiding principles and how she used them as a Tribal Leader.

Tribal Leaders need to keep digging until they find the values that, like Burnett's, can turn a group of professionals into a family. Frank Jordan, former mayor of San Francisco, recalled his early days as a police officer in the city. "I would only do something for a few years, and then I was done with it," he said. "After becoming a sergeant, I started doing community participation and crime prevention. How do you get interaction with the community and have everyone understand we're not foes? We organized neighborhood block clubs, where people would gather; a representative from the police would speak, and at some time during the two-hour meeting, the officers on patrol in that area would stop in and explain what they had seen and how they would respond to a call. It was great for community relations, and by the time we were done, we had three thousand neighborhood block clubs in San Francisco." When one listens for Jordan's values, they are obvious: "communication," "collaboration," "partnership," "making a difference," and "learning." Jordan introduced officers with the same values to the community, going a long way to foster a "we're great" vibe in the city. It's no wonder that he went on to become chief of police and then mayor.

Most companies hire for skills, not for values, and may thus find themselves without Amgen's values homogeneity. The key in this situation is to dig deeper and find values that unite people. For example, we watched one Tribal Leader in financial services whose department was cobbled together out of two mergers and an acquisition. Some people valued "innovation," others "collaboration," and some "independence." He asked why people valued each of these, and each in case, they came up with the same value: "accomplishment." People in his group took different paths—innovation, building teams, or working alone—to accomplish something they all felt was important. Often, the sense we get just before finding shared values is a sense of resonance—that your values and mine are not overlapping, but darn close. Keep digging!

COACHING TIP: Keep looking for new ways to express the values. *When a tribe commits to values, it makes those principles superior to the edicts of executives and managers. One of the pitfalls we caution company leaders to avoid is to identify values and then make decisions based on expediency, as if the values didn't exist. Such behavior depresses a culture, often all the way down to Stage Two, and creates a perception that values are created for the employees while executives are above the law. Instead, leaders of stable Stage Four tribes engage in a questioning process to find new ways to express the values. What projects do our values say we should begin? What initiatives do our values say we should kill? As Binder told us, a company's best hope for a "we're great" culture is that managers make values central. No executive, no matter how talented or quick-minded, can make all the decisions herself. An entire company that sees values as its bible, however, can move quickly, grow, and remain remarkably united—one of the hallmarks of Stage Four.*

The subject of values points out why so many high-profile businesses end badly. United Airlines and Delta both launched subsidiaries to compete with Southwest's business model, but while they could copy their systems, they couldn't replace their company's values with Southwest's values of "entrepreneurship," "fun," and, yes, "love" (the company trades under the ticker symbol LUV). Binder suggests that many mergers fail because analysts and executives do not consider values and culture but rather think only about compatibility of business models and balance sheets.

Turning Values into a Tribe

Once Tribal Leaders recognize shared values, they begin talking about them with people in the tribe, just as the middle manager at Amgen did. From our studies, others will agree or disagree, add viewpoints, or try to say you got it wrong, but in any case, the topic of conversation is now in the group itself.

It is at this moment—when a leader begins talking about everyone's values, as opposed to individuals discussing "my values"—that tribal magic happens. It reminds us of alchemy, when people searched for a way to turn lead into gold. In a sense, the moment when Tribal Leaders can speak to the members of the tribe about the tribe itself, a group of individuals gels, a common identity forms, and people dedicate themselves to the success of the group. This is what we call tribal alchemy—the first vision of Stage Three melting into Stage Four.

Note that behavior and culture reinforce each other. We asked Patrick Charmel, CEO of Griffin Hospital, about his best day in his company. "It's not a single day," he said, "but rather something that happens every single day. You see people doing something extraordinary that they wouldn't have done when they started working here. You see it in the valets, the housekeepers, physicians, nurses, everyone. My mother was a patient here recently, and she noticed it right away. We don't just talk about our values here; we live them." The test of whether a tribe is values-based is not just in its members' talk but in the alignment between their talk and the practices of the culture.

From our studies, this moment happens in many different ways. We saw Glen Esnard of CB Richard Ellis Private Client Group show a new business model on PowerPoint slides, causing a pocket of "we're great" to form out of a sea of Stage Three. We saw it happen in an aerospace company when an executive passed around photo-copies of an airline napkin he used to write down the values he heard from colleagues in another city during a business trip. We've even seen people get excited by e-mails that pinpoint tribal values, with people quickly forwarding the message to others.

In all cases, it was the tribe's reaction that made the moment one of alchemy: people recognized themselves in the message and said, "This is it!" In most cases, they also recognized the person who brought the message to them as a Tribal Leader.

COACHING TIP: Watch your blind spots! *In addition to having the honor of seeing the emergence of tribal identities, leaders, and collective language, we've also seen people operating at Stage Three attempt to make a group gel—and fail. Often, their approach is to say, "I think we all value . . ." or "I believe it's time for us to come together." Such attempts, based in "I," "me," and "my" language won't work for values, unless the "I" really means "we." Perhaps the most famous of these is Martin Luther King's "I have a dream" speech. On the surface, it is based in "I" language, but his "dream" was a distillation of thousands of discussions he'd had with people. In fact, his dream was really their dream, and the "I" was a rhetorical technique to make that dream personal and real in the moment. It had been a dream of many people since long before Lincoln, but he was challenging people to focus on the gap between that dream in the future and* now, *using "I" language to base it in time.*

TECHNICAL NOTE: *Values alone are not enough to elevate Stage Three behaviors to Stage Four. We've seen many tribes in our research where charismatic leaders come along, listen to core*

values, and repeat them, giving the appearance of "we're great."
When that leader steps down, however, the group descends
back to Stage Three. What happened? The individuals had not
gone through the personal epiphany of Chapter 7, so they ap-
proached joining the leader as a career move, not as part of a
values-driven cause. The point is that "owning" Stage Four re-
quires most of the tribe to be at that level.

In most such instances, the person the tribe recognized as a
leader had been working on the group's culture for months, if not
years, using the coaching tips we outlined in Chapters 4 through 7.
As they put these techniques into place, they upgraded the culture,
making it ready for the emergence of the Tribal Leader.

Finding Expressions of Core Values

Chapter 11 goes into what Tribal Leaders do once they identify
values—they construct tribal strategies to achieve important outcomes. Even before they get to this step, however, Tribal Leaders
guide the group's discussion to ways of making their values tangi-
ble. One of the strongest examples was Frank Jordan, who, when we
met with him, was special assistant to the president of the Betty and
Gordon Moore Foundation. The foundation is dedicated to funding
projects that make life better several generations out, and it rests on
the core values of communication, environmental responsibility, vibrancy, and innovation. At seventy-one, Jordan was the epitome of
health, looking as if he does 150 push-ups before going to bed. The
conference room where we met had an "Asian tech" look. The space
was warm and comfortable, inviting dialogue. The round conference table was surrounded by a two-foot-tall recycled brick wall,
above which was glass. A work area was visible from the conference

room, and vice versa. Everything about meeting the special assistant to the president screamed the foundation's values: bricks, the environment; the round table, innovation; the open space and visibility, communication; vibrancy, the fitness of Jordan.

Brian France, chairman and CEO of NASCAR, found a simple way to implement the company's value of teamwork. "We gave everyone a business card, from the janitor to the CEO," he told us. "The custodians felt so good when they got a card. It made everyone part of the company. Something to be proud of."

George Zimmer, CEO of Men's Wearhouse, built his company on a love of innovation, collaboration, and learning. Of the company's thirteen thousand employees, only a few hundred have graduated from a four-year college, and the bulk of people who work in the stores have only a high school education. "Retail is the factory job of one or two generations ago," he says. "We had to do something." "Something," in line with his and the company's values, is to make higher education available for as many people as possible. Zimmer set up and funded (out of his own pocket) the Zimmer Family Foundation, which gives five thousand dollars scholarships, renewable for up to four years, to children of employees. Last year, the foundation gave away $650,000—more than Zimmer was paid.

The Moment of Truth: When Living Values Isn't Easy

In 2001, an elderly woman was admitted to Griffin Hospital having trouble breathing. She lived alone, with little social contact. Despite her relative isolation from infectious diseases, doctors thought it might be anthrax, and the early tests confirmed it. Griffin alerted the authorities and arranged a staff meeting for 3:00 p.m.

to let the employees know of the development. Just a few hours before that time, the FBI ordered absolute secrecy until the final tests were in.

Several administrators, including Bill Powanda and Patrick Charmel, talked with high-ranking officials in the FBI, including an assistant director, and the FBI's order was firm and final: the staff must not be told. Minutes before the scheduled meeting, Powanda phoned Connecticut Governor John Rowland, whom he knew from his days in politics. "I'll support you no matter what you do," Rowland said. At 3:00 p.m., Charmel and other leaders spoke to the 350 employees and explained that the early tests indicated anthrax. Immediately after the meeting, Powanda phoned Governor Rowland and suggested he make a public announcement, so the news wouldn't trickle out from employees. Within minutes, the governor announced what the staff already knew, and an hour later the press began arriving at Griffin—first local TV and radio stations in Connecticut, then those from New York. Within a day, there were nineteen satellite trucks, nine radio station vans, and thirty-four print reporters at the hospital. Press conferences were carried internationally.

The final tests confirmed anthrax, and the woman died of the disease—the last of the 2001 deaths from the mysterious attacks. The morning after the staff meeting at Griffin, Governor Rowland went on the *Today* show, praising Griffin's handling of the situation.

Looking back, Powanda notes what the consequences of not telling the staff would have been. "We would have destroyed in twenty-four hours what it took ten years to create: a culture built on absolute commitment to values." He added, "It wasn't a decision at all. It was a no-brainer."

Gordon Binder told us that several times at Amgen, a manager had planned a course of action that an employee felt contradicted the corporate values. "I never heard of a case where such a manager didn't back down when an employee raised the contradiction with Amgen values," he said. Notice the courage it took on both sides: for the employee to confront the manager, and for the manager to admit that a plan was poorly thought out and let it go. A serious commitment to values requires courage.

Stories like those from Griffin and Amgen—when people followed the tribal values rather than doing what was easy—are remarkable because they are so common in companies truly dedicated to their values and so rare in companies that "pretend" to have values. Most of what employees told us about values is that executives publish a set of values, often derived from a consulting company and looking remarkably like every other list of values, as "our values." In an act that Scott Adams has ridiculed in *Dilbert*, the same executives often put values on the backs of employee badges and yet, in the minds of employees, don't follow them when faced with a tough situation. The single most important takeaway from Stage Four is that Tribal Leaders follow the core values of the tribe *no matter what the cost.*

Finding a Noble Cause to Unite the Tribe

If core values are the fuel of a tribe, a noble cause is the direction where it's headed. A noble cause captures the tribe's ultimate aspiration. Said differently, core values are what we "stand in" and a noble cause is what we "shoot for."

NASCAR's Brian France phrases the noble cause of his company this way: "Everybody's gotta win." "Everybody winning" is tough in a business where almost every aspect of the business model is run by an independent agent, from the tracks to the teams that field cars and drivers. "That's the toughest part," France says, "but everybody's gotta win. TV, the athletes, the track owners, everyone."

Because NASCAR aspires to a world where "everybody wins," it's been easy for them to work with "everybody." "People said we couldn't work with a movie studio to get things done, and we threw out all the rules and got it worked out." *Talledega Nights: The Ballad of Ricky Bobby* was coproduced by NASCAR.

That's the point of a noble cause: it sidesteps what people say can't work and finds a way for it to work. Said more technically, a noble cause leads to people "aligning." Not everyone agrees with NASCAR's allocation of race dates and rules for cars, but people can align on "everybody winning."

Bob Tobias, from Chapter 7, put together a single line to create alignment in the National Treasury Employees Union that he said was a cross between a mission and a vision. He had written an earlier document that used the words "dignity" and "respect," and he knew those words got to people's hearts and represented their aspirations. We asked him what the statement was. After taking a deep breath, he said, "We [the National Treasury Employees Union—NTEU] are about organizing federal employees to ensure that each federal employee is treated with dignity and respect." After he said it to us, he took another deep breath, as though he'd just said something important, which he had. Next to values, nothing is more important than the tribe's noble cause.

He added, "Even though it was technically imperfect, it worked well." Again, a noble cause represents the yearnings of a tribe, and technical accuracy isn't important. Most people aligned on the vision.

A noble cause is a pronouncement of a future state that a tribe will bring about through its coordinated action. It is bigger than what one person can do alone, no matter how many people are offering technical support; it requires people's best efforts and passions. It should arouse so much excitement in a tribe that even if people fail, the noble cause was worth the effort.

When France and Tobias voice their tribes' noble causes, they are speaking with their tribe behind them, and their resulting confidence conveys their status as Tribal Leaders. The reason tribes have a noble cause is that it gives them a common vision that cuts across individual differences and makes leadership possible. It produces alignment and often the ability to work with people who seemed to be enemies. People thought the NTEU could never work with an American president, but Tobias helped craft an executive order signed by Bill Clinton. People said NASCAR could never work with a movie studio, but *Talladega Nights: The Ballad of Ricky Bobby* was one of the box office hits of 2006. The film grossed $150 million within the first six weeks of its release. Additionally, several NASCAR sponsors received tens of millions of dollars in exposure value. Alignment made it possible, and alignment springs from a noble cause.

From our research, there are two ways to set a noble cause. First, keep asking "in service of what?" We worked with a department of business service professionals—consultants, architects, account managers, and IT experts. Each person wanted his or her profession to be the most important in the group; the consultants wanted the group to be known for consulting, and the account managers wanted everyone to focus on customer service. This disagreement—a hallmark of Stage Three—prevented them from forming a tribal identity: a requirement of Stage Four. If you have a similar group, then ask people to write down their version of the noble cause—a statement that expresses their highest aspirations for the tribe.

At first we heard profession-specific words: "making clients better through a combination of consulting and architecture" and "serving customers with a wide array of business services."

We asked what we'd learned from Tribal Leaders we'd studied. "In service of what?"

People in the group began to see that beyond the disagreement was a common objective: serving the client. That's a step toward the noble cause, but still not it. Again, "in service of what?"

People then penned lots of different versions of a higher-order statement: "helping customers and their stakeholders through all that we do," "building a stronger economy," and "building a better world."

Finally, one person in the group read a statement aloud: "building a better world through the power of design." "Power of design" cut across everything the group did: IT designed technology systems, consultants designed better organizations, account managers designed customer satisfaction, and architects designed physical spaces. "A better world" shows what people work *in service of.*

Almost to a person, people said "Yes!" and "That's it!" Here's the test of whether a noble cause is doing its job: agreement aside—people will always want to wordsmith it—there's a feeling that the tone of it is right, that it captures why they come to work instead of moving somewhere else. In short, they *align* on it.

The moment this group aligned on the noble cause was when they took a step into Stage Four. Prior to that moment, each was saying, in effect, "I'm great and you're not because I'm an IT professional and my area is most in demand" or "I'm great because I design the physical space where all work happens." After they aligned, their tone shifted to "We're great because we're building a better world through the power of design."

The second technique to setting a noble cause is to ask what we call the Big Four Questions. As we watched Tribal Leaders do their work, we noted that they tended to ask, "What's working well?" "What's not working?" "What can we do to make the things that aren't working, work?" and "Is there anything else?" These questions capture a group's current assessment of its situation and its aspirations about what should change and why.

Some people argue that the process of setting a vision (or a noble cause) is more important than the result, but that's not what we've observed. A Stage Four culture goes through the process of figuring out its highest aspirations *and* develops a sound bite that captures the discussion. While the tribe will benefit from any such conversations, "owning" Stage Four requires that the result of the quest for the noble cause produce words upon which people align.

COACHING TIP: Go from time management to space management.
In the Stage Three system, individuals rely only on themselves, so maximizing every minute is critical. Part of the epiphany to Tribal Leadership is seeing that the individual is incapable of winning alone, so establishing values-based relationships becomes the new focus. We refer to this as space management— managing the space between people. The next chapter focuses on how people at Stage Four structure their relationships. The basis of all "we're great" relationships are values and a noble cause. From a Stage Three perspective, it may appear that Stage Four tribes waste time by spending so much time talking. In fact, they are maintaining the tribal bonds that allow for bursts of effective, coordinated action that far outperform Stage Three behavior.

With only a few exceptions, Stage Four organizations don't print values and the noble cause on the backs of employee badges, emblazen them on company mugs, or hang them on the bulletin board next to the cafeteria menu. Instead, leaders talk about them, base decisions on them, and engage tribal members in discussions about what they mean. The advice from our research is simple: build the noble cause into ongoing communication, and don't resort to gimmickry.

Avoiding the Dark Side of Stage Four

When people learn how values function in a Stage Four tribe, they often ask the same question: What about al Qaeda, the Crusades, the Mafia, or the Spanish Inquisition? Aren't those Stage Four groups?

Each does share many of the characteristics of Stage Four: networked structures, independent cultures, and tribal strategies. They also share values. We spent years studying this point, talking with people in such cultures, and consulting those whose jobs it is to keep us safe from what we came to call rogue tribes—groups that benefit from some of the power of Stage Four but are capable of atrocities.

A rogue tribe is one in which people adhere to noncore values, which are values that don't have universal benefit. Likewise, a noble cause that benefits one group by disenfranchising another is a sign of a rogue tribe. "Integrity" is a core value only when people want it to apply to everyone—including their competitors. "Building a better world through the power of design" benefits everyone.

Al Qaeda has a "noble" cause, as its members see it, to further Allah's plan to build a world of freedom and enlightenment for true believers in Islam. The Nazi ideology was about building a Reich that would last for a thousand years and give a utopian world ruled by a perfect Aryan race. As such, both are nonuniversal. The dark side is when "core values" and "noble cause" are used as a justification for driving or excusing criminal or antisocial behavior. When this situation occurs, the core values aren't really core, and the noble cause isn't really noble. The result is the worst nightmare for the world—a group that has much of the power of Stage Four but with the intent of causing harm.

This statement might seem to contradict some of the Tribal Leaders' actions from earlier in this chapter. Amgen has a value of competing aggressively and winning. Is that a universal value? They don't want everyone to compete, do they?

Absolutely. Binder told us that Amgen was great because it played by all the rules, and that nothing spurred it to greatness more than a competitor that was competing just as hard. Mike Eruzione of the 1980 U.S. hockey team said that he loved playing teams that valued the work ethic as much as he did.

A noncore value is one that applies if only you have the "right" interpretation of it, and this links values to belief. Al Quaeda says it exists for Islam—but only *their* interpretation of it. The Mafia has loyalty as a value, but it's their interpretation of it—loyalty for the group and its leaders—not for everyone. The Mafia isn't interested in the rest of us having loyalty. It's a value on their terms, or not at all. A value that isn't for everyone undoes itself.

Let's look at one case where we have a lot of information to see how the pattern plays out—hundreds of years of data. Remember that tribes are a universal for human beings, so we can learn a lot by examining any cluster of people, whether from business or, in this case, world history.

The rulers and residents of sixteenth-century Spain looked as if they had followed a corporate playbook from the twenty-first century. Within a hundred years, they had conquered most of the known world, and their influence was about to become global. They had, arguably, the most powerful military in the known world, and their society had a rich diversity, including Jews and Muslims in important posts throughout the realm. In 1478, Ferdinand and Isabella wanted to ensure Catholic orthodoxy, so they established the Inquisition as an extension of the monarchy. In corporate terms, the inquisitors were like consultants who reported only to the CEO. According to Erick Langer, a history professor at Georgetown University, the Inquisition started with people who "asserted they were doing it because they were fighting for their ideals." One could argue it started with a focus on values.

David Burr, professor emeritus from Virginia Tech, has spent much of his career on inquisitions. "They were divided into various inquisitors [with] no overarching authority that was responsible. During the inquisition, there were some shared values, but on the whole, the inquisitors ran their own show." That's how it begins. Giving leaders the benefit of the doubt, it starts with a concern for orthodoxy—a specific interpretation of a set of values. In tribal terms, it starts with a concern for making sure we maintain our "we're great" status by purging anything that isn't in agreement (notice: not alignment) with the values and noble cause.

Burr highlights the work of one famous inquisitor, Bernard du Guise. Historians know a lot about him because he wrote a book that was preserved. "It gives his descriptions of what he believed heresies to be. It would be impossible to categorize the heresies based on a particular type, and so the inquisitors never quite had a clear idea of what they were dealing with." He adds, "In the end, inquisitors were working on a gut feeling of something wrong." As inquisitors do their work they often take a Stage Three approach: "I'm great because I have power and I get to decide what's heresy." The society is then made subject to this tyranny, and, as we saw in Chapter 5, people descend to Stage Two. Burr adds, "If a group of people take over and start conducting a purge within an organization, it's based on their insistence that these people are poisoning the atmosphere, and that decent collegial atmosphere cannot be established unless those others are purged." He adds, "It's always about something else . . . about power." Personal power is a hallmark of Stage Three, not Four. Ironically but predictably, a purge within a Stage Four tribe regresses the culture.

Many people were killed in the Spanish Inquisition, and many others fled the country. As a result of this official purge, two things happened. First, in an effort to keep its dominance, Spain lost its influence. The Inquisition was costly—financially, culturally, and morally. Second, the country lost its intellectual diversity, and so, in Professor Langer's words, "the Enlightenment largely didn't happen in Spain." The country was left behind as the Renaissance center of power shifted to Italy. Spain never recovered its international influence.

The Spanish Inquisition has two vital lessons for Tribal Leaders. First, values must be core, and that means universal. The moment a group withholds the benefit of a value from another, it is not universal, hence not core. Second, the unity resulting from core values and a noble cause must be *alignment*, not *agreement*. A value is a squishy concept, and that's part of what makes it so useful. Amgen saw its economic environment change radically during Binder's administration. Amgen was rigid in its adherence to its values, and its values did not change. Almost everything else changed, and many things changed more than once. Paradoxically, its values created a stable platform from which it could be flexible and change almost everything else.

Alignment, to us, means bringing pieces into the same line—the same direction. The metaphor is that a magnet will make pieces of iron point toward it. Agreement is shared intellectual understanding. Tribes are clusters of people, and people are complex and nonrational at times. If a tribe is united only by agreement, as soon as times change, agreement has to be reestablished. If people learn new ideas or see a problem from a new perspective, they no longer agree, so tribes based on agreement often discourage learning, questioning, and independent thought. Tribes based on alignment want to maximize each person's contribution, provided that they stay pointed in the same general direction like magnetized iron filings.

NASCAR is an organization where people often disagree about rule changes or revenue splits. Yet as long as they stay focused on "everybody's gotta win," they can work together. As long as the tribe remains aligned on core values and a noble cause, its unity is strong. When it becomes about agreement, purges often follow.

We asked Professor Langer what advice he'd offer to corporate tribes that had hired personnel for values overlap. He said, "You need to make sure that the positive part of values are what is enforced, and that the lack of diversity is not necessarily a good thing. Balance diversity with unity of purpose." He added, "Unity is good, but too much of it prevents us from seeing how the world is changing."

The Oil Change

Every Stage Four tribe we studied did regular "tribal maintenance"—airing grievances, ensuring alignment between activities and the touchstones of values and a noble cause, and deepening people's relationships. We came to term this process an "oil change," and we recommend that tribes schedule it at least once a quarter. The oil change is a chance for tribal members to revisit what's happened, understand events from all sides, resolve issues, and remove any process, system, or habit that's inconsistent with its values and noble cause. People report that an oil change "made me fall in love with my coworkers all over again" and "reminds me why I love working here."

The process of an oil change is for the group to talk through three questions: (1) what is working well, (2) what is not working well, and (3) what the team can do to make the things that are not working well, work. Tribes at Stage Two will voice grievances with no real desire to fix the problems. Groups at Stage Three will find that these questions lead to speech-making and attacks on others. Only when the tribe is aligned on core values and a noble cause (and has the other elements of Stage Four as described in the next two chapters) does it have a basis to assess its behavior, find shortcomings, and restore its focus on its principles.

The Endless Quest for Values and Noble Cause

Identifying values and establishing a noble cause is a process, not an event. Binder's tenure at Amgen shows the cyclical nature of the investigation. When the company revisited its values after a decade, it discovered that these same values still represented the feelings and attitudes of the employees. Unlike a top-down approach, Binder's process emphasized the tribe's values, not his own.

Likewise, a noble cause may shift over time and should be revisited every few years. While we were consulting at Amgen, a letter came in from a father whose son had died of cancer. One of Amgen's drugs boosted his red blood count during chemotherapy so that his end came at home, not in the hospital. The father thanked Amgen for its work and said that because of the company's product, his young son had eaten pizza at home on the last night of his life, and that, with his father, he had sipped beer for the first time. Binder handwrote a note of thanks to all Amgen employees, adding, "We renew life." Many who saw the note, including us, were moved by every part of what had happened. First, it is clear that Amgen is living its core value of adding value to patients. Second, Binder reacted to the note as a Tribal Leader does: by passing the credit to the tribe. Third, in that moment, Amgen saw itself and a noble cause formed in people's minds. Although it is not an official tagline, "We renew life" is still repeated at the company as the reason it's a great place to work. It found a new way to phrase its noble cause as a result of a tragic death from cancer.

● ● ●

Toward the end of our conversation with Scott Adams, the creator of *Dilbert,* he said, "I don't know if you read Steve Job's commencement speech at Stanford that went around the Internet." The comic edge to his voice was gone. "I didn't get him until that. He had a weird ability to influence people, and I read this and said, 'This may be one of the best things I've ever read in my life.' It completely changed how I felt the entire day. I thought, if you can, through your choice of words, make people feel different, and it even lasts awhile, you can change everything. You can get the best out of other people." (Our Web site, www.triballeadership.net, provides a link to the speech.)

While the efforts of such exceptional leaders cannot be reduced to a formula, they do share characteristics of finding shared values, aligning on a noble cause, establishing triadic relationships (the topic of Chapter 10), and building a strategy to make history (the subject of Chapter 11).

Without realizing it, Adams had given us one the best descriptions of Tribal Leaders we've ever heard: using words to get the best out of people, to change everything. "He's ruining the whole curve," Adams added, his comic tone back. Tribal Leaders tend to do just that.

Key Points from This Chapter

◆ Core values are "principles without which life wouldn't be worth living."

◆ There are two ways to seek core values. The first is for a Tribal Leader to tell a value-laden story, which triggers others to tell similar stories about their values.

◆ The second way is to ask questions such as "What are you proud of?" and ask three to five open-ended questions.

◆ The Tribal Leader's goal is to find shared values that unite the tribe.

◆ A noble cause is what the tribe is "shooting for." There are two ways to find a tribe's noble cause. The first is to keep asking, "in service of what?"

◆ The second way is to ask the Big Four Questions of people in the tribe. They are "What's working well?" "What's not working?" "What can we do to make the things that aren't working, work?" and "Is there anything else?" These questions capture a group's current assessment of its situation and its aspirations about what should change and why. The noble cause will often emerge out of people's answers to the questions.

◆ The goal of determining values and a noble cause isn't agreement; it is alignment, which produces coordinated action married with passionate resolve.

◆ *Anything* not consistent with the core values and noble cause needs to be reworked or pruned.

◆   The group captures the essence of Tribal Leadership when it asks, "What activities will express our values and reach toward our noble cause?" The answer becomes a reason to form networked relationships (Chapter 10) and the basis of a tribal strategy (Chapter 11).

CHAPTER 10

Triads and Stage
Four Networking

E very September, a remarkable party takes place at which people
in commercial real estate discuss and close more business than
perhaps on any other night of the year. At the center of the party is
CB Richard Ellis Vice Chair, Darla Longo.

In 2006, the party took up the entire fifteenth floor of the Clift
Hotel in San Francisco. Longo wore a turquoise silk dress and dia-
monds, sipping the same drink for hours. Many of the three hundred plus attendees showed less restraint, keeping the bartenders
busy. The event had the feel of a fraternity party, but with the attendees thirty-five years older and wearing gray pants and blue
blazers.

Longo's behavior was the most remarkable part of the event,
and most missed her magic. She didn't promote herself, talk about
her accomplishments, or say "I," "me," or "my," other than to say,
"I'd like you to meet . . ." Longo played matchmaker. She introduced
clients to brokers, senior brokers to successful rookies, and clients
to one another.

If we were to take any moment of the evening and watch it in
slow motion, we'd see three elements. First, Longo would have at
least two people around her. Second, she would talk to them *both*

at the same time, even if they didn't know each other. Third, if we listened to her words, we'd notice that they would have the effect of building or deepening the relationship between the other two people.

If we looked closer at this third element, we'd see that Longo is introducing people at two levels. First, she's going through résumé issues—who each person works for and what he's doing, why it is such a good idea for these two to meet each other. Second, and far more important, she's discussing what makes each great as a person—his or her core values.

As Longo snakes her way around the floor of the hotel—and as people shuffle around to meet her—the most remarkable aspect of this night becomes apparent. Once she leaves, people talk about her—her vision in setting up this event almost ten years ago, how it has grown to become one of the defining moments of the year in commercial real estate, how Longo runs her business within CB Richard Ellis, and what an accomplished leader she is. All the things that people at Stage Three might say about themselves, others say about her after she's left.

Longo emerged as one of the leaders in commercial real estate for many reasons: her drive, endless energy, talent, vision for the business, and focus on integrity and values. In our years of watching her, one simple act of behavior stands out: her ability to "triad"—to create business relationships *between* two people, based on core values and mutual self-interest, and then move on. She naturally receives the reciprocal benefit of this action by others saying good things about her, and her resulting reputation is a magnet for business. In essence, she receives loyalty and followership by creating relationships between other people. She is one of the most successful people in commercial real estate because her actions build triads, the foundation of a Stage Four tribal structure.

The Structure of Stage Four Relationships

We didn't invent the triad; we just recognized it. We saw many Tribal Leaders forming large networks of people—Longo's list of contacts would not fit in some PDAs and yet not seem to suffer from a lack of time. While those at Stage Three assume that these successful groups will fail as they get larger, they are always wrong in a Stage Four culture. Glen Esnard's early work in the Private Client Group caused some people to say that the group would collapse under its own weight when it hit fifty professionals. It's over 250 and growing. IDEO wasn't supposed to keep its special culture when it got larger than a hundred people. It's at 450. And Amgen was going to become just another big drug company culture when it hit a thousand employees. It's now over sixteen thousand. The triad is so powerful that it can link tribes together (remember the upward barrier on a tribe is 150 people, so many of these companies are tribes of tribes), creating an unlimited capacity for scalability.

The purpose of this chapter is to reverse-engineer what we saw thousands of Tribal Leaders doing: establishing three-legged relationships all around them. While the triad is the basic building block of Stage Four cultures, these blocks can be stacked to the sky, resulting in large, robust, dynamic, and growing networks of tribes at Stage Four. All are vibrant, values-based, and filled with people giving their best efforts—leading and being led at the same time.

● ● ●

As we saw in Chapter 6, dyads—two-person relationships—are the structural hallmark of Stage Three. People operating at "I'm great" tend to form a set of dyads, so that if they have to tell lots of people the same thing, they'll have a series of one-on-one conversations.

As a result, they hit several barriers. First, the person at the other end of the relationship often feels commoditized, valued only for her service or information. Second, the person forming the dyads feels he never has enough time or support, since the overhead maintenance required to keep a series of dyads together is enormous. Third, people are quick to spot inconsistencies in what the person says as he tells slightly different versions of the same thing to others, which damages his credibility and reduces their loyalty to him. (While most of these issues come down to simple misunderstandings, the sheer number of dyads within Stage Three tribes almost guarantees that such bungled communication will happen.)

As we saw in Chapter 7, the epiphany to Tribal Leadership doesn't require the person to lose any drive, passion, talent, or commitment to strategic thinking. Rather, everything that works well about Stage Three appears in Stage Four, but in a reorganized fashion. In the same way that ego shifts from personal to tribal at Stage Four, we don't see many dyads, but we see lots of triads.

In this chapter, we'll present the anatomy of a triad in detail, discuss its three main advantages—stability, innovation, and scalability—and show how it can become a launching pad to Stage Five.

The Anatomy of a Triad

At its most basic level, a triad has three parts. In its most stable form, the three parts are people, such as Longo, a client, and another professional from CB Richard Ellis. The triad can also function with groups brought together. The former prime minister of Malyasia, Tun Mahathir Mohamad, built the relationship between western academics and regional CEOs under the banner of an organization he began, the International Center for Leadership in Finance (ICLIF). He is wildly popular in his country and is often called "Dr. M" by his followers, usually as a term of endearment that also refers to his background as a physician. (While some of his comments just before he stepped down as prime minister aroused anger around the world, the overall effect of his leadership has been to establish Malaysia as a stable nation with a growing economy.)

Regardless of its parts, the three form a triangle, with each leg of the structure responsible for the quality of the relationship between the other two parts.

The Stabilizing Power of Triads

Bruce Cutter, CEO of Cancer Care Northwest, runs a remarkable organization. On the surface, Dr. Cutter is successful because he hires great people, has a sound business model, and is a dedicated physician executive. This surface view misses the remarkable part of his leadership: Cutter uses triads to resolve conflicts, develop his staff, and give everyone more time.

As we toured his facility a single moment showed how triads immunize tribes against spats. A staff member came up to him, glanced at us, and then looked back at him and rolled his eyes. "He's doing it again," the staff member complained. We learned later he was referring to another physician who wasn't following an administrative procedure, and as a result the staff had to do extra work. Cutter's steady voice said, "You and [the doctor] should work it out. You both want the same thing but see different paths for how to get there. You'll find a path that works for you both, and tell him I said that." With those few words, Cutter resumed our tour. We later learned that the two had met and resolved their dispute. In the process, both were reminded to work together (the most important element in employee development), they solved the disagreement in real time without having to wait for Cutter's involvement, and his time was free to

do what was most important: gaining respect for the tribe by showing it off to visitors.

When you use triads to solve problems, remind people of shared
values. Values, as we saw in Chapter 9, lead to alignment, which
trumps any disagreement. Just as Dr. Cutter did in this example,
Tribal Leaders remind people engaged in a spat that they're really
on the same page with what matters: values. If people don't see the
common ground, Tribal Leaders point it out. As we heard Glen Esnard say at an early Private Client Group meeting to two people
who disagreed on an issue, "You both signed an agreement that says
the team comes first. What's best for the team here?" With that, he
walked away—and the two people resolved their disagreement.

If Cutter had been operating at Stage Three, he would have said,
as we have heard thousands of times from thousands of managers,
"I'll look into it. Thank you for letting me know." He would then
have talked with the physician, gotten his side of it, and perhaps said
that the administrator didn't "get it," since he's not a doctor. He then
would have gone back to the staff member, heard his side of it, and
perhaps said that the doctor, while a brilliant clinician, doesn't "get"
administrative issues. Then he would have gone back to both with
his decision, and used tools of persuasion to get them to comply. In
essence, he would have dealt with the problem by creating dyads,
requiring his time and attention. Next time a spat happened, he
would have repeated the process, and thus his days would be con-
sumed by conflict management. He, like many people in our study,
would work late, going home to a midnight dinner and complaining
to his wife that he doesn't get enough support and that he's the only
one holding the office together.

Instead, a few sentences resolved the problem and restored the
relationship. Instead of staying late to work on the problem, Cutter

went to dinner, and we talked about his and the group's aspirations for the future, almost all of which have happened since our visit to Spokane. Stable triads resolve incidents and free the time of Tribal Leaders to focus on the topic of the next chapter: strategy.

Like many Tribal Leaders, Cutter didn't see this pattern until we interviewed him about it. "Wow, that's remarkable," Cutter said on the phone later, when we stepped him through what we had seen. "I never knew that I did that." Once he had the concept, he described how most of his day is spent building triads. He also saw that triads could involve bringing groups together. In an excited voice, he described a new initiative to identify the components of quality in his oncology practice. He realized that the initiative could work only if he was involved but if it was seen as owned by other stakeholders. He is actively building the relationship between two groups: healthcare professionals and staff, effectively creating a larger triad. As is always true in triads, each group builds the relationship between the other group and Cutter, meaning that he is always informed and that the relationship moves forward even when he is busy with other projects.

Once Tribal Leaders see the concept of the triad, they see them everywhere. Cutter pointed out that his career has been built on triads. Esnard began looking at the Private Client Group as a collection of triads, and he used his Saturday afternoons watching football as opportunities to invite new people into his triads. One person pointed out, after seeing the idea, that his family life is stable because he builds the relationship between his wife and his mother-in-law. Every time he and his wife fight, friends or parents-in-law remind them of how important the relationship is to both of them.

Triads are undermined when senior decision makers solve problems themselves. What's even worse is when they say, "Don't go behind my back," as this crushes triads before they form. Some people resist building triads because they think they'll lose control. Their thought is that this technique may encourage people to undercut them. However, the opposite is true. The rule of reciprocity implies, "Whatever you give out, you'll get back." If you build the relationship between two people and then walk away, most of them will praise your efforts. You've increased the respect you get by showing the same to other people. David Kelley describes the point this way: "I never mediate a conflict. If it's work for a client, let the client sort it out. What do I know?"

Not only do forming and nurturing triads save the Tribal Leader time, they encourage a level of followership that is unimaginable at Stage Three. A test of a true Tribal Leader is why people would come to their funeral: Do their words of praise stem from their hearts or from a desire to be politically correct? While we hope Darla Longo's eulogy is a long way off, one thing is certain: it will be standing room only, and the tears would be real. People don't value her just because of business she's sent their way but because she "gets" them: she knows them by their values, and she is known by hers—with "integrity" and "service" at the top of the list. The same is true for Bruce Cutter, Glen Esnard, Steven Sample, and David Kelley. When Gordon Binder's time comes, many people who never knew him will mourn his loss.

Thankfully, this level of loyalty, respect, and followership pays dividends while people are still alive. Most of the Tribal Leaders we studied are on the short list of candidates considered for CEO positions—or positions of even more prestige. One of the people we spoke to was Rafia Salim, who formerly ran the ICLIF program in Malaysia that brought together academics, bankers, CEOs, and government officials. She was recently appointed "Datuk" (roughly, the equivalent of a British knight) and a year later, the ninth vice chancellor (the day-to-day leader) of the Universiti Malyaya, the most prestigious university in the country. She is a much beloved figure in Malaysia, a role model in an Islamic country who happens to be female.

The triad provides a level of support that often comes as surprise to people who are used to dealing at Stage Three. Frank Jordan, referring to his work at the Gordon and Betty Moore Foundation, said about people who receive funding money: "It's not like we give you the money and walk away. We ask 'How can we help you get to the final finish line?' We're totally invested in these projects, and not just with our finances." Most Moore Foundation projects involve a triad between the foundation, the recipient, and the groups served by the recipient. In essence, the foundation is responsible for the quality of the relationship between the latter two groups. Funding is merely the mechanism to get started, not the final result. In a triad, no one is ever slogging through a problem alone.

Triads as Magnets for Innovation

In 1978, Angelica Thieriot was admitted to a large San Francisco hospital with a disease no one could identify. After almost dying several times, she was finally diagnosed with a rare but treatable virus. A native of Argentina, she marveled at the technological sophistication of American medicine but was appalled at the dehumanizing method of treatment. She complained about the nurses coming and going, paying her no more attention than they paid to the equipment. She spent hours alone, fearing for her life and often staring at a blank wall. Although the quality of medical treatment was superior in the United States, she said that in Argentina she would have been treated like a human being.

When she was discharged, she resolved to change the system. She approached the CEO of the hospital with her complaints and was given a polite brush-off. Although she was married to the publisher of the *San Francisco Examiner* (a fact the CEO apparently didn't know), she never used the power of her husband's influence to embarrass the hospital or the system. Later, Thieriot's father-in-law had a stroke and was hospitalized. In the words of a friend, "The insults kept coming—he was a powerful man, and he was being spoken to like a baby."

Thieriot then pulled together a group of visionary friends (the seed of a new tribe) and went to work. They imagined a medical system where patients could become partners and active participants in their treatment, not merely examples of biology. They started by clipping periodicals about disease, from gallbladder illness to cancer. Thieriot opened a small medical library, in a hospital, that was staffed with volunteers, and soon it had a steady stream of traffic. Patients learned about their diseases and thus could take a more active role in medical decisions. This initial success impressed the same CEO who had rebuffed Thieriot, and he now asked how she could take the model further.

Thieriot and a group of advisors formed Planetree, named after the type of sycamore tree in ancient Greece under which Hippocrates taught the first medical students. In 1985, the organization helped run a thirteen-bed medical/surgical department in the hospital. Planetree broke one piece of conventional wisdom after another by putting art on the walls, turning medical records over to patients, and opening kitchens. At the heart of the model is partnership revolving around the patients. This experiment, monitored by the University of Washington, was hugely successful. Susan Frampton, the current president of Planetree, said, "They then took this experience to four other hospitals—could you do it New York City? Could you do it in a community-based hospital? In long-term care?" Again and again, the Planetree model worked, as it triaded all the pieces of the healthcare model together: doctors, nurses, support staff, administrators, architects, and most especially patients. Planetree brings together everyone involved with care so that the patient feels informed and involved in medical developments and is treated like a whole human being.

Planetree now has 112 affiliate hospitals in North America and Europe. One of those hospitals is Griffin, the subject of Chapter 2.

As impressive as the Planetree story is, it's how Griffin used the organization—and contributed back to it—that shows how Stage Four tribes will almost always outperform Stage Three. CEO administrators, in the words of VP Bill Powanda, "seemed to go nuts—in a good way—for anything that would help" during their turnaround. CEO Charmel said, "When we started, people thought we were a little wacky." They brought in Planetree consultants, hired out-of-the-box architects, brought in Innovation Associates (a consulting group started by MIT's Peter Senge). Powanda told us, "If it worked, we tried it." They focused on process redesign, training, committing to values, and focusing on the patient. At each step, the administration helped form a triad, bringing together consultants (including those from Planetree) with hospital leaders. They ensured the quality of the relationships on all sides and then watched to see whether or not it worked. Most of what they brought in made an impact, so they retained it. When an approach hit the point of diminishing returns, they moved on. In each case, the organizations and people they brought in were left more capable for having worked with Griffin.

Ultimately, Griffin saw its ideal partner in the San Francisco–based Planetree, which was having its own problems at the time. Current Planetree President Frampton explains, "Membership grew to a point where the lack of experience and knowledge of the hospital culture became an Achilles' heel to the organization." Griffin had just joined as an affiliate and didn't want its guide to flounder.

Hospital executives eventually acquired the debts of Planetree, essentially acquiring the organization, and moving its headquarters to the East Coast. Over time, the board changed and now had more seats for affiliates. The transformation worked both ways, with Griffin now the model Planetree hospital, and Planetree gaining credibility from the buzz about Griffin. When people want to learn about one, they also learn about the other. Both are now integrating other hospitals into Planetree's affiliate program, resulting in better healthcare for everyone.

Many Stage Three organizations reject innovations they didn't originate—a situation often called the "not invented here syndrome." Stage Four organizations, like Griffin, will actively pull in resources, approaches, consultants, ideas, or anything else that will build the tribe. Planetree has been so successful in getting resources and keeping its members that it works on word-of-mouth buzz alone. In the language of Tribal Leadership, the organization relies on people triading them in, and so far, it's worked very well. "We don't advertise," Frampton notes. "Planetree is unique and requires buy-in from a largely altruistic care [perspective]. We have chosen to not spread the word but to let people find us." She adds, referring to the benefits of core values–based relationships: "We have low attrition, and it comes from buy-in from the heart as well as the head."

Again and again, we saw Stage Four organizations "triading in" innovation. IDEO brings in experts on almost any subject—provided they're *really* world-class—to see what learning emerges from the interaction. Men's Wearhouse George Zimmer added spiritual author Deepak Chopra to the board of directors of his publicly traded company. When we asked Zimmer how the other members of the board responded, he said, "One of our board members asked me, 'Who is [Chopra]?' I laughed and told him to go ask his wife. His wife told him, and now he's all for it. Chopra's great." Zimmer triaded an innovative person, and a new perspective, with the investment bankers on this board.

Triads and Business Development

Reid Hoffman, founder and CEO of LinkedIn, is one of the emerging experts on personal networking in the Internet age. The company allows users to request to join someone's personal network of contacts and thus gain access to their tribe. The system always asks permission of a connector before getting two people in touch.

Like most people at work changing the world, Hoffman connects his role in this new age to his values. "I am interested in what happens when you use the Internet as a force for massive change, creating viable economic benefits and improving people's lives." Hoffman bases LinkedIn on the belief that "lifetime employment is going the way of the dodo" and that in the new economy, "every professional in the world will have an electronic shingle that will be on the net."

He adds, "From a business perspective, eighty to ninety percent of the reason that a person would spend time with other people is based on referrals." He imagined a system that would allow a user to request an introduction to another user—a miniform of a triad.

We learned this lesson the hard way. In setting up interviews for this book, Hoffman was on our short list. We e-mailed, faxed, and called the LinkedIn PR office. A member of Hoffman's team saw our note and e-mailed Dave, suggesting that a good way to contact the founder might be through the system he founded. Duh.

Dave logged on to LinkedIn, requested a connection to Reid Hoffman, and learned that he was one person away—through Dave's best friend in high school, now a high-tech CEO. Dave requested that he introduce them—essentially building a triad—and two weeks later we were talking. In his introduction, Dave's friend referred to shared values as well as to personal accomplishments and what each would gain from the meeting.

> **COACHING TIP: How can triads solve your problems?** *The central theme of this book is that you are only as smart and capable as your tribe, and that by upgrading your tribe, you multiply the results of your efforts. We have yet to see problems that couldn't be fixed by a few good triads, such as the fact we couldn't get an interview with Hoffman. A great question for coaches to ask is this: "What triads, if built, will fix this problem?" The "black belt" version of the question (most useful in stable Stage Four cultures) is "What triads will help us spot and fix problems so big we can't even think of them?"*

"What most people don't understand is that if you manage your career, what you are doing is actually managing a set of relationships," Hoffman told us. "People need an infrastructure for that within their heads." He argued that the mental model of business-card networking isn't good enough for the new economy.

"What happens is that educational institutions have a serious break with the reality of modern careers," he adds. "The means about how to progress in a modern career [is lacking]. Things to do around building and managing and maintaining your career are simply not taught the right way, anywhere," he asserts. From our experience, he's right. A major part of business school career management is "industry nights," in which industry leaders—mostly alumni from the school—come and talk about what they do, and then network with MBA students. Most job seekers consider a great industry night one from which they walk away having made a good impression on people, and getting a stack of business cards. They then e-mail the industry leaders, often saying "It was great meeting you . . . I would love to help your company . . . can we continue talking?" An industry leader is deluged with such correspondence, and even the best-intended of them ends up not responding to many notes, which frustrates the students. It's a classic Stage Three model to get jobs. As Hoffman notes, dyads are ineffective in job hunting. We would add that two-person relationships are also incapable of running an organization, building new business, or achieving great results.

"The way business schools teach career management has to change," Hoffman continued. "It lacks the context for success." In fact, when Tribal Leaders discuss triading in business schools, they get looks of shock. "Why hasn't anyone taught us this before?" many students ask. The triad is one of those ideas that is obvious when you see it, but until you do, it's invisible.

All Longo has to do is introduce a new person into her community—such as introducing a prospective client to another broker within her company—and the group will describe the benefits of working with her. At Stage Four, the tribe closes new business—or gets jobs for people.

> **COACHING TIP: Next time you go to Starbucks, take two friends, not one.** *Once people see the value in a group of three, they often make three the minimum number for a meeting. Our clients have told us that it's changed their entire corporate tribes.*

In describing this facet of triads to MBA students, someone will often say, "That sounds like network marketing!" or "Isn't that how Amway works?" People usually laugh. Actually, it's exactly how multilevel marketing organizations work, and growing religions, and

expanding businesses, and booming law practices, and populist political campaigns. It's why so many people saw *The Blair Witch Project* and how successful business schools expand their applicant pool.
Dylan Stafford, the director of admissions for the fully employed
MBA programs at UCLA, turns information sessions into triading
events in which prospective candidates meet current students and
successful alumni. Stafford does what Tribal Leaders do: sets the
tone, trains the volunteers, leads the people doing the work, and then
lets the tribe grow on its own. His applicant pool is expanding geo-
metrically, as is the enthusiasm of prospects for a UCLA MBA.

Scaling Tribal Effectiveness with Triads

IDEO forms triads so quickly that what clients see is a blizzard of
networked activity, bringing together experts from many different
fields, everyone contributing ideas and leveraging off one another's
wisdom. Experts from the firm went to work with a healthcare service provider and noticed that physicians and medical assistants sat
too far apart. So IDEO worked to bring them together—literally
and figuratively. The consultants also saw that the clinical spaces
kept family members away from patients, making them feel isolated
and disconnected (Stage Two). IDEO human factors experts noticed
that patients often sat in exam rooms for quite a while, feeling vul-
nerable and alone. The IDEO design team asked executives to walk
through the system as patients, and they came to the same conclusions as the consultants: that all those systems had to change.

In essence, the IDEO experts didn't act as experts at all (a Stage
Three model) but as matchmakers: introducing physicians to assistants, staff to family members, patients to staff, and executives to
clinical employees. The result of all this "webbing" of relationships
was that the patient experience changed from one of isolation to one

of support. IDEO's original mission was to help design new facilities, but instead, they "triaded" groups to other groups. As a result, they fixed the problem without adding new facilities. Patient satisfaction scores increased. At the center of this effort, IDEO and the client redefined nurses' roles to include what Kelley calls creative responsibilities, adding, "And now they're happy as clams." By rapidly building triads, experts become partners, clients become teachers, and everything can change.

TECHNICAL NOTE: *From a Stage Four perspective, management consulting needs to be reinvented. Consulting, as a practice, borrows from the classic professions, such as medicine, whereby a family doctor would see a case that was beyond him and would bring in an expert for a consult. Note the dyadic relationship: the expert is greater than the primary care physician, has more knowledge, is better connected, and probably drives a more expensive car. Management consulting is built on the same model: a company is in crisis that is too big for an executive to deal with, so she calls in a consultant who has seen this problem before. It's a dyadic relationship, with the consultant living out "I'm great (and you're not) because I know how to fix this problem." Note how different the IDEO model is: consultants are peers, partners, and facilitators. They have graduated from "I'm great" to "we're great," and the "we" includes the client. It's time for consulting, as an industry, to transition from "consultant-as-expert" to "consultant-as-partner."*

Upgrading a Tribe One Triad at a Time

David Kelley has two professional passions: IDEO and Stanford. "Tending IDEO's culture is like falling off a log, compared to what's going on [at the university]." The traditional role of professor has been described as "sage on a stage." It's like a group dental practice, with experts living in separate offices. Getting people of all kinds to change their lifelong habits of operating independently and start to operate as a team is a big challenge.

> **COACHING TIP: Triad around Stage Three behavior.** *In an early chapter, we alluded to the most difficult question we ever get: "What if my boss [or my CEO] is at Stage Three?" Now that we've hit triads, we can now give a more complete answer. Stage Three derives its power from knowing more, being better informed, and hoarding information. If a person doesn't want to play in a Stage Four culture and you do, you have a choice: do it anyway, or give up. Assuming you want to try, then our advice is to be very careful. The Stage Three mind-set is threatened by triads, so it's important to think through the risks and rewards. If you want to move ahead, then begin triading with the people you need to work with—probably, people at late Stage Three—to accomplish something remarkable. Prove that Stage Four is more effective in terms of its results, and leverage the accomplishment into an invitation to join the emerging group at Stage Four. In short, taking great care to not offend people, triad around the Stage Three individual.*

Kelley says, "At Stanford design school, we're looking at the entire academic model. Stanford is winning the hell out of Nobel Prizes, and that's a great thing that comes from deep expertise. What we're trying to do is give students another tool, a tool we call design thinking. If you're using design thinking, you're inviting students to collaborate in the learning process. By having multiple professors in the classroom with different points of view, the students will need to make up their own minds about what matters to them, not what matters to the professors. I think this is ultimately going to change the fundamental way we approach learning in order to equip people with a broader set of tools for solving the big problems in the world."

As Kelley draws on his white board at IDEO he adds, "In universities, we build these deep disciplines of knowledge. Within each department, we're doing really well. But the innovation we're missing lies in between those disciplines. We need a new approach to facilitate collaboration between the departments. That's where design thinking comes in. We have world-class individuals, but the 'new world class' requires that these world-class guys talk to each other."

Kelley is using a triad of professors to turbocharge learning. With the blessing of Stanford University President John Hennessey, he is running a class with two other professors: a business professor and a social scientist.

In his signature Midwestern charm, Kelley describes what actually happens: "We're in the classroom. The business guy—a fantastic teacher—says he's working on a project in India to get rid of kerosene and use solar. He says, 'If you don't write it down, it doesn't exist.' I can't let him say that, so I bring up the importance of intuition and insight, which causes a heated debate to break out. After a while, the social scientist says, "What do you mean by 'exists'?" The learning is incredible. There's no right answer. These guys are really passionate. And then we have a more esoteric discussion. The students are watching the whole thing. Their nervousness is all about who is going to be doing the grading. At the end of every class, we debrief, with students all around us. This never happens when there is only one professor in the classroom. But here, these three guys debrief. Every once in a while, one of us will say, 'What do you think?' to one of the students. They have to decide for themselves what is the right thing to do."

Not only do the students in the course observe triads, but they are organized into groups of about five for class projects. (A group of five is ten potential triads if everyone is webbed to everyone else.) "It's a blast. You get a business student, an engineer, a social scientist, and each one gets to play the role of expert along with a couple of others. We put them through training so they can spot dysfunctional team behavior and deal with it." Kelley's experiment is a large network of triads. "The learning," Kelley says, "is incredible." It's also his attempt to change the culture of Stanford and become a model other universities follow. "These are really smart people [pointing back to his diagram of focused disciplines]; they're constantly benchmarking success. Stanford wants people to be trained in the deep thinking of their individual disciplines as well as collaborating with other disciplines to drive innovation. As we have more and more success with this, others will want to join . . . It's about changing the entire system," he says. We would add: one triad at a time.

> **TECHNICAL NOTE:** *At Stage Four, people assume trust; they don't earn it. At Stage Three, trust is earned. When lost, it has to be re-earned. At Stage Four, we observed a different phenomenon: people granted trust from the beginning. In fact, when we tried to set up meetings with people at Stage Three, many rebuffed us because they didn't know who we were. By contrast, many of the remarkable people interviewed for this book—those at Stages Four and Five—assumed we were who we said we were and granted us an interview because they said the project sounded important. The principle is this: where trust is an issue, there is no trust. Stage Four assumes trust. Stage Three says trust must be earned.*

Preparing for World-Class Triading

We're often asked how people can get the most out of triads. From our research, we'll offer four pointers.

First, know the values and current projects of every person in your network. Longo's introductions model the best practice—introduce people on both levels, and this is possible only by knowing about each person. There's no shortcut for knowing who is in your tribe, what's important to them, and what they're doing. As Longo told us a few days before the party, "We all want the same things. The rookies and clients are looking for personal growth, and how to be better at what we do." She speaks with confidence because she knows the interests and values of almost every person at her party.

Second, use what LinkedIn CEO Reid Hoffman describes as "the theory of small gifts." Before facilitating an introduction between two people, you have to have the credibility with both to pull it off. Hoffman describes the need for this practice to be systematic and ongoing: "Do little things for each person," such as sending them an article that is about one of their interests, remembering their birthday, and so on.

Third, be great at something, world-class if possible. We're often asked by people at Stage Two how they can triad with people who won't even return their calls. The answer is that they first have to go through Stage Three and become great at something, just as Kelley and his two Stanford colleagues all entered, and then graduated from, Stage Three. If someone hasn't owned Stage Three yet, world-class triading will be impossible.

Finally, there was a point in our research at which we believed that if people at Stage Three were to triad, they would automatically grow into Stage Four. We were wrong. Unless someone has had the epiphany of Tribal Leadership, triading looks like thinly veiled self-promotion. Effective triading requires a word that we heard people use again and again to describe real Tribal Leaders: "authenticity."

> **TECHNICAL NOTE:** *Triads lead to a blurring of roles between client, service provider, friend, mentor, and coach. Once the triad is established, all the roles merge and morph, requiring each person to contribute to, and receive contributions from, the other two.*

Launch Pad to Stage Five

Triading is a key not only to stabilizing at Stage Four but to beginning the leap to Stage Five: "life is great" and the subject of Part III of this book. Frank Jordan explains how it works at the Moore Foundation: "It's a whole third career for me [after chief of police and mayor], and it's so amazing to see. The Nobel Prize winners that come through this door in environment, science, technology, oceanography, education, health . . . to listen to them and then hear some of our people talk with them. The passion, commitment, vision, and 'have you thought about it this way or that way' approach . . . Next thing you know, we've completely redone our plans so we can get even better results, doing something no one has never done, really making history."

Triading brings together a group of people that can accomplish the nearly impossible: the history-making performance of Stage Five. First, though, they have to build a tribal strategy—the subject of Chapter 11.

Key Points from This Chapter

◆ Know the values, current projects, and aspirations of each person in your tribe.

◆ Use Reid Hoffman's "theory of small gifts" to build your relationship with people in your tribe as preparation for triading.

◆ Form a triad by introducing two people to each other on the basis of current projects and shared values.

◆ There's no substitute for going through Stage Three, so that you're known for some area of expertise. Doing so will give you the credibility to triad with others.

CHAPTER 11

A Tribal Leader's Guide to Strategy

Most business people think they know a lot about strategy, but their results say otherwise. Jason Ray's story is typical.

Several years ago, he formed a company, Explorati, around a dream for a new type of massively multiplayer online gaming system, involving thousands of people over the Internet. The problem with most computer games is that each character and scene needs to be sketched out and then programmed, drawn, animated, and woven together with the others. The development costs are huge, with most computer games costing five million dollars to twenty million dollars. To minimize these expenses, many games rely on common engines, the technology that creates a distinct game play, such as the physics of falling objects. A different skin—characters, setting, and "look and feel"—can then be put on the same engine, and the result is a completely different game. *Half Life 2* and *Vampire: Bloodlines* use the same engine, even though one is a futuristic shoot-'em-up game and the other is a role-playing game about the life of hellish creatures in search of blood.

Ray, working with his partner, Ed Halley, wanted to take engines and skins to another level. Instead of requiring everything to be laid out in advance, they would create an engine so powerful that it could sustain a "world." Within this world, the engine would make up the next move, so that the game would always play out differently. Not only would the start-up costs for a world be much lower than for today's games, but the games themselves would be much more compelling.

Ray describes his vision for a world based on the Fox television show *The X-Files*. Dozens of users would be playing in the same world, some as FBI agents (like Mulder and Scully) and others as those odd little extra roles that made the show so addictive. "Scully" might send a message to the assistant director for advice, and the system would see that the person playing his role wasn't online, so it would call his cell phone and ask for his move. If he didn't pick up, the system would improvise an answer, and play would continue.

The system would use nonplayer characters (NPCs) to actively move the story forward. If the plot ever stalled, NPCs would step in with a level of improvisation never before seen in computer games. Aliens might suddenly abduct Scully, or Assistant Director Skinner might recall the agents because of a threat to national security. The moves would be original, yet all consistent with the *X-Files* world. The same scenario would be captivating over and over, because different NPCs would always improvise different situations. Hundreds of parallel *X-Files* worlds would be playing at the same time, each inventing new combinations with the creativity of a screenwriter and the speed of Intel's latest chip.

Before Mulder could go after the evil Illuminati member who was hiding in an Academy Awards show, he would have to buy an Armani tuxedo and Gucci shoes. While this would all be make-believe, the user in the real world could also order these items from a real-life retailer with a right-click of his mouse, and a real-life FedEx driver would deliver them to the user's real-life porch the next morning—after charging his real-life Visa card. With time, the system would learn that its customer was more a Levi's-Hanes-Nikes guy, and offer game situations where these items would be the preferred choice—and the likely purchase in the real world.

Ray and Halley's vision was to merge Hollywood and video games. Advertisers would love it because they had a clear role that couldn't be TiVo'd away. Users would love it because the same world would be realistic and fun over and over again. Geeks would love it because they could create worlds in their garages, and the community of users would decide which were good enough to pay to enter, and which were the computer game equivalents of *WaterWorld, Show Girls,* and *Gigli.*

At the heart of their plan was Improvisational Computing, a new approach to interactive storytelling that made every user a star. Unlike others who tried to tackle the problem of giving each player choices within a story set, Ray and Halley believed they had a solution to a different problem: how to understand what each player was doing and making up an effective story around that player's actions. Ray related, "When a small child runs up to Scully (the player) and says, 'Please, please you have to help Betsy! Follow me!,' at that moment the player doesn't know who Betsy is, why she is in trouble, or who is responsible. Since the player doesn't know, the system doesn't have to make those decisions until they are needed, which makes it possible to make up the next events based on what the player does, instead of what the writer wishes."

Ray's strategy was to build two worlds that would show the power of Improvisational Computing, forming a new company, Explorati, to realize this dream. One would be for a soap opera and would demonstrate that improvisational story worlds would appeal to people who were not gamers. The other would be for the Playboy Mansion and would create media buzz. With these two worlds, their company would be the pixar of massively multiplayer games, some of which have profits rivaling blockbuster Hollywood movies. Explorati would then be the platform from which to build many more worlds, imagined by creative users or based on *The X-Files, Star Wars, Lord of the Rings,* or other "franchises."

Ray founded Explorati to bring his vision to reality, and he staffed it with a handful of people. With a small amount of seed funding, the Explorati tribe worked on the technical problems while Ray went out to raise more capital.

As investor money came in, Ray hired artists, more programmers, and system designers, including some highly talented and respected professionals, eventually numbering twenty-one. Some worked virtually from across the United States and others in the Explorati office.

The tribe working on the system didn't all share Ray's zeal for the idea. "I'm not sure this level of interactive game play is possible," his VP of engineering admitted, after reading technical papers on the problem and seeing the details of the founders' plans. Ray's response became "You just have to believe."

"I'm not sure I do believe," became the buzz in the hallways and over virtual chats. The tribe soon split, with half wanting to have the power to make key decisions and have others fall in line, and the other half wanting to make them through consensus. This tribal dynamic distracted people from the strategy.

As the buzz inside the company declined, it became harder to make real progress on the core technology and on the soap opera world that was under contract. In the wake of the dot-com implosion, raising money was getting harder, especially for early-stage companies. Although business development efforts were going well, everything else was feeling more fragile every day.

All the stress landed on Ray. He worked to prop up morale with impassioned speeches. He e-mailed and phoned investors as he continued to chase new money. Even his home wasn't a refuge—he was married to one of Explorati's writers, and they had taken out a second and third mortgage to finance their dream.

From a leadership perspective, there's a lot to admire about Ray. He put it all on the line for his dream. He led with passion bordering on charisma. As with his game system, he found a way to improvise when the funding didn't come through—often putting in more of his own money.

> **TECHNICAL NOTE:** *Most strategies are based on an understanding of the external environment, not the highest aspirations of the tribe. As a result, even the best plans often fail because people aren't giving it their all.*

Yet even with these advantages, Explorati ran out of cash and morale at about the same time, right after 9/11 caused the cancellation of the projects that were signed and dried up the last of the high-tech investor money. With no paying customers and investment money impossible to find even for stable companies, Explorati disbanded. Ray hoped to come back to the problem and make his dream a reality.

> **COACHING TIP: If a strategy fails, see what else—if anything—the tribe wants to do.** *Tribal relationships often survive the death of a strategy (even a company), although it's common for people to be at Stage Two in the wake of the failure. Many Tribal Leaders in our study rebuilt the tribal relationships and a new strategy at the same time, finding success the second, third, or fourth time.*

Ray's story is more the norm than the exception. Leaders seek the perfect strategy to excite employees and stock prices and to make history. This dream is as elusive as the hole-in-one, but that doesn't deter thousands of entrepreneurs from putting it all on the line, or large companies from spending an annual ten billion dollars on the top ten strategy consulting firms. As a *very* generous estimate, strategies fail 70 percent of the time, according to a 1999 study by Martin Corby and Diarmuid O'Corrbui. The problem doesn't play favorites; very few companies manage to sustain high strategic performance over time. Most entrepreneurs end up like Ray, although most lack his passion, tenacity, and sheer intelligence.

This chapter shows how Tribal Leaders can do it better, leveraging off the collaboration and innovation of Stage Four to set strategies that people want to implement and that are implementable. The result is an approach to strategy that is new, and almost embarrassingly simple.

TECHNICAL NOTE: *As with all the facets of Stage Four behavior, we learned by watching Tribal Leaders. In this case, however, we also were guided by a colleague who suggested that corporate tribes could learn from military tribes, so we began looking for military models that captured what we observed. The model we present in this chapter, which describes how many Tribal Leaders set strategy naturally, is a combination of strategy from applied economics (the basis of how the subject is taught in business schools) and military strategy, especially Carl von Clausewitz's* On War *and Robert Leonhard's* The Art of Maneuver: Maneuver Warfare Theory and Airland Battle.

The Essence of Tribal Strategy

People questioned Improvisational Computing, and Ray defended the vision. The result was a missed opportunity to refine the tribe's strategy. Just as important, people felt themselves to be the victims of inaction, and they were now solidly at Stage Two—"my life sucks." Even if Ray had been right, he still would have lost, since only a Stage Four culture could implement such an ambitious plan.

Throughout the history of tribes, most failed strategists weren't like today's entrepreneurs, who pick themselves up and try again. The edgier days of ancient history would have seen the person killed, as when the tribe of the Roman Senate took care of their upstart Julius Ceasar, whom they believed wasn't listening to them.

The more general the Tribal Leader was in taking things into account, the greater his chance of succeeding. It's no wonder that "general" and "strategy" have been linked for thousands of years, with *strategos* coming to mean "the art of the general." The history of successful tribes is the history of leaders learning to take the right things into account—which is what successful military generals do. One might say that the history of tribes gives us a compelling history of strategy. This tribal wisdom on strategy has been lost, and the result is lots of bright, ambitious people putting it all on the line, and failing when they don't have to.

> **TECHNICAL NOTE:** *Strategy, the way it's taught in business schools, is largely an outgrowth of research by Michael Porter and Peter Drucker. Taken together, their approach has proven extremely valuable and has fueled worldwide economic expansion for decades. However, we should consider that decades of research pales against the thousands of years of data from tribes and armies, so this chapter is an integration of*

traditional business strategy with what tribes have learned since the dawn of writing.

The Explorati tribe was split between people wanting to do it their own way (and management pushing them to focus on the company strategy, making them ticked off and passive—Stage Two) and those who bought into the vision (Stages Three and Four). Taking this into account would have meant stopping the action and dealing with the problem.

A similar situation happened at a public utility. The company was moving away from its hundred-year history of providing a staple product, and toward niche products with much higher margins. As part of the restructuring effort, an executive announced that the company would no longer consider itself a family.

That company had been built on the idea of family. It was common for a father to help get his son hired, who in turn would encourage his daughter to apply for work there. It was safe and stable, and people felt they were with their family from 8 a.m. to 5 p.m. The executive's remarks, to this day, are a stake in the heart of employees.

That executive failed to take the tribes in that company into account—their history, values, and identity. The employees simply crossed their arms and waited for him to fail—solidly entrenched in a condition of Stage Two ineffectiveness. It wasn't long before he left. The tribe is always more powerful than an individual, no matter what title is on his business card.

Tribal Leaders need a way of setting strategy that takes everything into account, *especially the tribe itself,* along with product life cycle, economics, technology advances, and market demographics. Such an approach might have saved Ray's company and the job of that utility executive. More important, it would have helped upgrade these tribes to the next level rather than eroding them to Stage Two.

The Five Components of Tribal Strategy

When we collected the best practices we observed from Tribal Leaders, and combined them with the results from a careful study of historical tribes, we came to the model in Figure 1, which has five parts: values, noble cause, outcomes, assets, and behaviors. The best practice is to go from values to outcomes, then proceed counterclockwise around the circle, asking the three test questions along the way.

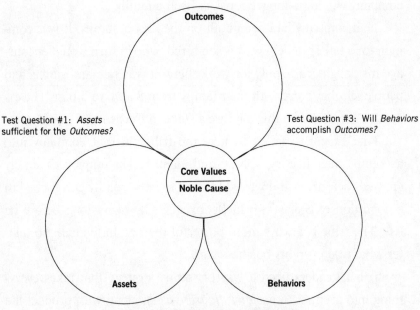

FIGURE 1: **THE TRIBAL LEADERSHIP STRATEGY MAP.** *START WITH CORE VALUES AND NOBLE CAUSE IN THE CENTER, THEN MOVE TO OUTCOMES AND GO COUNTERCLOCKWISE AROUND THE MODEL.*

Values and Noble Cause

Setting a strategy starts with recognizing the values of people who will implement it and the noble cause to which they aspire. As we saw in Chapter 9, these pieces give the tribe a boost in motivation and align it on a common purpose. They go a long way to owning Stage Four.

> **COACHING TIP: Point to the tangible benefits of shared values and a noble cause.** *Right away, the Tribal Leader may have a problem: the mention of values and a noble cause often sends eyes rolling, especially if the tribe has a dominant culture below Stage Three. These aspects of strategy are vital to inspiring people to put their all into work. We encourage people to remember the level of motivation the dot-coms had, with people often working twenty-hour days, fueled only by Twinkies and power naps. Such is the energy of basing a strategy on the core values and noble cause of the tribe. (Unfortunately, the dot-coms ignored most of the other aspects of strategy, such as markets, assets, revenue, and profitability, which is why so many Ferraris were repossessed in the early 2000s.)*

Explorati's noble cause was "a world of play and interconnection for everyone." People inside the company got excited about creating their own "worlds" (such as *Star Trek*)—a sign that the noble cause was in line with tribal aspirations. Their core values were "integrity," "open communication," and "fun."

The key to identifying these first two aspects of strategy is for the Tribal Leader to engage others in a questioning process about what the tribe stands for (values) and what it lives for (noble cause). This is not the time for an executive off-site retreat with a consultant, followed by eighteen holes of golf. This is the time to engage in the values discovery process described in Chapter 9 with as many people as possible.

Once the tribe has owned its values and noble cause, the Tribal Leader moves on to setting specific outcomes.

Outcomes: Success in the Moment

Once values and a noble cause are set, tribal strategy involves three conversations. The first is "what we want," or outcomes. The second is "what we have," or assets. The third is "what we will do," or behaviors. Many strategies go sideways by having two or even all three conversations at the same time—or skipping one of them completely. It's imperative that the Tribal Leader keep these three discussions separate.

Explorati's original outcome was "we will have created a playable proof-of-concept demonstration that uses Improvisational Computing by July 2001." This outcome is simple, clear, and in line with the tribe's values and noble cause. Note that any objections about whether this is achievable or not belong in a different discussion.

Outcomes vs. Goals

An outcome is different from a goal in one important way. Runner Carl Lewis showed this when he used to say that he ran while others raced. He described the race as already won before it started, and he then sought to fully experience each step of his unfolding victory. This is an outcome.

A goal is off in the future, so, to some people, it implies a failure in the present. "When we achieve the goal, we will have stopped failing" is how many people relate to the goal-setting process.

Many companies turn themselves around by setting goals to resolve a burning strategic problem, such as a pending bankruptcy, and it often works. Just as often, the tribe falls back into a crisis just a few months later. People are motivated by the goals in a crisis, but they lose their drive once the fire is out. Goals, when set this way, have diminishing returns as people become unwilling to spend their careers in a state of failure, scratching toward success. The unintended consequence of goal setting is often crisis management and adrenaline-inspired bursts of activity, followed by periods of letdown and burnout. It is unsustainable, and it does long-term damage to the tribe.

An outcome, by contrast, is a present state of success that morphs into an even bigger victory over time. The difference is the contrast between "I hope we make it—it'll be great when we turn this around" (setting a goal) and "we have already succeeded, and this is how it looks at this point in the process" (succeeding now with an outcome). The latter is much more in line with Stage Four; the former often unwittingly creates a Stage Two culture—"my life sucks because we're failing."

TECHNICAL NOTE: *A surprising number of Tribal Leaders in our study learned their most important leadership lessons in the military. Gordon Binder, for example, the former CEO of Amgen, credits his time in the navy with learning the importance of values and vision. As he told us, "if you walk on board a ship and the brass is polished, the guns will shoot straight . . . Walk on a ship where the brass is dirty, and that's a ship where we have to check the guns." Stage Four cultures tend to express their values in both big things (guns) and little things (brass).*

Keeping Outcomes at Stage Four

During the outcomes phase of strategy, people will often reveal which cultural stage they are in. The Tribal Leader needs to be highly attuned to this dynamic, knowing when to intervene and when to call a halt to the process. The objective is for the tribe (not just the leader) to set outcomes so compelling that people will want to form and maintain a Stage Four culture to accomplish them. A strong outcome will inspire the best in people and raise the dialogue above tribal politics. People operating at Stages Two and Three are often so immersed in politics that the outcome doesn't get enough attention.

A hallmark of Stage Two is the avoidance of ever being on the hook for anything, so people at this level will often suggest outcomes like "increase quality." Again and again, we saw Tribal Leaders pushing back: outcomes must be measurable, with a deadline. "How much, and by when?" was the response we heard from Tribal Leaders when people suggested vague targets. Some will offer sarcastic suggestions and then snicker, such as one person in a meeting we observed who said, "Buy a lottery ticket and win by August." The Tribal Leader needs to stay focused on tribal values and noble cause: "Any real suggestions?" was the the leader's quick comeback.

It's key to know when to push a tribe and when to back off and upgrade the tribal culture first. We are often asked, "What do I do when no one will say anything [in a meeting to set strategy]?" The Tribal Leader's first suspicion should be that the tribe probably has a large Stage Two contingent. Tribal strategy (as opposed to personal strategy) begins at Stage Four, and people can hear it and join in only if they are at Stages Three, Four, or Five. So in the case of a dominant Stage Two culture, start by upgrading the tribe before going any further. You might refer back to the coaching tips in Chapter 5.

People operating at Stage Three will engage, and argue for *their* suggestion. It will be measurable, and if you look closely, they will have to be in charge for that outcome to succeed. Again, this tactic is an attempt (perhaps unseen, even by the person making the suggestion) to divide the tribe.

The goal is not to take on Stage Three behavior (remember that people at this stage are often blind to the full effects of their behavior) but rather to look for what is valuable in the suggestion. Every comment is an addition, but not all additions are equal. The tribe determines the merit of "candidate outcomes"—which ones survive and which fall away. Here, the Tribal Leader must look for tribal will, not argue people into her point of view.

We saw this dynamic several years ago in working with a mid-sized software company. The CEO dominated the first hour of the strategy session by yelling his opinions and ridiculing other people's suggestions (classic Stage Three behavior), causing the tribe to divide into factions. He stepped outside to take a call. After a pause, one of the vice presidents said, "We're letting him push us into a strategy we know won't work." One person agreed, then another, and another. In that moment, the tribe began to form an early Stage Four culture, powerful but fragile. When the CEO came back in, the room fell silent. The first vice president to speak minutes before choked hard and said, "It's time we told the truth," and summarized the conversation that had just happened. To his credit, the CEO smiled and said, "Thank you for telling me the truth, finally . . . I was starting to think I had hired a bunch of weaklings, and now I'm proud to work here." The room filled with relieved laughter. The vice president had emerged as a Tribal Leader and set the stage for a great strategy session, and the CEO, to his credit, began thinking about why his behavior had created a Stage Two culture. It was his first step in the epiphany. The company implemented the strategy it set that day and saw a dramatic jump in its productivity. Years later, at the CEO's retirement party, people still talked of that day and of the guts it took for that vice president to speak for the tribe. He is now the CEO—a common career path for Tribal Leaders.

Nor is it necessary to be the one with the loudest voice. In the eighteenth century, delegates at the Continental Congress said that George Washington was the quietest man in the room and the best listener. He was looking for the emergence of outcomes that the tribe would own, and he came to see that independence from Great Britain was the will of the group. By becoming an advocate for what the tribe wanted to do (but hadn't clearly articulated), he became its leader.

Again and again in our research, we saw specific ideas inspire people, and the conversation kept returning to these suggestions. This is a sign that those "candidate outcomes" are in line with the tribe's core values and noble cause. For a tribe of employees from the company's construction division, the outcome was to build research facilities that were flexible enough to "turn on a dime, overnight" to accommodate clinical breakthroughs as they happened. This construction group, far down from the boardroom, had found its way to further the Amgen noble cause of "renewing life."

Once the tribe is excited by one or more outcomes, it's time to turn to the next phase of strategy.

Assets: The Potential for Continued Greatness

After identifying values and setting preliminary outcomes, the tribe should turn to identifying assets in a conversation focused on "What do we have?" An asset is anything the tribe and its people have right now, and it includes equipment, technology, land, relationships, good-will, brand, public awareness, reputation, culture, and drive. The classic blunder in identification is considering only physical assets but ignoring people's education, passions, and interpersonal networks. During this conversation, the tribe must look itself in the mirror and say what it has now—not what it had, will have, or wish it had. It should find all assets that are appropriate to the outcomes.

Explorati had some to-die-for assets, including some of the best gaming talent in the industry. When Ray led the assets discussion, it was an upbeat meeting. People started piling on asset after asset, and it was hard to record them as fast as they were sent zinging around the room. Quickly, though, the conversation turned to "We don't have enough money." This is not an asset conversation. Once again, the Tribal Leader needs to keep the group focused. The assets conversation is *only* "What do we have?"

There are two special types of assets that the leader needs to make sure the tribe considers. The first are core assets, which we define as "assets so central to the tribe that they may be invisble to people inside." The American soldiers in the Revolutionary War had learned guerrilla tactics from the Native Americans, and this asset helped to win the most important battles. At first, though, these tactics were seen as ungentlemanly. Similarly, in our day, tribes within Apple have sometimes not considered the cultlike support from core users, seeing the constant e-mail and calls as borderline guerrilla harassment. But by taking it into account, the entire company lever-aged itself to profitability, making die-hard Appleheads the network that spread the word about the iPod. This is Apple, leveraging its built-in tribal asset of true believers. Former Apple executive Kathy Calcidise said, "At an opening of an Apple store, there was a crowd around the block, chanting 'Apple, Apple, Apple.' That is when I drank the Kool-Aid."

One of the major unexploited core assets in most companies is the resources inside each and every person's network. While some at Explorati did not like to work in a virtual company, the situation actually created space for employees to become a part of more tribes than they would in a traditional building. This increased the resources available to the company through these networks. However, the employees will do so only if they are fully aligned with the values, noble cause, and strategy of the tribe (as they were in the early days at Explorati). These issues have never been more relevant, with virtual teams now affecting millions of employees.

We suggest that Tribal Leaders ask the question, "What do we have a knack for doing better than anyone else?" This question will often reveal core assets.

COACHING TIP: Ask outsiders what your tribe's core assets are. *Since core assets, almost by definition, are hard to see, outsiders can often see them more easily. Tribal Leaders often bring in outside experts for their perspective—not just as experts but as people with a different perspective.*

The second special type of asset, almost always ignored, is critical to strategic success: "common ground." It answers the question, "How are we seen by those with whom we want to transact?" If the tribe and the audience see the same thing, common ground exists. It's important to establish common ground—or the lack of it—with customers, vendors, and the larger organization. If it is lacking, the tribe needs to take this strategic situation into account, and fast.

Here, Explorati had a challenge. They were seen as odd gaming people by many advertisers. They were trying to take online gaming to the masses, which alienated them from hard-core gamers. Looking back, Ray admits he was trying to do too much on too small a budget. "You can't evangelize a new idea for non-gamers and sell a specific game contract to a specific game publisher at the same time." A focus on common ground would have revealed that problem sooner and given Explorati a larger potential customer base, which might have given them more options when their primary contract was canceled.

It's easy to see how common ground works when we look at entire companies, as long as we tie the lesson back to tribes. Microsoft saw itself as unlocking people's potential through technology, while many corporate customers, developers, and consumers were worried about what they saw as predatory behavior. This lack of common ground continued to slip, and the anger festered, until the company was labeled as a greedy, unfair monopoly. Wal-Mart is boycotted in some Middle American neighborhoods because they see it as a destroyer of Main Street economies, while the company sees itself as giving the consumer an edge in price and selection. For corporate tribes, lack of common ground has four predictable results: being ignored by the market, boycotts, legislation and regulations, and lawsuits.

To test whether your tribe has common ground, ask outside stakeholders (especially customers or external executives) how they view it. One of the most famous strategic blunders in history rested on a tribe not having common ground with its parent company. This was Xerox PARC, which had invented a revolutionary type of graphical interface, using a mouse and desktop. Today, that invention is at work in every computer running Windows and on every Macintosh. The upstart R&D tribe saw its members as developing the future of technology, while corporate leaders looked at them as out-of-touch nerds who were wasting money. Xerox ignored its own tribe's work, so they opened their doors to anyone who wanted to see their invention. A young entrepreneur from Silicon Valley saw the value in their technology, though, and immediately called all the members of his tribe. That person was Steve Jobs, and the tribe he brought in to see this amazing advance was the R&D group at Apple. Jobs got the technological breakthroughs of the decade in exchange for a few shares of Apple stock.

In summary, the assets discussion needs to take all the assets of the tribe into account, including the core assets and whether it has common ground with outside stakeholders. The tribe should also consider the cultural stage of the tribe, and people's commitment to core values, as assets, since these are the fuel that will drive extraordinary performance over the long run.

Test Question #1: Enough Assets for the Outcomes?

Before a strategy can be successfully implemented, the tribe must answer "yes" to three critical questions. Until that happens, the strategy is unfinished. The tribe can't be sure it will work, and just as important, people won't have the confidence required to take a strategy to success.

The first question is whether the tribe has enough assets to accomplish the outcomes. There is nothing wrong with answering "no," as long as the tribe then deals with the consequences; in fact, the answer is "no" for most corporate strategies in the first round of planning meetings. It's the same in the military, when the answer is almost always "no" when a war begins. The United States didn't have enough naval assets in the Pacific theater after Pearl Harbor, or military assets in the Middle East immediately after 9/11 for the strategy to invade Afghanistan.

In the case of Explorati, we've come to the fork in the road.

The answer to the first question was clearly a "no"—the tribe lacked technology, money, and common ground with most advertisers and game publishers. Could the company have made it anyway?

It could, if things went well, and Ray describes how things almost clicked—including being ultrashort-listed for the *The Lord of the Rings* game. The problem with under-resourced ventures of any kind—from military operations to runs for political offices to start-up businesses—is that things do not usually go well. While history has some examples of inventors who went for their dreams without enough resources and eventually made it work, the same history has many more examples of people not making it and having a reasonable explanation for why it didn't work—a downturn in the economy, changing customer tastes, or a competitor who seemed to appear out of nowhere.

Our model encompasses ten thousand years of tribal wisdom that says it's not smart to proceed *as if* things will go as planned. As Field Marshal Helmuth von Moltke said, "no battle plan survives contact with the enemy." If all limitations are not taken into account (stopping the action and confronting the problem), eventual failure becomes likely.

In the event the answer to this first test question is a "no," the strategic discussion changes to "How do we build our assets?" This new focus then takes the place of the desired final outcomes as an interim outcome. At this point, the new interim outcome is to accumulate appropriate assets or common ground until the first test question becomes "yes." When this happens, the strategy shifts back to the original outcomes. Figure 2 shows an interim strategy.

Regardless of whether the answer is "yes" or "no," the tribe should move forward to the last of three discussions.

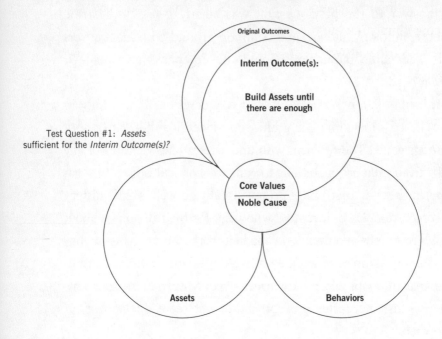

FIGURE 2: AN INTERIM STRATEGY

Behaviors: Strategy in Action

In the behaviors discussion, the tribe asks the question, "What should we do to accomplish the outcomes?"

What does a tribe do that answered "no" to the first test question? This is the situation our friends at Explorati were in. In this case, write down the behaviors that will build the assets your tribe needs. One approach that might have worked for Ray's tribe was to take the existing talent to produce "kick-ass multiplayer games" and focus them on building something more salable to the regular game publishers. These games wouldn't use Improvisational Computing, but the revenue from them could fund continued R&D until Explorati completed its breakthrough. With a temporary shift in strategy, Explorati might have survived, flourished, and still been the first to put Improvisational Computing on the map. In the end, the company simply ran out of cash.

If your tribe answered "yes" to the first question, then it should get specific about the behaviors that will accomplish the outcomes. These outcomes need to be put in order of implementation, with each being specific. One of our clients, for example, has an IT strategy with the outcome to build a real-time, Web-based executive information system (EIS). The behaviors that flow from it are to (1) locate the best three EIS installations, regardless of industry, by June 1, (2) complete a needs assessment of all business units by November 1 and present this to senior management by December 1, and (3) finish a tactical plan for implementation, including hiring/redeploying talent and maintaining funding for this initiative by December 15.

The process of writing down behaviors is deceptively simple, and people are in constant danger of making two classic mistakes. The first is writing down what people are already doing, rather than focusing on behaviors that will bring the outcomes to life. The conversation should be about what the members of the tribe will do to be successful.

The second mistake is assuming that everything will go perfectly. It won't. Whenever practical, the strategy should include at least two behavioral paths to accomplishing each critical outcome. When this two-path model is too inefficient, it may be useful to start both paths and see which leads to the outcome first. This approach has been the basis for countless tribal victories in times of war. In World War II, for example, American military plans in the Pacific assumed that some battles would be lost.

An effective behavior focuses people on covering ground quickly. When the unnecessary issues are set aside, it's remarkable how much progress people can make, even on outcomes that seem like major stretches.

As the tribe puts these behaviors together, individual leaders will step forward. It's a lot like what ancient tribes did around a campfire, or in a cave sheltered from the storm. For the good of the tribe, a leader would say that his family, a subset of the tribe, would start a farm, and another person would step up to lead the hunt for game. Today, a person may say she will take the lead on financial models, and another will put together the PowerPoint deck for the CEO. The content of the conversation is different, but the process of tribal heroes stepping forward is the same.

Once the tribe has recorded its behaviors, and the list seems complete, it's time for the last two test questions.

Test Question #2: Enough Assets for Behaviors?

Most often, the answer to this second question will be "yes." If the answer is "no," the tribe has two choices. First, it can add assets to the strategy. A good question to ask is, "What assets do we have that we haven't identified yet?" Second, the tribe can modify its behaviors so that they require fewer assets (often, time, money, and people). A good question is, "Is there a faster, cheaper way to get this done?"

When the answer to the second test question is "yes," the tribe can move on to the last question.

Test Question #3: Will Behaviors Accomplish Outcomes?

Here, the tribe looks at the behaviors from a critical eye. Will they work?

In Explorati's case, and perhaps yours if your tribe has an interim strategy, the question is, "Will the behaviors produce the missing assets (the interim outcome)?" Ray's version of this test question might have been, "Will our behaviors make enough money from 'kick-ass games' without Improvisational Computing to fund our development efforts of this new technology?"

There's a danger in this third test question: the same tribe that developed the plan is now evaluating it. The "we can do anything" euphoria that comes from these three strategic conversations may prevent a fair evaluation.

To get around the problem, Tribal Leaders should ask every person in the tribe to answer this test question as if he were sitting on a jury. No one gets to abstain, and if someone thinks the behaviors will fail, she has to give details. It is vital that these contrarians be able to freely express their skepticism, but do not ask the naysayer for solutions. Doing so will make people feel that it is not safe to disagree with rest of the tribe. Once all have expressed their thoughts, the tribe needs to take the concern or objection into account. The pitfall here is that members of the tribe may start attacking the person with the objection. To allow this is as critical a mistake as not asking the test questions at all. The Tribal Leader has to make sure the objection is heard and considered. She might ask another person to repeat it back until the naysayer is satisfied that the objection, concern, or point of view has been fully expressed. Only at this point should the tribe consider what to do about it, if anything.

If the answer to this third question is a "no," the solution is to ask the tribe what else it can do to achieve the outcome. Often, it's simply a matter of brainstorming a few more action steps, and then the answer rolls over to "yes." At this point, the tribe has finished the interim outcome. The concern is now resolved, and the tribal focus returns to the original outcome. It produces a new list of behaviors, utilizing its new assets, to accomplish it.

We saw this situation in a high-tech start-up in 2001. Their interim outcome was to raise capital, but they lacked a patent on their core idea, and this missing asset was a concern to potential investors.

To the credit of company executives, they stopped asking for money and concentrated all their efforts on obtaining the patent—a nerve-wracking process, as they were then burning through their meager reserves. Once they had done so, they went back to the original plan and found raising money much easier. Instead of denying the problem, they dealt with it via an interim strategy.

This test question also guards against behaviors that are not relevant. One small biotech company we studied—a single tribe—set an outcome of advancing a line of drugs through Phase III clinical trials by a certain date; yet its stated behaviors included recruiting benefits experts, erecting new buildings, and adding IT functionality. The small impoverished research group would have gotten to Phase III clinical tests eventually, but no thanks to the stated behaviors. The behaviors were off task to the outcome and therefore not relevant. The company floundered and eventually filed for bankruptcy.

This test question forces the tribe to pick only behaviors that will accomplish its outcomes.

Getting Started with Tribal Strategy

Explorati had two strategic problems: part of the tribe was at Stage Two, and it was under-resourced (as most start-ups are). The Tribal Leadership approach would say to form an interim strategy right away and, at the same time, upgrade the tribe.

Looking back, Ray notes that he hired the best people around, all with the right résumés. All were on board for the vision, but people weren't aligned on how to get there. He notes that if he had it do over again, he would have hired people who were on board with the whole strategy, and he would have been more responsive to the concerns of team members. That's Stage Four thinking.

Next time, we think he'll pull it off.

Cascading Strategies

The system of strategy in this chapter works at every level we've studied, from top corporate strategies through individual plans. The last question we need to address is, How do all of these strategies work together?

This history of tribes shows a process of coordinated, networked strategies so that high-level behaviors flow down to the outcome of the next level. In the military, a general's behaviors become the outcomes for colonels, and their behaviors become the outcomes of captains, and so on. Amgen's top strategy included a behavior step of hiring and promoting people with the eight Amgen values, and this flowed down to its own outcome within human resources.

In tribes, unlike corporations of the 1950s, strategies also cascade up. People in direct communication with the customer—often at the bottom of hierarchies—are often in the best position to suggest top-tier strategies. Within the context of a Stage Four culture, every person, every group, and every department all have their own strategies, and these all interlock together. This feature of strategies—that they network together and are interdependent—becomes the basis for partnership. It's not that the "top" strategies are dependent on the strategies at the "bottom"; it's that all require one another, so without a culture of mutual accountability (part of a Stage Four culture), the system will underperform.

Fulfilling the "We're Great" Pledge

Griffin Hospital didn't move through these steps as systematically as we have presented them in this chapter; yet, their story shows the discipline of tribal strategy. As VP Bill Powanda recounts it, "In every business, profit is price times volume minus expenses. It doesn't matter if you're selling mayonnaise or selling cars. In a hospital, price and expenses are fixed [by the managed healthcare system], so the only thing we had control over was volume. We looked into it and saw that volume was a function of patient satisfaction, and that meant we had to become a patient-centered facility [the outcome]. We looked around and realized we didn't know how to do that [we were missing assets], so we went looking and found Planetree [an interim outcome]. They provided part of the answer, but we had a lot more work to do [behaviors]." In just a few sentences, Powanda summarized the method of a tribe coming together and setting its own strategy—and since it was the *tribe's* strategy, people were invested in it. Both because of the strategy and in preparation for it, the culture became Stage Four.

As happened at Griffin, tribes need to respect the different "dialects" of outcomes, assets, and behaviors. Tribal Leaders need to ensure that the tone of one discussion doesn't slop over into the next. Outcomes is all about measurement. Assets focuses on making a long and exacting list of everything the tribe can bring to bear on the strategy. Behaviors is much like a to-do list. For example, many tribes we observed (after some basic training in this approach to strategy) had lively discussions on assets, with people throwing out ideas faster than they could be written down. This same free-for-all spirit doesn't work well in a behaviors discussion, however, as it requires exactness of action.

Once the tribe has set its strategy based on values and its noble cause, firmed up its outcomes, surveyed its assets, gotten specific about behaviors, and tested whether the three major parts connect, it will most often have a palpable sense of excitement. If the tribe was on the border between Stages Three and Four, this process usually pushes it over the top into "we're great." People will begin networking (through triads) to fulfill this dynamic, and they will actively bypass people who refuse to budge off Stage Three behavior. Every member of the tribe knows exactly how to succeed and what each person must do to make the tribe effective.

That's the promise of tribal strategy.

Key Points from This Chapter

◆ A tribal strategy is nothing more than three separate but interlocking discussions, all flowing from values and a noble cause.

◆ In outcomes, answer the question "What do we want?"

◆ In assets, answer the question "What do we have?"

◆ Before moving on to behaviors, ask the first test question: "Do we have enough assets for the outcomes?" If the answer is "yes," move on. If the answer is "no," construct an interim strategy.

◆ In behaviors, answer the question "What will we do?"

◆ Ask the second test question: "Do we have enough assets for our behaviors?" If the answer is "yes," move on. If the answer is "no," add more assets or revise behaviors.

◆ Ask the third test question: "Will the behaviors produce the outcomes?" If the answer is "yes," you have a strategy. If the answer is "no," add more behaviors, making sure you're leveraging all available assets.

◆ Once you have a strategy, focus only on the behaviors. Restrategize every ninety days.

Leverage Points for a Person at Stage Four:

◆ Stabilize her at Stage Four by ensuring her relationships are based on values and mutual self-interest of current projects.

◆ Encourage her to form more triads, the subject of Chapter 10.

◆ Encourage her to use the strategy process in Chapter 11 with her team. In particular, encourage her to run sessions that explore the team's core values, its sense of a noble cause, outcomes that would inspire the team, its assets, and then its behaviors (who would do what). In short, encourage her to pick projects that are more of a stretch and that accomplish bigger and bigger results, by working more in partnership with other people.

◆ Once she is fully stable at Stage Four (which you can measure by her use of "we're great" language and her networked triads of relationships), encourage her team to take advantage of market conditions to make history.

◆ If the market doesn't offer the right conditions, engineer an opportunity.

◆ Recruit others to the tribe who share the values of the group's strategy.

◆ When the team hits difficulties, point people to others for solutions. Encourage her to not solve problems, as doing so is consistent with "I'm great (and you're not)."

◆ Perform regular "oil changes" with the team. In this process, she should lead a discussion about (1) what is working well, (2) what is not working well, and (3) what the team can do to make the things that are not working well, work.

Success Indicators

◆ She will use "life is great" language rather than "we're great (and they're not)."

◆ She will seek out ever more challenging projects, and her network will include an almost stunning amount of diversity—but mostly people who, like her, have owned and then left Stage Three.

◆ She will make decisions about how to spend her time based on the tribe's core values and noble cause.

◆ She will appear to be an embodiment of the tribe's strategy, especially its values.

PART IV
Toward Vital Work Communities (Stage Five)

CHAPTER 12

Early Stage Five: Life Is Great

Gordon Binder, former CEO of biotechnology giant Amgen, didn't
know it at the time, but his company delayed publication of this
book for almost five years.

In the early 1990s, we only knew about tribal Stages One
through Four, and we had lots of examples of each. On the basis of
our observations, we believed that Stage Four's "we're great" language was the top of the mountain. Then, thanks to Amgen, everything turned upside down, delaying the publication of this book.
The discovery was worth the wait.

We expected Amgen to demonstrate a cultural mood of tribal
pride—a hallmark of Stage Four—with people congratulating one
another for a job well done. Profits and revenue were up, and employees were making a *lot* of money off options. We expected a
"tribal vibe" not unlike the end of the movie *Rudy,* with thousands
of Notre Dame fans going nuts with joy over the victory.

We walked into Amgen in the 1990s and asked who their competitors were. We expected "Genentech" (another biotechnology firm)
or maybe—if people were ambitious—"Pfizer" (a fully integrated
pharmaceutical company). It was even possible that people would be
so ill informed about the marketplace that they wouldn't know. All of

those answers would be consistent with what we expected to find, and they would help verify our hypotheses and make us happy researchers.

"We're in competition with cancer," we heard from Amgen employees. *Huh?* No mention of a company.

The same people went on to say, "Maybe [our competitor] is inflammatory disease, such as arthritis. Obesity, Parkinson's." We weren't happy. In fact, our four-stage model couldn't explain what we were hearing.

One person added, "We might be in competition with untimely death—human disease. I guess we're not really targeting starvation or war."

Again, our reaction was *Huh?*

To make our situation worse, we didn't see any evidence of tribal pride. No high fives, no "We're #1" banners (which they were in growth, although not in revenue or market capitalization).

"It's amazing," one person in engineering told us. "A few good experiments, and now we're sitting on billion-dollar patents. It makes me think of all the human diseases we'll beat in the next few years." His tone was what perplexed us more than his words. It wasn't pride. It was almost a whisper, said like a prayer of thanksgiving. It's a mood we came to call innocent wonderment.

We had stumbled across our first example of Stage Five, and it was as much a leap forward as Stage Four was from Three. It is, we believe, the future of business.

At Amgen in the 1990s, and in most other organizations at this stage, the culture oscillated in and out of Stage Five. After a burst of history-making activity, the group fell back to the "we're great" language of Stage Four, assessing their performance relative to competitors. Then another market opportunity, or possible discovery, would come along and catapult them back into Stage Five again. If we graphed out the Amgen of the early 1990s, the culture would be like waves on the beach: the crests in Stage Five and the troughs in Stage Four.

Stage Five

Stage Five accounts for just under 2 percent of workplace cultures. It's marked by "life is great" language, devoid of any competitor. It's not that competitors don't exist; it's that they don't matter. Values, which are important at Stage Four, are vital—a word literally meaning "life-giving." Without them, the tribal culture would collapse to Four and keep falling. A noble cause—critical at Stage Four—is the group's only compass. Without another tribe to study and beat, "renewing life" was Amgen's only direction, and values were its only way to know who they were. (At Stage Four, tribes know who they are by their competitor.)

Since Amgen, we've found dozens of organizations with Stage Five tribes. Some are for-profit companies, like Amgen. Others are not-for-profits: some local Boys & Girls Clubs, several think tanks, and a few wildly successful technology start-ups. What they all have in common is Tribal Leadership taken to its next level, and a level of performance that makes history.

Not-for-profit organizations have an advantage in seeing beyond the competition and aligning themselves on a noble cause. Mindy Watrous, CEO of Colorado Special Olympics, said, "These people [the staff] support anyone. They make me better. They elevate people within the organization and elevate the athletes. They celebrate everyone." The noble cause of the Special Olympics is "creating opportunities for all athletes." They believe they are making history every time athletes compete.

People who have ever been part of a Stage Five tribe—or even seen one at work—often describe it in the same tone of reverence and gratitude they use to tell stories of their kids.

All things being equal, Stage Five will always outperform Stage Four. At Amgen, the focus was on curing disease. Making money wasn't the goal, and rewarding investors didn't motivate this group. That said, Amgen *was* making money, with analysts at the time saying that the company had a "license to print money." *Fortune* picked Amgen as one of just a handful of companies that had made investors truly wealthy.

The purpose of this chapter is to pass along what we know about early Stage Five: how it works, and what Tribal Leaders can do to elevate their companies to this zone of peak performance.

Graduation from Stage Four

Jim Clifton, the CEO of the Gallup Organization, is a Tribal Leader on steroids. "Over the years, people have called Gallup a cult—our detractors I mean—but I have always considered that a great compliment."

In fact, Clifton has long referred to the organization he heads as a tribe. He explains, "We have a lot of common values in our organization that remind me of a tribe." Clifton formerly ran Selection Research, Inc. (SRI), a marketing research company that conducted structured psychological interviews to identify individuals who would fit a designated position in an organization. The SRI brand wasn't well known, and the group searched for a way to make a global impact. It needed something more.

"Something more" turned out to be Gallup—the organization started by Dr. George Gallup in 1935 (originally called the American Institute of Public Opinion). Clifton explains, "We [at SRI] worked hard to acquire Gallup from the family, because people latch on to symbols. When we were at SRI we couldn't develop global pride until we had a global symbol. We don't wear it like pro teams, but here at

Gallup we wear a *lot* of label clothes." With the world-famous name and organization part of the tribe, everything began to change. (It's important to note that acquiring Gallup wasn't the ultimate goal but rather an interim strategy, as described in the previous chapter.)

With the resources of both SRI and Gallup, now under one name, Clifton moved the organization in a new direction, establishing the Gallup Path, a model that ties individual contribution to the organization's bottom-line performance. Under his Tribal Leadership, Gallup moved the group more toward consulting. All that work set the stage for the organization's jump to Stage Five.

"We developed a belief, based on our research of three hundred thousand people, that a person's strengths are at the very base of it all. We believe any individual can be extremely valuable or even has a shot at being a world leader if they will pull it off using their own strengths instead of trying to become a Jack Welch or a Ted Turner," Clifton argues. The core value we heard in his statement is "potential," and everything the organization has done is based on unlocking it—in individuals, clients, and even the entire world. Furthermore, the Gallup tribe has developed research and procedures to assess and develop this potential, basing such efforts on natural ability. Although Clifton had not seen the strategy model in Chapter 11, he already had a noble cause, a set of core values, and core assets (research abilities, global brand, and research on unlocking potential).

In addition, Clifton saw the value in the tribal culture: "The kind of people we attract to our organization are the kind of people who are driven by mission and purpose—that sets our tribe apart." When we explained our research on tribes and the five cultures, he added, "Many of our activities are at Stage Five, but it wasn't always that way."

He said, "We asked the question, 'Are we helping six billion people or just the best corporations in the world?' The honest answer was that we were helping the best corporations—and schools and universities," Clifton said. "We weren't doing much for the six billion people."

From our research, companies that are engrossed in warfare with a competitor don't consider questions like the one Gallup asked. They are generally focused on winning market share and new customers—and thwarting the rival at the same time. At best, an early Stage Four "we're great" culture develops, focused on beating that competitor. Gallup had owned Stage Four and was ready to move on. As a result, it could recognize the insufficiency of the Stage Four culture. In a sense, the group had a realization that is a more advanced version of the epiphany to Tribal Leadership—the subject of Chapter 7. The result was a new appreciation for their ability to contribute to global concerns—an all-inclusive view.

Gallup set its new noble cause "as improving the well-being of our clients' organizations *and* improving the lives of the six billion people on the earth." The group didn't let go of its competitive edge, but the drive to win lost its sense of a competitor. No one has to lose in the service of six billion people.

One of the outcomes the organization set is a "world poll," which, according to Clifton, "represents ninety-seven percent of the world's population." For the first time in history, the world will speak with a single voice, thanks to Gallup building on its values and strengths in research. Furthermore, the research will reveal what Clifton calls the soul of over a hundred individual countries.

Nobel Laureate Daniel Kahneman, who works with Clifton—and has a reputation for honesty—told us, "The Gallup organization is unlike anything I have seen. In some ways the way their culture emphasizes the positive is relentless . . . The true positivity of their culture permeates everything."

Stage Five tribes use all the subtleties of Chapters 9, 10, and 11. Although Clifton hadn't read our work or seen the strategy model, what he volunteered about Gallup showed all the elements: a noble cause, a set of shared core values, an outcome (the global poll), core assets (research abilities, a global brand, top talent, a highly nimble and networked tribe), and behaviors (the steps people would take to conduct and popularize the world poll). His description of the company's culture included triads, and Gallup works with clients as partners. Note that once a tribe establishes stability at Stage Four, it can either take advantage of a market opportunity or engineer such an event (as Gallup did with its world poll) to pop into Stage Five.

> **COACHING TIP: Bring together the tribe and ask the following question: "What would propel us to the next level?"** *One way we've found that sometimes works is to think of adding assets on the "big deal scale," which we abbreviate BDS. The question is, what asset would be a one or two (out of ten) on the BDS? A five? An eight? A ten? Moving to Stage Five becomes real when a group commits to a strategy (usually with several interim strategies to build its assets) that they think is beyond them—and beyond any competitor—that would have an impact on the entire world.*

Moment of Transcending Stage Four

Stage Five tribes often describe a moment when they transcended the "we're great" culture and emerged somewhere else: in a culture so different that many didn't have the words to describe it.

Mike Eruzione, captain of the 1980 U.S. Olympic hockey team, encountered Stage Five when his team beat the Soviet Union. His story starts with the prerequisites of Stage Four. He describes the people he played with: "There were twenty players on this team, and nineteen of them were captains at some time." He named the people, referring to high school or college teams. Eruzione was a captain among captains.

Despite some press to the contrary, the coach was not loved by the team. "It was always us against him. As [Coach] Herb [Brooks] used to say, there was a method to his madness, and we always tried to figure out what that method was, and when it was done, we all said, 'Wow, he was right.' He helped orchestrate it, he helped plan, he knew he had the type of players [we were]."

Eruzione's tone toward his old coach never changed. "I can remember ten years ago, the phone rang, and my wife told me it was Herb, and I thought, 'Oh my God, he's going to yell at me.' I have three kids running around the house, and I'm worried that Herb is mad at me. It's crazy."

The coach of the famous team has since died, but his method is now clear to Eruzione: "Herb didn't care if we liked him; he cared about our respecting him. . . . We never saw Herb off the ice. He did what he did and left us alone." Off the ice, players often grumbled about his tactics, including his relentless practice sessions. The culture became Stage Four: "We're great and Herb's not" (a rare case wherein the enemy of a group is a single person).

The stage was set. Players knew their roles, had the talent, and knew one another by their values, not just their abilities. They had put in the time and effort. As with Amgen and Gallup, all the pieces were in place. The 1980 U.S. team was stable at Stage Four, waiting for the right opportunity to move to Stage Five.

The team's time came in the game with the Soviets. When Herb told the team it would all come together, what they didn't realize was that he was giving them the stage and their opportunity to become the team he knew they could be. In that moment, the U.S.

Olympic Hockey team took a quantum leap. They jumped from a successful Stage Four tribe and became something more, playing not against Herb or a competitor but for something much bigger. They played for the love of sport, for themselves, and for all the old-fashioned values that united them.

It was a moment when everything came together, and the sense of wonder didn't set in until the game was over. Eruzione told us, "The countdown: five-four-three-two-one. . . . The puck could have gone in. Everything could have changed so quickly. So then when the buzzer sounded . . ."

We asked him about his mood at that moment. "The first thought I had was 'Wow.'" He said it to us in a whisper, very much like the people at Amgen in describing clinical breakthroughs. His tone conveyed the sense that people had done the impossible. It wasn't about beating the Russians (Stage Four); it was about doing what people thought could not be done (Stage Five).

The next scene was not tribal pride but innocent wonderment overwhelmed with gratitude. "We went back into the locker room, and guys were hugging and crying. We just couldn't believe it," Eruzione told us.

In that game, the group transcended its self-imposed barriers and emerged as a fully functional Stage Five tribe, guided only by its values and its noble cause. In so doing, it shocked everyone, even itself.

The word "miracle" has become associated with the 1980 victory. It's also a word we heard again and again from organizations that were operating with a Stage Five culture. We interviewed one corporate team that had been contacted by the White House to join a summit with then President Bill Clinton. "It was a miracle—someone like me meeting a U.S. president," the team leader said. We heard the word at Amgen in reference to their clinical breakthroughs and to their always seeming to be one step ahead of the competition. Our view is that the emergence of Stage Five feels so unfamiliar to most of us that we go to religious or spiritual language in describing it.

"Wow" was what we heard when we talked with people who were part of the Apollo missions in the 1960s, leading to the first manned mission to the moon. The mood was the same, despite the tribe members' scientific orientation and the years of preparation. "We couldn't believe it," we heard from people, now long retired. "It just didn't seem possible." And many times: "Wow."

At this point, groups often stop us. "What if it's not real?" people ask. In the early 2000s, we collected data from other Stage Five organizations—dot-coms—many of which don't exist any more. At the time, principals said how they were "changing the business model of retailing," and "inventing a new world of business service." As we pointed out in other chapters, culture and strategic performance move together. When these companies didn't have the follow-through, their cultures degraded, one stage at a time. At Stage Four, people said, "We're better than our competition because we have enough cash to last nine months, and they'll be out of business in six." At Three, they said, "I still have my job, but I'm sorry you lost yours." At Two, "I have no job and no prospects, and I don't know what to do." Some went all the way to Stage One and committed suicide, the ultimate tragic act of "life sucks." A tribe should attempt a Stage Five outcome (like the Gallup "world poll") only if it's stable at Stage Four and has the business results to keep it there.

COACHING TIP: Engineer an opportunity that produces a Stage Five culture. *IDEO's David Kelley tries to engineer this mood—what he calls child's mind. "It's been there when we had some of our greatest breakthroughs," he said, recalling Stage Five moments. As with the U.S. hockey team, the moment of "wow"* *comes when a stable Stage Four tribe meets a history-making opportunity.*

Resonant Values

A tribe operating at Stage Five acts like a magnet for other groups that can help in their pursuit of its noble cause. Amgen and Gallup are both famous for their tendency to partner with organizations and individuals, many of whom do not share their values. At the same time, both organizations are famous for their *commitment* to shared values. Is there a conflict?

No. At Stage Three, the focus is "my" values. At Four, it's "our" values. At Five, it's "global"—or "resonant"—values, so the only important factor is that values can work together. IDEO values "collaboration" and what David Kelley calls "child's mind." Apple values "elegant design." Amgen values, above all, "being ethical." These values, while not the same, resonate with one another, so the organizations could work together. None would partner with a corrupt government or with organizations run by what Gordon Binder calls crooks.

A Stage Five tribe can work with any group that has a commitment to values that are core and that apply to everyone, even if those values are different from its own. At Stage Five, these three organizations could network together in the service of a noble cause that is bigger than what any company could pursue alone.

The Emergence of Tribal Elders

In our study of Stage Five, we also noticed that Tribal Leaders tended to "graduate" to a position of brokering "treaties" between tribes. Bill Gates, Warren Buffet, U2's Bono, Jimmy Carter, Nelson Mandela, Desmond Tutu, and people of their ilk often go on to contribute to global—not just tribal—causes. As they do, the tribes they once headed wish they would stay—and some even accuse them of becoming traitors.

If we look closely, however, we see that their commitment to values has shifted to (or perhaps always was) resonant values. They often refer to their corporate, political, or organizational tribe in the same way many of us think of our hometown—it will always be home, but we have outgrown it.

We asked many of the Stage Five leaders we met whom they admired, and most mentioned people of global influence. The Moore Foundation's Frank Jordan gave us a typical answer: Dr. Albert Schweitzer. "He had everything," Jordan said (meaning success at Stages Three and Four) "and gave it all up to go to Africa to help because he saw such tremendous need. All he said is that I don't know what your destiny will be, but this I do know, those who will be truly happy will be those who sought and found how to serve others."

People at Stage Five find themselves in a unique role. Their Stage Four and Five successes make them celebrities, but most shun the spotlight. In time, many go to work for a cause in which they bring together multiple tribes to achieve an outcome far greater than any single one could do alone.

The Future of Business

These examples of early Stage Five are the highest tribal cultures we have ever seen. However, it is our hope and belief—based on the extrapolation of our research and the opinions of experts—that there is a way to stabilize a tribe at Stage Five. Just as few people would have bet on the people, teams, and organizations in this chapter, the Tribal Leaders involved defied what others (and they) thought was achievable. As the purpose of this book is to report on our research, we've made our speculative thoughts about what stable Stage Five would look like on our Web site: www.triballeadership. net. In short, we're looking for the emergence of stable Stage Five tribes: groups that continue for years without falling back to Stage Four.

Simply put, the future of business is Stage Five—either frequent leaps into it from Stage Four (as several companies in this study are doing) or breaking new ground by finding stability at this level. Our company, and our professional lives, are dedicated to giving everyone the opportunity to be a part of a Stage Five group. We hope that as you do, you'll let us know, so we can spread the wealth from your discoveries.

● ● ● ● ● ●

A Tribal Leader's Cheat Sheet

Overview Questions

What Is a Tribe?

◆ A tribe is any group of about 20 to 150 people who know one another enough that, if they saw another walking down the street, would stop and say "hello."

◆ They are likely people in your cell phone and in your Outlook address book.

◆ A small company is a tribe, and a large company is a tribe of tribes.

◆ What makes some tribes more effective than others is culture. Each time people speak, their words exhibit the characteristics of one of five tribal stages. Stage Five outperforms Four, which accomplishes more than Three, which gets more done than Two, which is more effective than One.

◆ A medium to large tribe (50 to 150 people) usually has several cultural stages operating at the same time.

What Is Tribal Leadership?

◆ Tribal Leadership focuses on language and behavior within a culture.

◆ It does not seek to address cognitions, beliefs, attitudes, or other factors we cannot directly observe.

◆ Each cultural stage has its own way of speaking, types of behavior, and structures of relationships.

◆ Tribal Leaders do two things: (1) listen for which cultures exist in their tribes and (2) upgrade those tribes using specific leverage points.

To Listen for Which Cultures Exist in Their Tribes, Tribal Leaders Must Know the Following

Summary of Stage One

◆ The person at Stage One is alienated from others, expressing the view that "life sucks."

◆ When people at this stage cluster together, their behavior expresses despairing hostility, such as in a gang.

Summary of Stage Two

◆ The person at Stage Two is separate from others, although unlike Stage One, Stage Two people are surrounded by people who seem to have some power that they lack. As a result, their language expresses "*my* life sucks." Unlike Stage One, a person at Stage Two communicates the view that others' lives seem to be working.

◆   When people at this stage cluster together, their behavior is characteristic of being apathetic victims.

Summary of Stage Three

◆   The person at Stage Three is connected to others in a
series of dyadic (two-person) relationships. The language
of this stage expresses "I'm great," and in the background—
unstated—is "and you're not."

◆   When people at Stage Three cluster together, they attempt to outperform one another (on an individual basis)
and put one another down. Although this is often done
under the veil of humor, the effect is the same: each is
striving for dominance. Individuals' behavior expresses a
"lone warrior" ethos, and collectively, the culture becomes
the "wild, wild west."

Summary of Stage Four

◆   The person forms structures called triads, in which
they build values-based relationships between others. At
the same time, the words of Stage Four people are centered on "we're great" and, in the background, "and they're
not." The "they" is another tribe—in the same company
or in another.

◆   When people at Stage Four cluster together, they ra-
diate tribal pride.

Summary of Stage Five

❖   A person at Stage Five expresses "life is great." Five shares the same characteristics of Four, except that there is no "they." As a result, these people form ever-growing networks with anyone whose values resonate with their own. The only Stage Five cultures we have observed (in corporate settings) exist as long as a history-making project lasts or as long as the tribe is so far ahead of its competitors that they are irrelevant.

❖   Once the situation changes, the culture regresses to Stage Four, where it can move forward once a new opportunity arises or is engineered. The behavior of Stage Five expresses innocent wonderment.

Tribal Stage	Collaboration	Communication	Structure
5	Team	"Life is great"	
4	Partnership	"We're great"	
3	Personal	"I'm great"	
2	Separate	"My life sucks"	
1	Alienated	"Life sucks"	

FIGURE 1: SUMMARY OF TRIBAL LEADERSHIP LANGUAGE AND STRUC-
TURES. NOTE THAT THE PERSON IN QUESTION IS THE CIRCLE ON THE
RIGHT COLUMN—GOING FROM ALIENATED AT STAGE ONE TO PART OF AN
EVER-GROWING NETWORK AT STAGE FIVE.

Leverage Points and Success Indicators to Upgrade Tribal Culture

For a Person at Stage One

◆ If the person is willing to move forward, encourage him to go where the action is. This means having lunch with coworkers, attending social functions, and going to meetings.

◆ Furthermore, encourage him to notice ways in which life itself works. For example, a person can notice that your life is pretty good, so it's possible that his may improve.

◆ Encourage him to cut ties with people who share the "life sucks" language.

SUCCESS INDICATORS

◆ He will use *"my* life sucks" language, as opposed to "life sucks." In other words, his concern has shifted from a generalized gripe to a specific set of reasons why *his* life doesn't function as it should. In particular, he will compare himself to others' abilities, social advantages, and, most of all, interpersonal connections.

◆ He will exhibit the passive apathy of Stage Two, as opposed to the despairing hostility of Stage One. This shift may appear as a setback to people who aren't familiar with Tribal Leadership; in fact, it is a major step forward.

◆ He will cut his social ties to people who are in Stage One.

For a Person at Stage Two

◆ Encourage her to make a friend. Then another friend. Then another friend. In other words, encourage her to establish dyadic (two-person) relationships.

◆ Encourage her to establish relationships with people who are at late Stage Three. Such individuals can be identified by their eagerness to mentor others into becoming mini-versions of themselves. (However, the same individuals will not tolerate another's becoming greater than they are.)

◆ In one-on-one sessions, show her how her work *does* make an impact. In particular, show her areas where she is competent and where her strengths are. In the same meeting, point out abilities she has that she has not yet developed, but be careful to make the tone of these discussions positive.

◆ Assign her projects that she can do well in a short time. These assignments should not require excessive follow-up or nagging, as this behavior may reinforce her "my life sucks" language.

SUCCESS INDICATORS

◆ She will use "I'm great" language, as opposed to "my life sucks." She may name-drop, point to her own accomplishments, and brag. Many of her sentences will start with "I."

◆ She will exhibit the lone warrior spirit of Stage Three, often comparing herself with her coworkers and using disparaging language like "What's wrong with them?" and "If they tried, they'd succeed."

For a Person at Stage Three

◆ Encourage him to form triads (three-person relationships). In particular, he should introduce his contacts to one another by pointing to (1) shared or resonant core values, (2) overlapping self-interest, and (3) a specific opportunity where each can contribute to the work of the other. For example: "I've been wanting to introduce you for a long time. You both share a love of the arts and are focused on integrity, and you're aboveboard people. You're both working on marketing plans, and I thought you may want to compare notes because you're using different approaches. Also, Jack here is an expert on market segmentation, and Kathy is a master of promotion plans, so I thought you each might be able to save the other time."

◆ Encourage him to work on projects that are bigger than anything he can do alone. In short, assign him work that requires partnership.

◆ Point out that his success has come through his own efforts, but that the next level of success is going to require a totally different style. In other words, show him that what's brought him to this point will not be enough to move him forward.

◆ Describe role models (ideally in the company) that are exhibiting Stage Four behavior. You'll know these individuals by (1) their focus on "we," (2) the number of triads in their networks, and (3) the success that comes from groups.

◆ When the person complains that he doesn't have time and that others aren't as good (the two chief gripes at Stage Three), show that he has crafted his work life so that no one can really contribute to him.

◆ Tell stories about the time you made the transition from Stage Three to Stage Four.

◆ Coach him that real power comes not from knowledge but from networks, and that there is more leverage in wisdom than in information. Compliment his successes—and they are likely numerous—and convey that you're on his side. Also help him to notice that his goals require getting more done than he is able to do alone, no matter how smart and talented he is.

◆ Encourage him to manage using transparency, as much as is possible under corporate policy. Coach him to not follow the Stage Three tendency to tell them only what they need to know. Rather, encourage him to over-communicate.

SUCCESS INDICATORS

◆ He will substitute "I" language for "we." When people ask about the secret of his success, he will point to his team, not to himself.

◆ He will actively form triads, and his network will expand from a few dozen to several hundred.

◆ He will work less, and yet get more done.

◆   His complaints about "there's not enough time" and "no one is as good" will cease.

◆   The results for which he is accountable will increase by at least 30 percent.

◆   He will communicate with transparency.

◆   He will communicate more information, and more often.

For a Person at Stage Four

◆   Stabilize her at Stage Four by ensuring that her triads are based on values, advantages, *and* opportunity.

◆   Encourage her to use the strategy process in Chapter 11 with her team. In particular, encourage her to run sessions that explore the team's core values, its sense of a noble cause, outcomes that would inspire the team, its assets, and then its behaviors (who would do what). In short, encourage her to pick projects that are more of a stretch and that accomplish bigger and bigger results, by working more in partnership with other people.

◆   Once she is fully stable at Stage Four (which you can measure by her use of "we're great" language and her networked triads of relationships), encourage her team to take advantage of market conditions to make history.

◆   If the market doesn't offer the right conditions, engineer an opportunity.

◆   Recruit others to the tribe who share the values of the group's strategy.

◆ When the team hits difficulties, point people to others for solutions. Encourage her to not solve problems, as doing so is consistent with "I'm great (and you're not)."

◆ Perform regular "oil changes" with the team. In this process, she should lead a discussion about (1) what is working well, (2) what is not working well, and (3) what the team can do make the things that are not working well, work.

SUCCESS INDICATORS

◆ She will use "life is great" language rather than "we're great (and they're not)."

◆ She will seek out ever more challenging projects, and her network will include an almost stunning amount of diversity—but mostly people who, like her, have owned and then left Stage Three.

◆ She will make decisions about how to spend her time based on the tribe's core values and noble cause.

◆ She will appear to be an embodiment of the tribe's strategy, especially its values.

Goal of Tribal Leadership

◆ Tribal Leaders upgrade as many people—and clusters of people—as are willing and able to move forward to Stage Four, the zone of tribal pride.

◆ Figure 2 shows an actual corporate tribe before a Tribal Leader began using the leverage points.

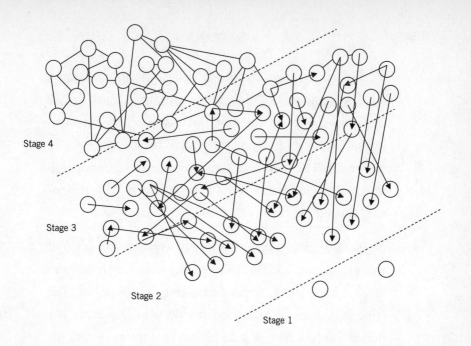

Stage 4

Stage 3

Stage 2

Stage 1

FIGURE 2: AN ACTUAL TRIBE BEFORE TRIBAL LEADERSHIP.

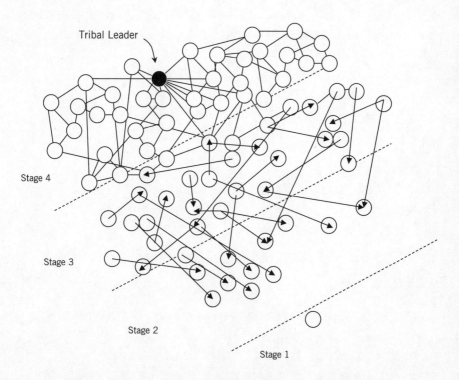

Tribal Leader

Stage 4

Stage 3

Stage 2

Stage 1

FIGURE 3: THE SAME TRIBE AFTER TRIBAL LEADERSHIP.

◆ Figure 3 shows the same tribe nine months later. All key measures of effectiveness jumped, most by 30 percent—a typical outcome. Measures of engagement, job satisfaction, and expectations of future success also increased. The tribe also took advantages of opportunities that made history in its industry, forming a temporary Stage Five culture.

◆ While Tribal Leaders do their work for the good of the group, not for themselves, they are rewarded with loyalty, hard work, innovation, and collaboration. The tribe gets work of higher quality done in less time. The person is often seen as a candidate for top organizational jobs or for positions in government.

APPENDIX B

The Story of Our Research

Big ideas emerge by synthesis: bringing together areas of thought that have previously been separate. Albert Einstein, Sigmund Freud, and Abraham Maslow all started by combining diverse fields and deriving new principles from the combination. While we don't consider ourselves on the same level as these individuals, this work, too, began as a work of synthesis. John's background in athletics, coaching, and chaos theory[1] were combined with Dave's academic study of rhetoric and organizational theory[2]. The big idea that got us going was that one could view a culture as a self-correcting system of language. This perspective, we thought, would complement the more common approaches of cultural inquiry as anthropological, psychological, or sociological. (We later came back to embrace the sociological view once we had the communication framework worked out.)

---

1 Wheatley, Margaret, *Leadership and the New Science: Discovering Order in a Chaotic World.* San Francisco, CA: Barrett-Koehler, 1999.

2 He is especially indebted to the work of his dissertation advisor, Patricia Riley, and her work in corporate culture on structuration theory; and many chats in his first year at USC with Eric Eisenberg about the conflict between coordination and creativity. The list of people in organizational communication we are indebted to is literally too long to mention, as this entire field has attempted to understand organizations through the lens of communication variables. The two people he most credits in understanding Kenneth Burke are Peter Marston and Thomas Hollihan.

Without explaining where the origins of our thoughts began, we cannot accurately describe how we developed our methodology.

Rhetoric and Its Relationship
to Organizational Culture

Our foundation for the study that took more than ten years is rhetoric, especially the writings of Kenneth Burke. Burke's idea of "terministic screens" was the lynchpin. He suggests that a "web of words" (our way of expressing his idea) exists in everyone's mind, and, in his words: "Even if any given [terministic screen] is a *reflection* of reality, by its very nature . . . it must be a *selection* of reality; and to this extent, it must also function as a *deflection* of reality."[3]

This notion sounded a lot like how cultures worked. It is literally true, Burke's groundbreaking arguments suggests, that if people change their words (or, more accurately, their words and their words' relationships to one another), they change their perception of reality. As they change their reality their behavior changes automatically. Instead of people using their words, they are used by their words, and this fact is unrecognized.

Armed with this framework, we then studied how systems of language segment themselves. Going back to very old ideas in rhetoric (especially Aristotle's rhetorical view of values), we hypothesized that there are four common cultures: (1) a negative tone with an individual focus, (2) a negative tone with a group focus, (3) a positive tone with an individual focus, and (4) a positive tone with a group focus. For each one, we expected to find a consistent "web of words" that became the basis of a culture, and a reality.

---

3 Burke, Kenneth, *Language As Symbolic Action: Essays on Life, Literature, and Method.* Berkeley: University of California Press, 1968, p. 3.

Our first research subject was a major healthcare organization on the West Coast. Working with an intact tribe of forty-five people, we taught people the principles of the themes of each level and coached them into using "we're great" language. At the time, we didn't know about the structure of relationships, such as dyads and triads. To measure the group, we modified standard questions from USC's Center for Effective Organizations so that we'd measure the constructs of the four levels of culture. Specifically, we focused on four factors: listening environment, problem solving, ongoing support in jobs, and participation/engagement in work projects. We operationally defined what each culture would look like on a scale of one to four. Researchers interested in our tools can contact us at www.triballeadership.net.

We ran an initial pretest on the forty-five people, many of whom were in the process of transitioning out of the department when we started. We then ran sixteen months of teaching, training, and coaching based on the leverage points mentioned in this book, meeting with the group six times for all-day sessions and with smaller departments once a week for sixty- or ninety-minute coaching sessions. We then let nine months go by during which we had no contact (other than informal social events) with the group, after which we performed a posttest using the same instrument, narrowing the pool of people to twenty-five after the scheduled staff changes had taken place. The results are below:

FACTOR	PREINTERVENTION LEVEL	POSTINTERVENTION LEVEL
Listening environment	3.17	4.38
Problem solving	3.79	4.54
Ongoing support in jobs	2.92	3.72
Participation/engagement	3.83	4.58

All changes are statistically significant with $p < 0.05$.

A 3.5 would indicate a stable Stage Three tribe, and a 4.5 would indicate a stable Stage Four tribe, as defined by theories from organizational rhetoric. What's most noteworthy about this first study is that the culture moved to around a stable Stage Four on three out of four measures, showing us that when a tribe changes its language, it stays changed.

We went on to repeat this practice in six organizations from 1997 to 2000, amassing a database of 472 people. Every study showed similar results: that a nine- to sixteen-month intervention could reliably raise the self-report of culture by one level, and that the changes were lasting.

We began using our consulting engagements in organizations as an opportunity to see if this finding could be confirmed. We also gathered data from organizations in which we did not consult, although we found that our access in these companies was usually limited. We did see these four cultures again and again. We also expanded our use of tools, most notably recording open-ended interviews with tribal members and meetings in which we asked similar open-ended questions. As is often the case in research, our methods became more focused, so that from 1999 to 2006, we had interviews involving over one thousand people in six companies (both individual and group). We used the Burkean method of cluster analysis to make sense of these, in which one looks for which words are said in close proximity to other words.

STAGE	SAMPLING OF WORDS THAT CAME IN CLOSE PROXIMITY TO OTHER WORDS
One	Life, sucks, f----, break, can't, cut, whatever
Two	Boss, life, try, can't, give up, quit, sucks
Three	I, me, my, job, did, do, have, went
Four	We, our, team, do, them, have, did it, commit, value

However, the process of collecting these data was interrupted, time and time again, with our attempts to incorporate established theories. When we found data that didn't make sense, we stopped and tried to figure out what was going on.

For example, the relationship between individual and group turned out to be complex, much more so than we expected. In particular, our research showed that many workplace discussions were collective-negative (what we later called Stage Two), but the person in charge often spoke with an individual-positive (what we later called Stage Three) set of vocabulary. We paused from our data collections to try to figure out this dynamic from well-established theories, especially those derived from, or consistent with, systems theory and development.

Systems Theory and Development

In particular, we wondered about a group's general tendency to move forward, but also back. Why would that happen? As we read theories of development, no backward movement is possible. We were drawn to developmental psychology and to "layering" from systems theory. We later combined these fields with more avantgarde approaches, such as those in *Spiral Dynamics*[4] and later Ken Wilber's view of "holons."[5] What we learned from this study is that the communication cultures we had found seemed to present a sequence, and that if we looked at the overall chronology of humankind, societies appeared to evolve. Still, the question remained, why did we see backward progress—Stage Four became Stage

---

4 Beck, Don Edward and Christopher C. Cowan, *Spiral Dynamics: Mastering Values, Leadership and Change.* Malden, MA: Blackwell Publishing, 1996.

5 Wilber, Ken, *Sex, Ecology: The Spirit of Evolution.* Boston, MA: Shambhala Publications, 1995.

Three, for example—especially when Wilber argues that for a stage model to be valid, no backward movement will ever happen. While we found his readings insightful on this question, it was finally a discussion with him that resolved the issue. He said, "Cognitive development wouldn't regress. However, the self center of gravity can bounce around." To put it more simply, a person cannot think beyond her level of development: a child cannot think as an adult. However, an adult's sense of self can regress to childishness. To put it into our language context, a person with a level of development can use language from a lower developmental stage. Thus, a world-class leader could be dropped into a Stage Two culture and could learn to speak the Stage Two language. Doing so doesn't cognitively regress the person. As Wilber told us, "You can see [language] regression quite a bit, but cognitively, if you shift down two levels you have brain damage." The question was answered: leaders can speak all five stages of language without losing any of their own development. In fact, doing so would be a key to effective leadership.

Furthermore, Wilber, informed by integral studies, had come to the same conclusion we had, informed by rhetoric and chaos theory, about the relationship of person to group. He told us, "Let's say you have six people in a poker game. Five are at Stage Five, and one is at Stage Three. What do you call this darn group? If half are at Stage Three and half are at One, what comes out of that? Alfred North Whitehead distinguished it by saying that an individual has a dominant monad and a group doesn't. . . . A group doesn't have anything close to that . . . Groups have a dominant mode of discourse, and discourse tends to slot into a given stage because people try to settle in on the same wavelength. The leader's dominant mode of discourse tends to become the dominant mode of discourse for the group." Our research notes that Wilber's assertion holds in new groups, but most work groups form over time, with the leader's voice being one of many.

Putting all these theories and perspectives together, we had a series of hypotheses: that language "chunks" into four unique sets, marked by different terministic screens; generalized terministic screens exist on this one-to-four scale; groups generally forward through the stages, although they may get stuck along the way; people will form unique roles within a social group that will be consistent with the relationship between their character armor and the dominant terministic screen—resulting in several cultures existing within the same social group.

This last point was especially important. A person's relationship to a social group is imperative in understanding the person: take the social group away, and the person has no one to approve his character armor. We realized that our unit of analysis had to shift from the individual to some social group, which we came to call a tribe. Thus, tribal culture and a person's sense of self are inseparably locked together. One cannot be understood without the other.

This focus solved a lot of problems. Peter Senge's assertion that the "hero-CEO"[6] is a myth is put into context. A tribe and its leaders create one another, in a relationship that is "mutually arising." Also, most of us who have tried to redefine ourselves know that the social group pushes back on our efforts. We saw from this tribal framework that the tribe literally tells us who we are, although, with all five canons of rhetoric at one's disposal, it is possible to change not only oneself but the entire tribe's cultural stage. This goal became our focus: to produce a series of leverage points that would upgrade

---

6 Senge, Peter, Art Kleiner, Charlotte Roberts, and Rick Ross, *The Dance of Change: The Challenges of Sustaining Momentum in Learning Organizations.* New York: Currency, 1999, pp. 10–15.

a tribe, no matter which of the four cultural stages were at work. (At this point, we hadn't identified Stage Five.)

In recent years, since the publication of Jim Collins's *Good to Great*,[7] we're often asked how our scheme compares to Jim Collins's Level 5 leadership. Ken Wilber explains the difference in his four-quadrant model, which can be viewed on the Web at www.integralinstitute.org. The upper right quadrant is the domain of individual behavior—that which is observable. Most books on management (processes, rules, tips, and procedures) are written to boil down to this zone—what should I *do*.

Wilber's lower right quadrant is collective behavior and includes a company's systems, processes, and structures. Process redesign and quality initiatives are examples of corporate activity in this quadrant.

His upper left quadrant is where we'd put Collins's Level 5 leadership—the zone of individual intentions, motivations, emotions, etc., and it is where most books on leadership focus (ideas, values, attitudes, and transformative notions). Collins's argument that Level 5 leaders show a "paradoxical combination of will and vision" is clearly individual "interiority"—what is in the leader's mind.

We're fans of Collins. However, some people as they read his description wonder where these exceptional leaders come from. It appears to some that they descend out of the sky when needed. (In fairness, the origination of Level 5 leaders wasn't the focus of Collins's study, although he's paid considerable attention to this question since the publication of his landmark book.) The tribal framework answered that question: their leadership constructs are born out of

7 Collins, Jim, *Good to Great: Why Some Companies Make the Leap . . . and Others Don't*. New York: HarperCollins, 2001.

language and culture, which is set and reinforced by the tribe. Level 5 leaders emerge from the dynamics of tribe, terministic screen, and character armor as people advance through the cultural stages.

Our work started in Wilber's lower left quadrant—the zone of interior collective, which is language and culture. As we got going, we also observed the structure of relationships of people (such as dyads and triads), which is the lower right quadrant. Finally, we correlated all of this to what individuals do—the upper right. The only zone we didn't focus on is the upper left—individual psychology.[8]

We described our approach to Wilber as an "on ramp to integral thinking," and that's what we hope it is. Wilber's research, which builds on psychology, systems, sociology, and even spirituality, shows a correlation between all four quadrants. Level 5 leaders and late Stage Four cultures create each other, and Stage Five cultures (which we hadn't yet identified) create a level of leadership that business is only beginning to recognize—something possibly beyond Level 5.

Return to Data Collection

We then returned to our data collection and had to deal with the fact that we were beginning to see cultures that didn't fall into the

---

8 We should add that Wilber had two arguments with our five-stage model. First, he argued that what we call Stage One and Stage Two are pathological versions of what we call Stage Three. However, as we review our data, organizational cultures do appear to advance from Stage Two to Three, just as they advance from Stage Three to Four. We concede that this phenomenon may be a factor unique to workplace cultures, but we stand behind the data we've collected. Second, Wilber argued that we should add a Stage Six and Stage Seven, which would correlate to higher levels of consciousness he described. We dealt with this concern in Chapter 11. We should add that at the time of writing this book, we are collaborating on a paper that will be posted through the Social Science Research Network, detailing our hypotheses for Stages Six and Seven, with Ken Wilber's guidance. The links for all such papers are available from our Web site: www.triballeadership.net.

four cultures we expected to see. (The first was Amgen.) Here Dave and John had an argument that lasted for years. John argued that it is possible for a business culture to have no discernable rival and to outperform a culture that was focusing on "besting" another company. With Dave's focus as a business professor, this made no sense to him. A culture that ignored its competitors was doomed to failure, Dave argued.

What finally convinced Dave that John was right was that Warren Bennis and Patricia Ward Biederman confirmed a similar finding in *Organizing Genius,*[9] when they looked at great groups down through time—ones we could consider having a late Stage Four or early Stage Five culture.

The data supported John, as well. Throughout the late 1990s, we saw more and more cultures that were what we came to call Stage Five—having a mood of innocent wonderment and a level of performance that was history-making.

From reviews of recordings and transcripts, the "terministic screen" of Stage Five becomes visible. The words people at that stage tend to use together include "wow," "miracle," "lucky," "vision," values," and "we." Although we weren't assessing tone of voice in any formal way, our anecdotal observations were that people in Stage Five organizations spoke more softly and reverently, and in Stage Four they were more boisterous.

Review of these interviews, mostly transcribed, revealed the four cultures in their detail and correlated to our surveys. Almost right away, we hit a problem. In the early 2000s, we saw an aberration: Stage Five cultures with no discernable business expertise. Many weren't making money but did have large infusions of investment

---

9 Bennis, Warren, and Patricia Ward Biederman, *Organizing Genius: The Secrets of Creative Collaboration.* New York: Perseus, 1997.

capital. Even more puzzling was that many of these companies were publicly traded, and at multiples far in excess of companies generally considered world class. What was going on? The end of the dot-com bubble produced the answer: over the long term, culture and strategic performance correlate, with the higher factor falling to the level of the lower. Thus, a company with a great culture and low strategic performance will, over time, find that its culture erodes: good people leave, and a "my life sucks" language begins to dominate.

With the five cultures in place, we searched for simple ways of summarizing them. While the process was informal, in hindsight we had followed the same system that focus group facilitators use: we walked into a culture, summarized it in our language, and then recorded the reactions. Over time, we noticed that the "life sucks," "my life sucks," "I'm great," "we're great," and "life is great" labels simply worked. We have used them for eight years. After collecting data on a culture, we share the data with the people in it, along with the title, and we can think of only two occasions when people said the title wasn't a fit. Both organizations had idiosyncratic issues (a leader with a terminal disease in one case, and a successful subsidiary being shut down by its owner in the other).

The next major breakthrough came in structures. For years, we had been studying informal networks, mostly from secondary sources. We then began having workshop participants draw the structure of the relationships around them as they also rated the cultural stages of individuals. We began to notice that structures and cultural stages correlated to an amazing degree—also over 90 percent. While the structure of relationships has been extensively studied in communication studies, the field is often divided into interpersonal and group communication. Triads, described in Chapter 10, seemed to fall in between these two areas and thus didn't receive as much attention. We spent several weeks looking at research mentioning "triadic," "triune," or "three-person" communication, and while we read hundreds of articles, none captured the insight that is built in Chapter 10: that a person is responsible for the quality of the relationship (anchored in values) between the other two people. However, once the insight is made, it is obvious, so we're fairly certain someone somewhere has come to the same conclusion, despite our best efforts to locate their research.

In 2001, we saw that we could peg a culture on the one-to-five scale very quickly (often in minutes) on the basis of their language. Our initial reads correlated with our surveys more than 90 percent. On this basis, we dropped surveys and began using expert assessment. We ran some early interrated reliability studies using some of Dave's graduate students at USC, and we learned that people within the organizations were almost as good as outside observers in categorizing the cultural stage of their coworkers (the correlation was over 0.9). We also noticed that people are not as accurate in noticing their own cultural stage. The dynamic we observed is that people at Stage Three often say that they are at Five; people at Two generally say they are at Four. Aside from this self-reported (on the basis of individual behavior) two-stage increase, people are very competent at rating the culture around them. In other words, people are accurate in saying they work in a Stage Three culture, but they will often describe themselves as Stage Five leaders.

We then trained groups, as part of workshops and in coaching sessions, to categorize (anonymously and confidentially) the people they worked with. We have five separate databases, each reflecting a different measurement system, and our percentages of the working population are drawn from these sources. It should be noted that these data do not represent random sampling, and our populations were slanted toward the educated, affluent, and urban. Furthermore, as our work expanded we began to ask people—now numbering just

Summary of Research Tools

TIME	TOOL, NUMBER OF DATA POINTS	RESULTED IN
1997–present	Surveys based on established organizational development factors, 472	Proof of concept that cultures operate at consistent levels across cultural factors (e.g., a Stage Three culture is consistent across listening, problem solving, ongoing job support, and participation/ engagement). Furthermore, when a culture changes, it tends to stay changed.
1999–present	Recorded/transcribed interviews, eventually resolving down to the "Big Four Questions" (discussed in Chapter 9), interpreted with Burke's cluster analysis and standard content analysis techniques, 1061	Generalized "terministic screens," showing which words came up in relation to other words. When these were correlated with surveys, we understood that each stage had a standard way of talking that cut across technical areas and the education level of its members. This gave us the worldview of people at each cultural stage.
2004–present	Sociograms (diagrams of people's working relationships), 241	Ninety percent correlation of structures (e.g., dyads) with language of tribes (e.g., "I'm great").
2003–present	Training on the stages, then anonymous and confidential self-rating of department, divisional, and organizational cultures, 22,418 (Note: we trained people in their organizations to train and then collect data, accounting for 15,420 of these data points.)	An understanding of the prevalence of cultures. When this is combined with training and consulting, proof that cultures can be changed with the leverage points in this book.

under 24,200—to rate themselves, their immediate work group, and their organization's "center of gravity." Since we had already established that people in organizations were effective at "pegging" their culture, we felt confident that this method of data collection had utility. (We took people's ratings of one another as our guide and eliminated self-reports from our study.)[10]

By the end of our work, we had data on over twenty-four thousand people in our databases. It is important to note this study has turned into one involving tribes of tribes, with people armed with the framework reporting their data to us. While we can't guarantee the quality of their observations, we are more than convinced by the data we have collected from over seven thousand people in two dozen organizations since 1997.

Going Deep

The final step we took was to "go deep" with a single client (it had been years since the first 1997 study), where we could easily measure results. Starting in 2001, we chose CB Richard Ellis, the world's largest commercial real estate services firm, because the effectiveness of teams can be measured in revenue. We took two approaches at the same time. First, we worked with "producer teams" and implemented the techniques in this book, mostly with teams that were considered problematic by management. As of the last public measure we saw (March 2005), out of seventy-five major national teams, six of our client teams ranked in the top fifteen. (Most of the credit for this achievement goes to the clients, most of whom were exceptional per-

---

10 We also searched for verification of this tendency from other stage development theorists. Don Beck, author of *Spiral Dynamics*, has noticed the same effect, which he calls aspirational error. As he explained the phenomenon to us, "I aspire to it [the stage], therefore, I am it [the stage]."

formers before they started working with us.) Second, we worked with the Private Client Group, a start-up in the company, which produced significant revenue (starting at basically zero) in thirty-six months.[11]

Other Conclusions

It is interesting that people in companies where we consulted and gathered data often reported using Tribal Leadership in their relationships: in their marriages, with their families, in their neighborhoods, and so on. It appears that the system reflects that these nonbusiness relationships work the same way, but it's important to note that this use went outside the boundaries of our study. Thus, our points on broader relationships should be considered folk wisdom, but we have not seen data that contradict anything in this book being applied to relationships in general.

For some academic colleagues, our research methods may seem imprecise. However, it should be noted that the cultural stages are worlds unto themselves, with each one being as different from another as Germany is from Missouri. It becomes easy to spot which stage people are in. Even with minimal training, people's interrated reliability was over 0.85.

Final Words

Our final conclusion is the most important one. This book was written by a tribe. While the words are ours, the ideas came from all around us—from clients, research subjects, graduate students, world-class scholars, CEOs, union leaders, government officials, friends,

---

11 Exact revenue is confidential.

and family. Our role was a simple one: ask questions, figure out what the answers meant by talking it through with experts from different fields, and then asking more questions. It is to our tribe that we offer our gratitude. We hope that as you read this book you'll decide to contact us with your experiences and stories, and thus build all of our tribes.

● ● ● ● ● ●

How to Reach Us

O ur goal in writing this book is so you don't have to hire us—to transfer the gems that we've learned from twenty-four thousand people into a single volume that anyone can use to upgrade his or her corporate tribes. However, our tribe, including our editor at HarperCollins, suggests we include information about how to contact us, in case our presence in your tribes would make a difference.

About CultureSync

CultureSync is a management consulting firm specializing in cultural change and strategy, resulting from the principles in this book. CultureSync's clients include dozens of Fortune 500 companies, governments around the world, and not-for-profit organizations of all sizes. It also provides coaching expertise derived from the Tribal Leadership methodology.

Dave Logan

Dave Logan is cofounder and senior partner of CultureSync, where he heads major engagements in healthcare, commercial real estate, high technology, and government.

In addition, he is on the faculty at the Marshall School of Business at USC. From 2001 to 2004 he served as associate dean/executive director of executive education and corporate programs. During that time, he started the Master of Medical Management (MMM), a business degree for midcareer medical doctors. He also initiated new executive education programs with dozens of organizations, from aerospace to high-tech start-ups to financial services. He has taught in the Marshall MBA since 1996, including courses in management consulting, organization design, negotiation, principles of management, and leadership. Dave has a PhD in organizational communication from the Annenberg School at USC.

He lives in Los Angeles with his wife, Harte. He can be reached at dave.logan@culturesync.net.

John King

John King is cofounder and senior partner of CultureSync. He is in demand as a keynote speaker and is nationally recognized as a senior teacher, coach, and program leader. He heads major engagements in emerging technologies, government, and real estate. He also heads CultureSync's coaching efforts and its research and development initiatives.

John is part of the leadership development team at Sierra Health Foundation and is on the faculty of several corporate universities and the California Leadership Institute. John is also a frequent guest lecturer in executive education programs at USC. Clients of his coaching practice, and graduates of his training programs (numbering over twenty-five thousand), have been featured on all major television networks and in *The Wall Street Journal*.

He lives in Marina del Ray, California. He can be reached at john.king@culturesync.net.

Halee Fischer-Wright

Dr. Halee Fischer-Wright is a partner of CultureSync who began her career in pediatrics and has since become a leading expert in not only healthcare but also general business and management circles. Prior to joining CultureSync in 2005—where she heads up projects related to financial services, education, high-technology, healthcare, and entrepreneurial ventures—Halee spent the previous ten years wearing multiple hats as an owner, manager, and physician at Foothills Pediatrics and Adolescent Medicine in Denver, Colorado. She has served on several executive hospital boards and is currently president of a 400-physician group in Denver.

With a focus on balancing quality with profitability, Halee initiates programs that build values-based partnerships in client organizations. She also helps businesses create high-performance teams with energy, purpose, and motivation. She holds an M.D. from the University of Colorado, a Masters of Medical Management from USC, and a Certificate in Executive Leadership Coaching from Georgetown University. Dedicated to her passions in both medicine and business, she continues to serve on faculty at the University of Colorado as an assistant clinical professor, as well as teach executive programs at USC.

She lives in Denver with her husband, Michael. She can be reached at hfischerwright@culturesync.net.

INDEX